Economic Analysis and Evaluation of the
Gulf Cooperation Council (GCC)

European University Studies

Europäische Hochschulschriften

Publications Universitaires Européennes

Series V

Economics and Management

Reihe V Série V

Volks- und Betriebswirtschaft

Sciences économiques, gestion d'entreprise

Vol./Bd. 1783

PETER LANG

Frankfurt am Main · Berlin · Bern · Bruxelles · New York · Oxford · Wien

Simon Koppers

Economic Analysis and Evaluation of the Gulf Cooperation Council (GCC)

2nd Edition

PETER LANG
Europäischer Verlag der Wissenschaften

Bibliographic Information published by Die Deutsche Bibliothek
Die Deutsche Bibliothek lists this publication in the Deutsche Nationalbibliografie; detailed bibliographic data is available in the internet at <http://dnb.ddb.de>.

Zugl.: Bonn, Univ., Diss., 1995

D 5
ISSN 0531-7339
ISBN 3-631-51992-3
US-ISBN 0-8204-6552-6

Printed in Germany 1 2 3 4 6 7

www.peterlang.de

Economic Analysis and Evaluation of the Gulf Cooperation Council (GCC)

List of Figures, Graphs, Map, Tables

List of Appendix Tables

List of Abbreviations

ACM	Arab Common Market
b/d	barrels per day
CIF	cost, insurance, freight
DUP	directly unproductive (activities)
EC, EEC, EU	European Community, European Economic Community, European Union (since 1 January 1994)
EFTA	European Free Trade Association
FGCCC	Federation of GCC Chambers
GATT	General Agreement on Tariffs and Trade
GCC	Cooperation Council for the Arab States of the Gulf
GIB	Gulf International Bank
GIC	Gulf Investment Corporation
GOIC	Gulf Organization for Industrial Consulting
IMF	International Monetary Fund
KIA	Kuwait Investment Authority
KISR	Kuwait Institute for Scientific Research
NCB	National Commercial Bank
OECD	Organization for Economic Cooperation and Development
OPEC	Organization of Petroleum Exporting Countries
PPP	Purchasing Power Parity
SABIC	Saudi Basic Industries Corporation
SMO-GCC	GCC Standards and Metrology Organization
UAE	United Arab Emirates
US, U.S., USA	United States of America

A. Introduction

The world faces a growing regionalization and the establishment or revival of preferential trading blocs. One of them, the 'Cooperation Council for the Arab States of the Gulf' (Gulf Cooperation Council, GCC) was founded in 1981 and groups Bahrain, Kuwait, Oman, Qatar, Saudi Arabia and the United Arab Emirates (the UAE). Among developing countries, the Gulf Cooperation Council is one of the Big Four in terms of combined GDP and it is viewed as the most successful in terms of implementation of free trade measures (Torre / Kelly 1992, pp. 26f). The analysis (part B of this study) and evaluation (part C) of the GCC's economic dimension – not only with regard to free trade – is the focus of this study, framed by the introductory part A and by part D with summary and perspectives.

In brief, the three chapters of part B provide insight into the main development problems of the GCC member countries, into the possibilities and limitations of cooperation and into the steps which the GCC has taken to cooperate. Part C evaluates the outcome of the actions and is devoted to an ex post assessment of the GCC, as well as to explanations for major failures.

The rationale for the six member countries of the GCC to engage in economic cooperation was their belief that this could substantially augment their internal markets and international bargaining power. Together they want to achieve development, mainly in the industrial sector. Their fear of staying behind is best expressed in their Working Paper (1981): "[H]umanity is pushing into space and the development of modern nuclear physics, using fast and direct communications. Whoever lags behind remains among the backward states and nations." The appropriateness of the GCC members' development strategy to push for industrialization is investigated in chapter B.1; the viability of achieving higher growth paths by regional cooperation is the subject of chapter B.2.

From the beginning, the GCC declared its readiness to pursue economic cooperation in all its aspects. In general, economic agents can in many cases considerably improve their economic situation by cooperation (i.e., by exchanging their endowments, such as goods and services, and by coordinating their production and consumption plans). In the case where agents are sovereign, they always have the option to take unilateral action in refusing to cooperate. Hence, cooperation takes place through negotiations and subsequent agreements. A special case is economic cooperation between sovereign countries, such as the six GCC members. Governments may not only try to directly achieve the above-mentioned improvements (e.g., through common investment projects), but also by setting the 'rules of the game' for other 'players'. The economically important decisions of the GCC to influence the various agents (mainly investors) are grouped and analyzed in chapter B.3.

All of part B – GCC's development problems, appropriate regional cooperation and actual cooperation decisions – provides the basis for evaluating the GCC's actual impact on the member countries' economies in part C. In chapter C.1, the measurable economic success or failure of the decisions is laid down. As is known from the literature, some experts on the GCC believe it has performed well in the economic sphere while others do not subscribe to this view. Therefore, an opinion survey has been conducted to study the opinions of some thirty experts in detail. Because the GCC Free Trade Area has been in force since March 1983 and the data and reasoning which are presented by the GCC Secretariat General to prove that it has performed well is questionable, the Free Trade Area's impact on intra-GCC trade is analyzed with the help of a macro-economic model. In addition, influences on factor movements and international bargaining power are evaluated.

Having studied the economic performance of the GCC, it is necessary to ask for the reasons for failures. First, the design of the GCC is put to the test of economic theory in chapter C.2. Next, the underlying reasons for this design have to be found in chapter C.3.[1]

---

[1] Obviously, this last subject touches the spheres of other sciences as well (e.g., political science, sociology, psychology, history, ethnic studies, religious studies) and only limited insight can be provided in the present study.

B. Economic Analysis of the GCC

B.1. Development Problems of the GCC States

Before analyzing the chances and drawbacks of various cooperation schemes within the GCC in chapter B.2., it is important to first analyze the economic chances and problems which the GCC countries are facing.

In addition to providing data on the GCC countries, theoretic implications will also be considered. In particular, the theory of Dutch Disease (sections B.1.1. and B.1.2.), the problems of rentier states (B.1.3.), and the chances of exploiting comparative advantages and of exporting down-stream products on the world market (B.1.4.) will be analyzed. Most GCC economists and politicians are well-aware of the problems which result in rentier states. However, the concept of Dutch Disease is more important, but less understood: obstacles to industrialization result from a real appreciation which is due to high levels of oil (i.e., rent) income. Therefore, and for the reason that the theory is not immediately applicable to the GCC and its economic integration, a relatively large part of this chapter is devoted to the theory of Dutch Disease.

It should be kept in mind that not all GCC member countries are facing the same chances and problems. There are important similarities, such as the present dependence on oil (cf. Tables 2 and 3) and the economic order: market economy with private ownership; strong central government which guides industrialization by indicative and supportive planning. Arabic is the common language, Islam is the common religion and they have similar desert cultures and geographies. Nevertheless, the GCC is a grouping of unequal partners. This can be seen from Table 1, which may also give the reader a first impression of the GCC.[2] In terms of per capita GNP, the GCC is divided in two

---

[2] Three general remarks on the data are called for. First, '$' and 'US$' both refer to US Dollar in this study. Second, data from 1989 have often been chosen in this study instead of the latest year available. This is due to Iraq's occupation of Kuwait from August 1990 to February 1991. Therefore, the GCC countries would have been misrepresented if data from 1990 to 1991 had been chosen to point out some persisting structures. This is not to say 1989 is a representative year for the future, especially given rapid changes in the world (e.g., breakdown of the communist systems, Palestine-Israel Accord, world-wide recession etc.), but it is preferable to 1990 or 1991. Third, official data from the GCC countries are limited and sometimes not reliable, as well as difficult to compare. For example, IMF's Government Finance Statistics do not cover Qatar and Saudi Arabia, and IMF's Balance of Payments Statistics do not cover Qatar and the UAE. As an example of extreme problems with reliability, Oman reported 1988 exports to the UAE of US$ 1,871 million; but the UAE reported it received imports of only US$ 10 million from Oman. In this case, import data are

Table 1: Economic Strength of the GCC Members, 1989

	Share in Total GNP (in %)	Population mid-1989 (in million)	Share in Oil Revenue (in %)	GNP per Capita (in US$)
Saudi Arabia	53.2	14.43 *	47.7	5,967
Kuwait	19.3	2.05	17.7	15,220
UAE	17.0	1.55	21.6	17,742 †
Oman	4.5	1.45	7.2	5,034
Qatar	4.0	0.34	4.5	19,118 †
Bahrain	2.0	0.49	1.3	6,735
GCC Total	*100.0*	*20.31*	*100.0*	*7,971*

Notes: * population of Saudi Arabia based on Saudi figures "which are widely considered too high" (Economist Intelligence Unit 1992, p. 3). It is "more likely around nine million" (Twinam 1992, p. 25); † GNP values are not available; therefore, GDP values have been chosen (however, according to United Nations Development Programme (1992, p. 174) the difference between the UAE's GDP and GNP is less than 1%)
Memorandum: GNP added up to $161 billion in 1989
Sources: International Monetary Fund (1992b); Arab Monetary Fund (1991a); NCB Economist (January 1992); NCB Economist (February 1992)

groups. The richer countries are Qatar, the UAE and Kuwait, the poorer ones are Oman, Saudi Arabia and Bahrain. However, Saudi Arabia dominates in terms of overall GNP, population and oil income. As the assigned IMF quotas are related to economic indicators, it is interesting to look at the relative shares of the GCC countries: Saudi Arabia 74.2%, Kuwait 14.2%, the UAE 5.7%, Qatar 2.8%, Oman 1.7% and Bahrain 1.2% (International Monetary Fund 1992d). Saudi Arabia is also dominating in geographical terms. In the economic context it is less important that Saudi Arabia is the largest country. More important is the fact that Saudi Arabia participates in all borders between GCC countries, the only exception being the Omani-UAE border (cf. Map 1).

Advantages and disadvantages in the GCC region with respect to development of a diversified and strong economic structure are manifold. The primary sector aside from oil and gas is not able to serve as a growth engine in the

---

more reliable (cf. section C.1.2.). In cases where serious doubts about quality of data persist, this is pointed out (as is done, e.g., in the notes to Table 1 for Saudi Arabia's population figure).

Map 1: The GCC Region

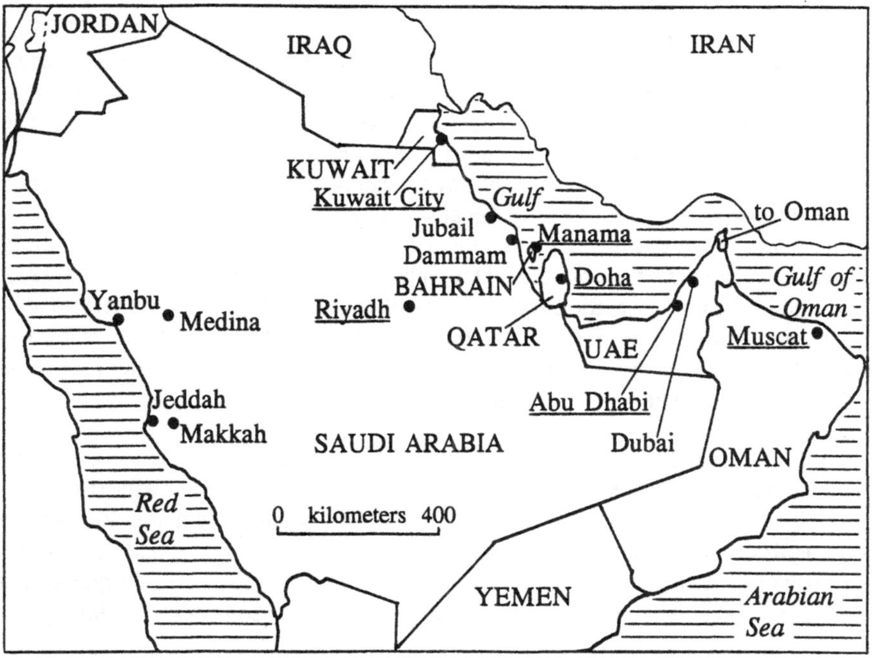

medium and long run, although fishing plays a significant role in Oman and provides some future potential. There is general agreement that agriculture is not a long-run option for economic growth in the GCC countries due to climate, soil and water reasons. Oil and gas revenues are subject to high and unpredictable fluctuations. The "GCC region is not rich in known mineral deposits" (Industrial Strategy 1985, p. iv). The secondary and tertiary sector, as well as the outlook for oil and gas, will be dealt with in the following.

B.1.1. The Fundamental Dilemma: Dutch Disease

In this section Dutch Disease theory and its implications will be examined one by one and linked to the situations in the member countries of the Gulf Co-operation Council. In brief, since the 1970s, the oil-exporting countries received high oil income from abroad. The associated economic rent led to a real appreciation and a drop in the production of tradable goods other than oil. The shift from tradable goods (i.e., mostly manufactured goods) to nontradable goods (i.e., mostly services) because of an increase in rent income from abroad is called *Dutch Disease*. 'Dutch,' because this explanation has first been applied to the situation in the Netherlands after its discovery of the Groningen gas field in the early seventies (Benjamin / Devarajan / Weiner 1989, p. 72).[3] 'Disease,' because the real appreciation reduces non-oil exports, and policy-makers as well as economists believe that a large and diversified production of exportables is essential for a country's welfare in the long-run.[4] Government intervention is often called for when Dutch Disease persists.

It is a stylized fact that the GCC's member countries experience an inflow of rent income from abroad through oil revenues. This is especially true since the 1970s, when oil prices increased considerably and when the foreign oil companies were nationalized. However, oil revenues are not equally important for all six GCC economies as Table 2 shows. In addition, Table 2 suggests that the importance of crude oil and gas has diminished considerably during the 1980s, from 2/3 of GDP to 1/3.

---

[3] The phenomenon itself is not new, of course. Historians have noted long ago that Spain's development process was slower than England's because of Spain's high gold transfers from South America. Today, Dutch Disease is one explanation for the difference in development between East Germany and other former Socialist countries in East Europe. In 1992, consumption and investment is about twice as high as production due to transfer payments from West Germany (Schlesinger 1993). East Germany's industrial base shrunk much faster than that of the other countries, and it was the only country with a real appreciation. (For a brief summary of the situations in East Europe at the end of 1992, see Fischer 1993.)

[4] As van Wijnbergen (1986, p. 130) puts it for the case of development aid: "[S]ubstantial amounts of aid [or rental oil income] will put upward pressure on the real exchange rate and will in that way counteract the export promotion schemes often recommended by aid donors."

Table 2: Share of Mining, Quarring and Fuel in GDP at Market Prices, 1980 and 1989 (%)

	1980	1989
Bahrain	30.5	15.5
Kuwait	65.6	40.3
Oman	62.1	45.8
Qatar	67.2	30.1
Saudi Arabia	66.1	27.6
UAE	64.4	38.7
GCC Total	*65.2*	*32.4*

Source: Arab Monetary Fund (1991b)

However, exports of crude oil constitute still the lion's share of total exports, as Table 3 shows.[5]

Table 3: Share of Crude Oil Exports in Total Merchandise Exports, 1976 and 1989 (%)

	1976	1989	1976-1989 *
Bahrain	77.2	75.2	83.5
Kuwait	92.5	90.7	89.8
Oman	98.7	89.2	93.0
Qatar	96.7	94.0	94.0
Saudi Arabia	99.7	84.9	94.9
UAE	96.7	66.3	85.6
GCC Total	*97.4*	*74.5*	*91.8*

Note: * simple arithmetic average of annual shares
Sources: King Fahd University of Petroleum & Minerals (1991); Arab Petroleum Research Center (1992)

[5] In the World Bank's World Development Report 1992 (1992, p. 308), Bahrain and Kuwait are grouped as "[e]conomies in which no single export category accounts for more than 50 percent of total exports" during the period 1987-1989. This is due to the inclusion of services as a category. In particular, Kuwait received high service receipts due to its investments abroad. According to the International Monetary Fund (1992), the net factor incomes from abroad as % of GNP (i.e., (GNP-GDP)/GNP), were in 1989 as follows [in square brackets data from United Nations Development Programme (1992)]: Saudi Arabia 4% [10%]; Kuwait 26% [29%]; the UAE n.a. [0.4%]; Oman -15% [1%]; Qatar n.a. [n.a.]; Bahrain -9% [n.a].

To understand the implications of the predominance of the "black gold" for the structure of the rest of the economy, the seminal model of Swan (1955) and Salter (1959), known as the *Australian model* of a small open economy with nontradable goods, will be extended. One of the major assumptions is that the domestic economy has no international market power in the sense that "[v]ariations in the terms of trade – although frequent and often disastrous – are determined almost exclusively by conditions abroad" (Salter 1959, p. 226). This *small-country assumption* will be maintained for all goods except oil. The other essential assumption is *openness to consumer goods*. In general, this assumption states there exists no artificial trade barriers, such as import tariffs, export taxes, quotas or domestic industry subsidies. In addition, natural trade barriers such as transportation costs are assumed to be negligible. This assumption is changed only slightly in allowing for some goods to be prohibitively protected, such that none of these goods can ever be imported or exported.[6] This assumption is not in strict accordance with reality in the GCC, but the conclusions do not depend on this assumption which facilitates the analysis. In reality, there exists natural barriers (e.g., transportation costs) for all goods, and the artificial trade barriers which are present in the GCC do not prevent all goods from being traded.

In contrast with the openness to consumer goods, factors of production are assumed to be only nationally mobile, but internationally immobile (Enders / Herberg 1983, p. 477; van Wijnbergen 1984, p. 44; Benjamin / Devarjan / Weiner 1989, p. 74). The next section (B.1.2.) investigates the consequences of assuming international mobility of factors of production.

The non-oil consumer goods of the GCC economies are grouped into two categories: *tradables* (T-goods) and *nontradables* (N-goods). Purchasing Power Parity (PPP) is assumed for tradables: the domestic price of a tradable good is equal to the price of a perfect substitute on the world market times the nominal exchange rate.[7] A nontradable good has either no close substitute on the world

---

[6] This is in accordance with Salter (1959, p. 556) who distinguishes between "sheltered and unsheltered industries," only the latter consisting of exportables and importables, and with Enders / Herberg (1983, p. 474) who distinguish between a "sheltered" and an "exposed" sector.

[7] For identical goods this can be justified by the "law of one price" under the no-arbitrage assumption. However, PPP is applied in the current context to price indices for tradables. It is obvious that PPP will not hold if the weights in the index functions are not equal, which is generally the case due to differences in the consumption structure in different countries. Theoretically, this can only be avoided if one assumes identical weakly separable utility functions which are homothetic for the tradable goods part. In this case, the consump-

market, or competition is prohibited by natural or artificial trade barriers. Tradable goods are in general either *imported goods* (M-goods) or *exported goods* (X-goods). There exists three exemptions from this rule: a) in rare cases, domestic production just equals domestic consumption; b) in other rare cases, not the good itself is imported, but a perfect substitute; and c) the third case is very common, whereby a good is imported *and* exported. Such intra-industry trade exists due to the practically unsolvable problem of classification; or due to the existence of high transportation costs between distant parts of a country; or due to a lack of information; or due to a change in international competitiveness of the domestic industry within the reporting period. In the present model, these three exemptions are not considered.[8]

Tradable goods are mostly manufactured goods, whereas nontradable goods are mostly services (e.g., wholesale and retail trade, transportation, communications, finance and business services, insurance, real estate, social and personal services, public security and defence, public administration). However, it has to be noted that some manufactured goods are nontradables (for example due to high transportation costs), and some service sector goods can be internationally traded (tourism, transportation, insurance, finance).

In the present GCC model economy, four sectors are of importance: producers, consumers, government and the rest of the world. Producers are characterized by their aggregated production possibilities curve (assumed to be concave) and profit maximization. Consumers are characterized by the aggregated indifference curves (assumed to be convex) and by maximization of the aggregated utility function. Government ensures free trade, sells oil or imposes trade barriers. Assuming that the no-arbitrage condition holds, the rest of the world determines the prices for the imported and for the exported good.

---

tion structure of tradables will be identical in all countries even if the prices for nontradables differ internationally. Because this is mainly a technical point which has no influence on the general results, it is assumed that PPP holds for tradables. In the present models, this difficulty is often avoided by introducing only one traded good.

[8] One could think of changing the terminology from "tradable good" and "nontradable good" into "world-price good" and "nonworld-price good." This could be justified because the one-to-one dependence on world prices is *the* distinguishing criterion for grouping of goods in this model. One can think of cases in which a good is nontraded, but its price is nevertheless determined on the world market (e.g., when the domestic value added is almost negligible – an issue which achieved significant prominence in the GCC in connection with the free trade agreement). In addition, there are services such as tourism which are "exports" and "imports" in national accounting, but their price is not determined in a one-to-one way on the world market. However, the rise in exactness seems to be too small to justify the change of well-introduced notations.

Figure 1 depicts these relationships.

Figure 1: Equilibrium in a Small Open Economy with Tradable Goods (Exportables and Importables) and with Nontradable Goods

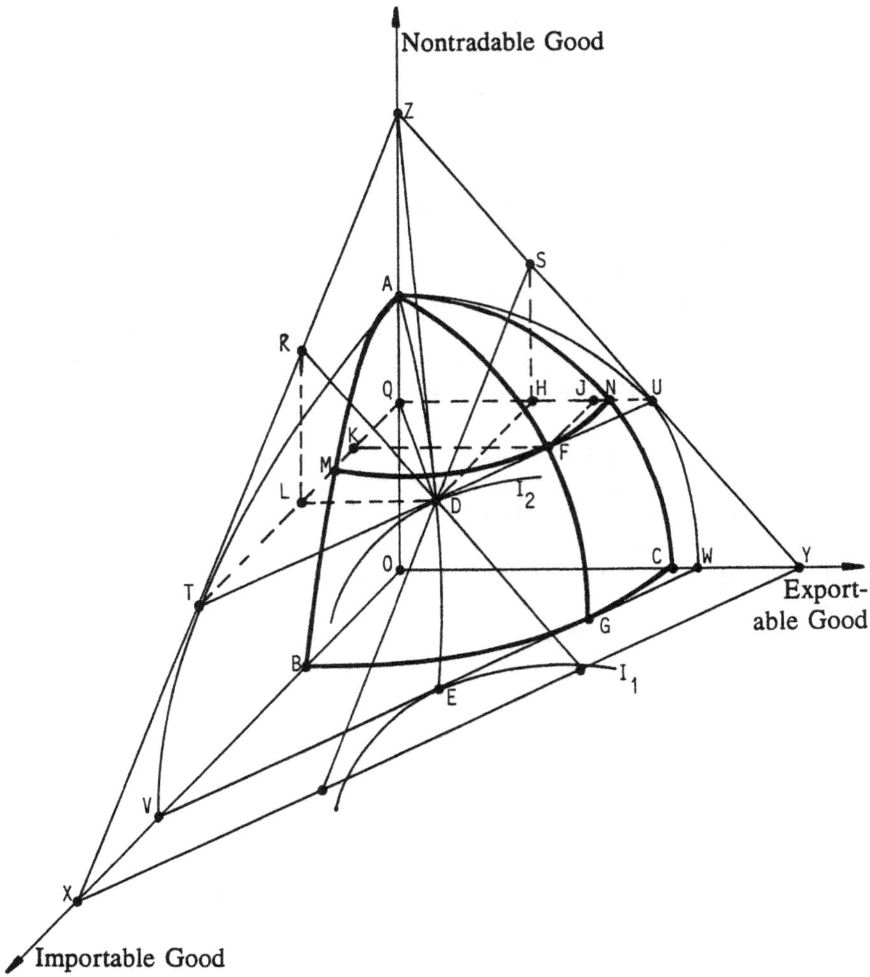

Note: explanations are provided in the text

The production possibilities are depicted by the sphere ABC (excluding wasteful use of resources, such as "producing" O). If no N-good would be produced, the production possibilities frontier would be BC. The consumption possibilities frontier would be VW; utility would be maximized at E at the level I_1. Similarly, with fixed production OQ of the N-good, TU would be the consumption possibility and D would maximize utility at the level I_2. TU and VW are parallel because their slope is the terms of trade (OV/OW), which is constant by the small-country assumption. The line ADE is the set of equilibria conditioned on fixed production of the N-good. Of course, the overall equilibrium lies on this line. Let this be D, which implies $I_2 > I_1$. The production of the N-good is OQ; the production of the X-good is QJ, and HJ will be exported; the production of the M-good is QK, and KL will be imported.

In equilibrium (D), for any of the three pairs of goods the following well-known marginal conditions are satisfied: equality among the marginal rate of transformation, the marginal rate of substitution and the ratio of prices. To be specific, for the pair X-M this ratio is OV/OW (terms of trade), for X-N it is LR/LD (real exchange rate of the exported good), and for M-N it is HS/HD (real exchange rate of the imported good). For the use of the expression *real exchange rate* for the ratio tradables' price to nontradables' price ($e = p_T/p_N$), see Aghevli / Khan / Montiel (1991, p. 8).[9]

The real exchange rate (this term is commonly used although one should speak of a real exchange rate index in the present context) which can be derived from the two individual real exchange rates is QZ/QU. Proof: To calculate a real exchange rate (index) first express both individual rates in 'units of N-good per unit of X-good.' This is done by converting HD into HU. As the weight for the X-good's real exchange rate its expenditure share is chosen, which is QH/(QH+HU). Similarly, for the imported good, one minus this share is HU/(QH+HU). With QH+HU=QU and LD=QH, the real exchange rate is (QH/QU)(LR/QH) + (HU/QU)(HS/HU), which amounts with LR+HS=QZ to QZ/QU.

From Figure 1, the common Figure 2 can be derived.

For any given amount of the nontradable good, the value of domestically produced tradable goods is expressed in terms of the exported good alone. Note

[9] Another definition of the real exchange rate takes the product of the world market price index and the country's nominal exchange rate index and divides it by the domestic price index. Here, when assuming Purchasing Power Parity for tradable goods, the general results are not changed by employing one definition or the other.

Figure 2: Equilibrium with Inflow of Rent Income from Rest of the World in a Small Open Economy with Tradable and Nontradable Goods

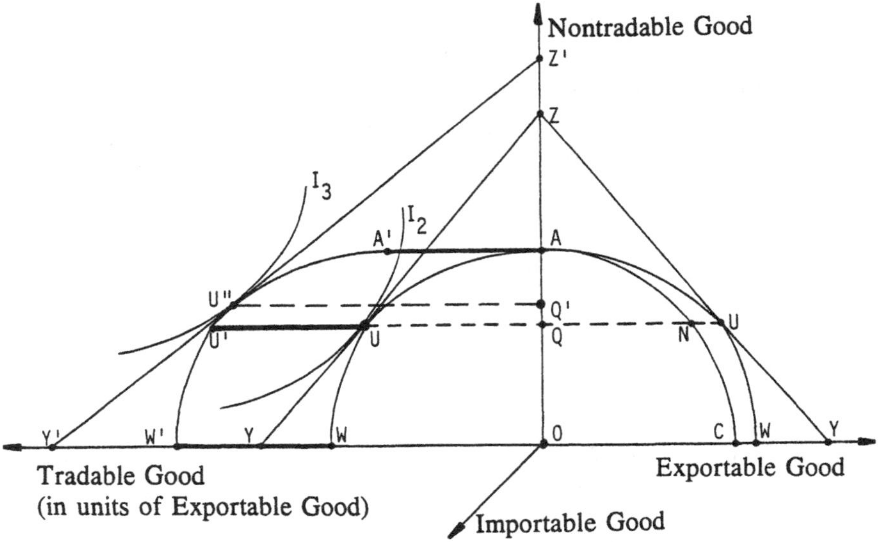

Note: explanations are provided in the text
Sources: adapted from Salter (1959, p. 227); Edwards / van Wijnbergen (1989, p. 1487)

that it is possible to achieve this specific value for any given amount of the nontradable good because the terms of trade are not influenced by the specific amount of exports or imports from the model economy. Thus, the transformation curve AUW for tradable and nontradable goods in the N-X-plane (nontradable good - exportable good plane) is achieved, which is mirrored onto the N-T-plane (nontradable good - tradable good plane) to avoid confusion with the labelling of indifference curves. The aggregate utility value associated with any point on this curve is taken from the ADE line of Figure 1. Because in almost all cases these utility levels can only be achieved by trade, the line AUW in the N-T-plane is not the usual autarky production frontier. Thus, it is not correct to label this line "production possibilities frontier" (Edwards / van Wijnbergen 1989, p. 1486) or "transformation curve, which traces out all possible combinations of traded and non-traded goods which may be produced" (Salter 1959, p. 228, who acknowledges this inaccuracy in his footnotes 5 and 7). Rather, it should be labeled "consumption possibilities frontier."

How will production and consumption react to an inflow of rent income from the rest of the world (e.g., higher oil revenues)? Three assumptions have to be made to facilitate the analysis. First, no domestic factors of production are needed to generate the rent income flow. (More on this in the context of the discussion of the economics of exhaustible resources below). The production possibilities sphere is left unchanged in the short run. Only if this increased income leads to new net investment this curve will change in the medium and long run. However, the consumption possibilities frontier is shifted into the exportable good direction and into the importable good direction of Figure 1, as will be discussed in detail when presenting Figure 3 at the end of this section. In terms of Figure 2 this shift is in the tradable good direction, e.g., by the amount AA'=UU'=WW'. The resulting new consumption curve is W'U'A'A.

The second assumption is that additional income is spent on all types of goods. It is natural to make this assumption of positive income elasticity for all goods. Only if the state, who is the primary recipient of the oil income in the GCC countries, spends it exclusively on foreign goods, foreign services or shares in foreign real capital, may the demand for nontradable goods not increase (if the export multiplier between the rest of the world and the home country is zero). However, even the Kuwait Investment Authority (KIA), which invests the means of Kuwait's 'Future Generations Fund' et al., received only part of Kuwait's oil income for investment abroad.

Third, the economic agents assume the oil revenue to be permanent; they have static expectations.

According to Figure 2, an excess demand for the nontradable good results (QQ'), which increases the relative price of this good to the prices of the imported and the exported good. Thus, the oil revenue creates a *real appreciation*. As was shown above, the initial real exchange rate is the absolute value of QZ/QU. Similarly, the new rate can be calculated as Q'Z'/Q'U'', which is clearly smaller than QZ/QU. The next effect is the shift of production from tradable goods to the nontradable good.[10]

---

[10] What happens to wages in this model of Dutch Disease? Because factors of production are domestically mobile, wages are always equal in both sectors. It is easy to show that in terms of achievable utility, wages are higher under the new production scheme and the new prices, at least if labor receives a constant share of production and the aggregate utility function is homothetic.

How does this correspond to the observed reality in GCC countries? Data on real exchange rates is almost not available. However, at least for the 1980s and for Saudi Arabia, the link between oil revenues and real exchange rate is shown in Graph 1.

Graph 1: Real Crude Oil Revenues (in $ 1985 billion) and Real Effective Exchange Rate (1985 = 100) for Saudi Arabia, 1980-1991

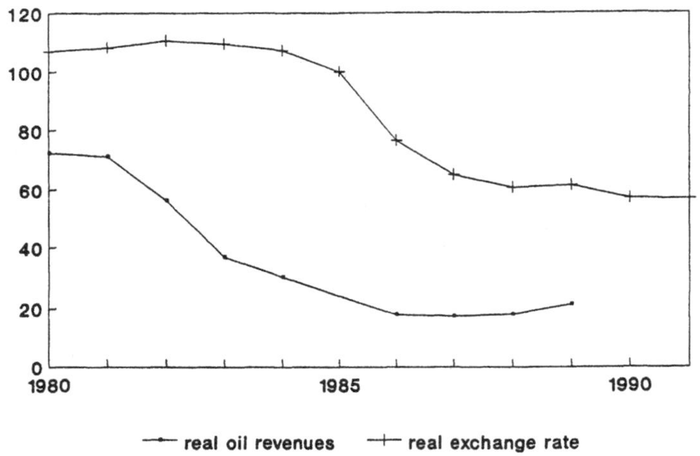

Source: International Monetary Fund (1992c)

Thus, the real depreciation due to the sharp fall in oil revenues came after a lag of several years.

Has there been a shift from the production of manufactured goods to the production of service sector goods? Again, data are hard to obtain. As is shown by Graph 2, in Saudi Arabia the share of the private service sector in GDP relative to the share of manufacturing was positively correlated with the real contribution of crude oil and gas to GDP.

Another indication is the change in the sectoral distribution of the labor force towards the service sector. At least for Saudi Arabia, the UAE and Oman there are complete data available, as is reported in Table 4. It has to be noted, however, that there has also been an increase in the share of industrial labor. While this may be regarded as contradicting the Dutch Disease theory, other explanations are possible, as will be outlined immediately when discussing industrial subsidization.

Graph 2: For Saudi Arabia 1969-1987: Contribution of Crude Oil and Natural Gas to GDP (billion 1984 Saudi Riyals); Private Service Sector in Relation to Manufacturing (%)

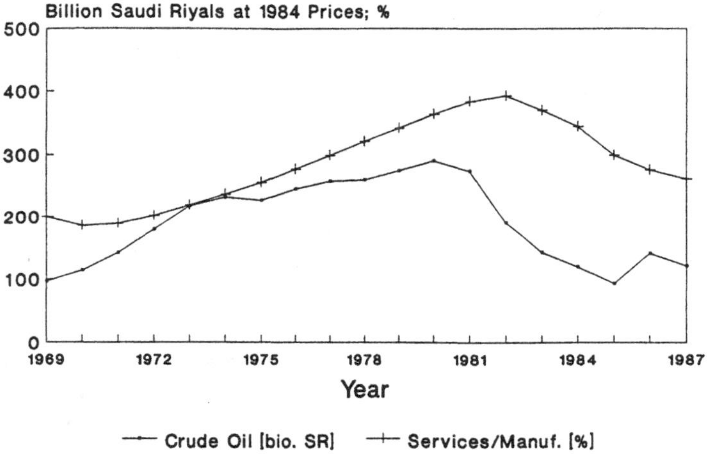

Notes: private services comprise wholesale and retail trade, transportation, communication, finance, insurance, real estate, community services (without electricity, gas and water); manufacturing comprises petroleum refining, petrochemicals, other non-oil manufacturing
Source: Saudi Arabian Monetary Agency, Central Department of Statistics

Table 4: Sectoral Distribution of Labor Force, 1965 and 1986-89 (%)

	Agriculture		Industry		Services	
	1965	1986-89	1965	1989-89	1965	1986-89
Saudi Arabia	68.0	48.5	11.0	14.4	21.0	37.2
Kuwait	2.0	-	34.0	-	64.0	-
UAE	21.0	4.5	32.0	38.0	47.0	57.3
Oman	62.0	50.0	15.0	21.8	23.0	28.6
Qatar	-	3.0	-	28.0	-	69.0
Bahrain	-	3.0	-	35.0	-	62.0
West Germany †	*8.5*	*4.0*	*46.8*	*38.0*	*44.6*	*58.0*

Notes: "-" means "not available"; † data for Germany are for 1970 and 1988
Sources: United Nations Development Programme (1992, p. 158); Institut der deutschen Wirtschaft Köln (1991, Table 8)

Overall, the figures suggest the growth in the service sector has been higher than in the manufacturing sector. However, these data have to be interpreted very cautiously. Dutch Disease models are static. A dynamic version for the GCC countries could be based on the notion of *absorptive capacity* (Eckaus 1989). The basic idea is that "capacity sets a limit to the amount of efficient investment physically possible" (Eckaus 1989, p. 18). This would set a ceiling on period-by-period investment and growth, not on total investment. It may be conjectured that such dynamic versions of Dutch Disease would also predict that growth in the secondary sector is slower than in the service sector if the economy receives increasing rent income from abroad.

However, the prediction of a slow growing secondary sector is also achieved in models of economic development which are not based on oil revenues or the like. As the data for West Germany in the above Table 4 shows, the trend toward nontradables can also be observed in countries without a sudden increase in the inflow of rent income from abroad. The reason is the following: Industrial countries experience a real appreciation in the course of industrialization. This is due to the fact that the productivity growth is much higher in the traded goods sector than in the nontraded goods sector. Under the assumption that wages in the two sectors do not match this difference (as is the case in neoclassical models as well as in the Scandinavian model with centralized wage bargaining, where wages would be equal in the two sectors) the relative price of nontraded goods will rise.[11]

The GCC governments may have implemented subsidies to support the industrial sector. The subsidy structures in the GCC countries will be analyzed in section B.1.4. One result is that subsidies for the industrial sector exist, but it is difficult to judge whether they have been higher than those for the service sector. Export promotion schemes are designed to diversify the sources of income as "most economists and politicians [in the GCC] believe that it is dangerous for an economy to rely on the income from one resource and not to industrialize in order to diversify and stabilize export earnings" (Koppers 1991, p. 117). The underlying assumptions are that citizens are short-sighted, capital markets are not perfect and/or industrial production has positive external effects. The vulnerability of the GCC due to the reliance on oil revenues was

---

[11] This argument has been used in the early 1990s by the International Monetary Fund to calculate purchasing power adjusted GNP figures. These figures serve to compare real income levels in countries at different stages of development. For every expenditure category a "true" exchange rate is calculated which in the case of nontraded goods not necessarily equals the nominal exchange rate (for details cf. Williamson 1983, pp. 213f). China has been moved up from position 8 under the traditional GNP ranking to position 3.

demonstrated in the 1980s when the GCC experienced a sharp drop in real GDP during the so-called oil-price war (cf. Graph 3).

In any case, GCC governments are convinced that industrialization is an important goal for their economies. In the "uniform strategy for the industrial development of the GCC States" the Ministers of Industry spell out the GCC members' commitments toward industrialization and toward subsidies and incentive schemes for investments in the manufacturing sector (Industrial Strategy 1985). Industrialization shall bring about diversity of sources of income, steady economic growth and prosperity. In the preamble of the document which was approved by the heads of state in November 1985,

> the GCC confirms that it is "[c]onvinced of the need to proceed with the option of economically viable industrialization, not only to diversify sources of income but also in order to create an industrial society that is aware of the importance of industrialization in the life of nations, the members of which society strive to acquire technical skills and absorb modern technology and adapt it in a manner conducive to a steady growth of economic development, and to the prosperity of the peoples of the GCC states" (Industrial Strategy 1985).

How likely is a sharp drop in oil revenues for the GCC member countries? Each GCC member country has to look at two factors to be able to predict its future oil incomes: (a) the future oil price and (b) its expected individual quantity supplied.

ad (a) Concerning the question of the future oil price, theory would start with stating the "r% rule" or "Hotelling rule" of *optimal depletion* (Hartwick 1989, pp. 3-5). For the marginal ton of oil supplied in each period the net profit in real terms rises at the real interest rate:

$$p_{t+1} - mc_{t+1} = (1 + r)\,(p_t - mc_t)$$

where p is the price for one ton of oil, mc is the cost of extracting the marginal ton, and r is the real interest rate. A smaller rate of expected price increase would make immediate extraction the best policy.

Assuming that extraction costs are constant, the real oil price would rise at the real interest rate. This is unrealistic. As Harberger (1993, p. 11) pointed out, with a nominal interest rate of 7% p.a. the r% rule would predict a 100% increase in nominal oil prices after 10 years and a 1800% increase after 50 years. No exhaustible resource exhibited such a steep price pattern in the past. Possible reasons are the following:

- extraction costs declined considerably;
- demand may have increased at a slower path than expected; nowadays the European Union and the US administration think about introducing energy taxes to reduce CO_2-emissions (this would reduce demand for oil); specifically, the EU is considering the introduction of an energy/carbon tax "to stabilise CO_2 emissions at 1990 levels by 2000 after which time Europe wants emissions to be cut" (MEED 1992); the plans are not yet implemented because the EU has promissed its industry to wait for the USA moving first;
- stocks have increased more rapidly than expected due to new discoveries;
- backstop technologies (i.e., production modes which do not use oil as input) have been developed faster and at lower prices than expected, thus reducing the optimal depletion time and price of oil (Hartwick 1989, pp. 36-39);
- governments may feel more secure to have the resource "at home" in the ground instead of having financial deposits abroad. They may feel that these deposits are at risk if foreign governments wanted to extort them for one reason or another; or the institutions which control earnings may fear that the institutions which decide on expenditure may spend the money on unproductive activities once it is on the country's banking accounts.[12]

It is often argued that OPEC has been able to increase prices because it is a monopolistic supplier. True, a monopolistic supplier of nonrenewable resources who faces a linear demand curve would extract at a slower rate and at higher prices than competitive suppliers. The appropriate r% rule would still apply, but marginal revenue is not equal to price minus marginal cost. When increasing the quantity the monopolist has to take into account intramarginal income changes due to changes in price.[13] However, models with a monopolistic supplier (OPEC) and several competitive fringe suppliers are more useful (Hartwick 1989, pp. 68-72). They show the monopolist will start production *after* the exhaustion of the fringe, at least if both face the same extraction costs. OPEC did not follow this prediction exactly. One reason may have been the wish to smooth out the intertemporal consumption path, combined with the inability to borrow for development using stocks in-ground as

---

[12] Khalid M. Abdulla (1991, pp. 32f) believes that, due to "excessive consumption," exhaustion of oil resources at a very high rate takes place. One might argue this is not correct for Saudi Arabia, but for Bahrain (the primary focus point of Abdulla's study). At the very least it shows that such fear exists.

[13] If demand exhibits constant elasticity with respect to the oil price (i.e., $q=p^{\epsilon}$), and extraction costs are zero, then the monopolist and the competitive solutions are identical.

collateral. However, deliberately or not, OPEC and GCC ran down their stocks at a slower rate than the competitive fringe countries, as Table 5 might suggest.[14]

Table 5: Oil Reserves of OPEC and GCC as Share of World Total, 1970 and 1992

	1970	1992
OPEC	66%	76%
GCC	39%	47%

Source: International Petroleum Encyclopedia ([1992], p. 318)

To conclude, because OPEC members are likely to become predominant oil suppliers in the following years and decades, OPEC may be able to act as a monopolist and raise prices. This depends on a business-as-usual assumption for demand, backstop technologies, known reserves and the willingness of important OPEC members to stay in the oligopoly and not to become fringe sellers.

This willingness to adhere to the cartel's decisions is not very high. True, the only country that quit OPEC up to now was Ecuador at the end of 1992, but often members could not resist the temptation to produce beyond the quota. The best example was the "price war" in 1985/86. In the 1980s, it took the GCC countries by surprise that OPEC's influence on oil revenues was much lower than expected. In the early 1980s OPEC had to cut sales to maintain the high oil price (i.e., although commodity terms of trade remained high until 1985, income terms of trade in the GCC countries experienced a sharp drop since 1981; for a discussion of the different terms of trade cf. El-Shagi 1991, pp. 25-28). The failure of OPEC to simultaneously control prices and maintain a high share in the oil market led to the 1985/86 "price war." As Graph 3 shows, this led to a further decline of prices and revenues (see also Bild / Cranfield 1990). Thus, even though oil exhibits some characteristics which would favor the building of an effective cartel (e.g., its homogeneity and the controlability of sales activities), the temptation to deviate is high.

ad (b) Concerning the question of quantities the GCC countries may supply, Table 5 already gives an indication: quantities are bound to increase. To analyse this in more detail, a closer look at the GCC members is taken. Table 6

---

[14] The figures in Table 5 are no proof of the statement because they do not take the different growth rates of oil discoveries into account.

Graph 3: Oil Price (US$, and real 1982 US$), GCC's Oil Revenues (US$ 10 billion)

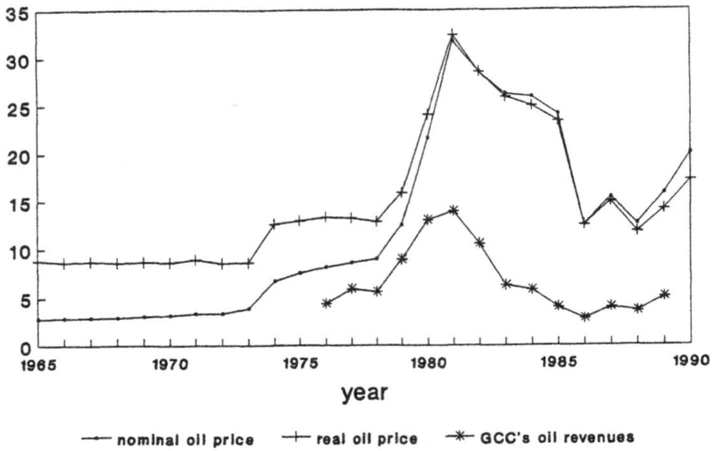

Sources: International Petroleum Encyclopedia ([1992], p. 309); King Fahd University of Petroleum & Minerals (1991, p. 59)

Table 6: Reserves/Production Ratio for Oil and Gas, 1976 and 1991 (years)

	Reach of Oil Reserves			Reach of Gas Reserves		
	1976	1991	(%)	1976	1991	(%)
Bahrain	14	5	0	49	20	1
Kuwait	90	177 *	20 *	87	126 *	8 *
Oman	23	17	1	23	121	3
Qatar	31	26	1	263 †	571	26
Saudi Arabia	48	87	57	39	95	30
UAE	44	109	21	41	192	32
GCC Total	**53**	**95**	**100**	**56**	**151**	**100**
World Total	30	46	219	49	63	749 ‡

Notes: (%) percent of GCC's total reserves at the end of 1991 (oil: 461 billion barrels; gas: 617 trillion cubic feet); * 1989 instead of 1991; † 1977 instead of 1976; ‡ 1990 instead of 1991

Memorandum: GCC's total oil reserves in 1976 were 262 billion barrels and gas reserves 157 trillion cubic feet, which accounted for 41% and 7.22% of world reserves, respectively; 1 cubic foot = 0.028 m^3

Sources: King Fahd University of Petroleum & Minerals (1991); Arab Petroleum Research Center (1992)

shows the reach of crude oil and natural gas reserves at current production levels to be more than 100 years for the GCC as a group.

It is most probable much more oil and gas is awaiting discovery under the Arabian Peninsula and Gulf; in fact, most of the reserve figures are already revised upward. Because the GCC's current world production share of oil is far lower than its world reserve share (22% vs. 46%), the GCC region will be a major player in the oil market in the decades lying ahead. However, Bahrain, Oman and also Qatar are constantly faced with the problem that their oil wells will run dry at the beginning of the next century. This seems to explain the aggressive dispute between Bahrain and Qatar over the barren but potentially oil-rich Hawar group of islands (Egyptian Gazette 18 August 1991; New Arabia No. 7, 1991). However, in Qatar the situation is less serious due to the high gas reserves. "With its enormous reserves of LNG [liquified natural gas] the emirate's economy is gradually being transformed into an almost wholly gas-based one" (Knipe 1993, p. 42). Bahrain has a secure income because it receives half of the oil from the Saafa offshore oil field between Bahrain and Saudi Arabia which is managed by Saudi Arabia. Estimated reserves of the field are 6.6 billion barrels, which will last for another 120 years at the 1990 production level of 150 000 barrels per day (Bild / Cranfield 1990, p. 161). Recently the oil handed to Bahrain has been increased to 100,000 b/d (Jordan Times 11 February 1993). This compares to only 42,000 b/d, which Bahrain produces itself. Because the seven Emirates of the UAE are relatively independent in their economic policies, it is interesting to note that only Abu Dhabi, Dubai and Sharjah have substantial oil reserves; Abu Dhabi's reserves will last for more than 125 years and Sharjah's for 117 years, but the reach of Dubai's oil is only 27 years (Bild / Cranfield 1990, p. 161).

Even for the countries with good prospects of future oil income (i.e., Saudi Arabia, Kuwait and the UAE), there are good reasons for a strategy of diversification. This fits into the old debate about diminishing factorial terms of trade for primary commodities. The debate was initiated by articles of Prebisch and Singer in 1950 (Palma 1989a, 1989b; Singer 1989, 1991). In the case of oil, they would argue that even if the r% rule would apply and prices as well as rent income would rise over time, another fact points to the inappropriateness to rely on the production of oil: positive external effects are low. Increases in productivity of oil production don't add much to the productivity of other sectors. Thus, spill-overs are at best the usual income multiplier effects; "at best" because this effect will be smaller if the economy runs near full-employment.

The additional problems a rentier state faces will be discussed in the section B.1.3.

The previous discussion of the economics of exhaustible resources allows to be more specific on the assumption that oil sales will produce a considerable inflow of rent income. There are three reasons why the GCC members' net profit from selling oil is much higher than the profit from selling renewable goods. First, the r% rule implies ever increasing net profits. These profits are called "royalty" or "dynamic rent" or "Hotelling rent." Second, to the extent they have lower costs than competitors, they receive the usual producer rent, which is called "differential rent" or "Ricardian rent." "[B]etween 1974 and 1978, the cost of finding and developing a barrel of oil in the United States was 4.06 U.S. Dollars, while, the equivalent cost in the Middle East was a mere 12 cents" (Abdulla 1991, p. 22).[15] Third, to the extent that the OPEC cartel establishes a monopolistic situation, oil sales include a "monopol rent." For details see Hartwick (1989, pp. 1-7, 59f).

It pays to analyze the Dutch Disease situation not only with the common Figure 2, but also with the three-dimensional graph in Figure 1. The result is shown in Figure 3.

The oil income leaves the production possibilities frontier ABC unchanged. However, it shifts the consumption possibilities frontier into the importable good direction and into the exportable good direction. Assuming as before that the income elasticity for the demand of all goods is positive, then in the new equilibrium D'' the consumption of all three goods will be increased. The real appreciation can be seen from the smaller slope of the line tangent to U'' than the slope of the line tangent to U' (which equals the slope of the line tangent to U). Furthermore, it becomes clear that exports will diminish considerably, even if production of the formerly exported good doesn't change. First, under zero-production and consumption of the nontradable good, the assumption of convex indifference curves means the additional income is spent on both the formerly exported and the formerly imported good. The new consumption point is E'. Following the general belief that domestic producers will first serve the domestic market before exporting, it is evident exports will diminish considerably. Second, allow consumers and producers to adapt to the new situation. Actually, in this concrete example with D'' being the optimal solution, no more non-oil goods will be exported even though some tradables are produced. This is always the case if the optimal solution lies in A'A''G''G'.

---

[15] If one takes all suppliers of energy sources as being the "relevant competitors", oil suppliers receive an even higher Ricardian rent. This producer rent shrinks the higher oil taxes and coal subsidies. Although economically unsound, production of coal with low or even negative gains is supported with arguments such as national autarky, supply security, social and employment structure or cultural heritage.

Figure 3: Equilibrium with Inflow of Rent Income from the Rest of the World in a Small Open Economy with Tradable Goods (Exportables and Importables) and with Nontradable Goods

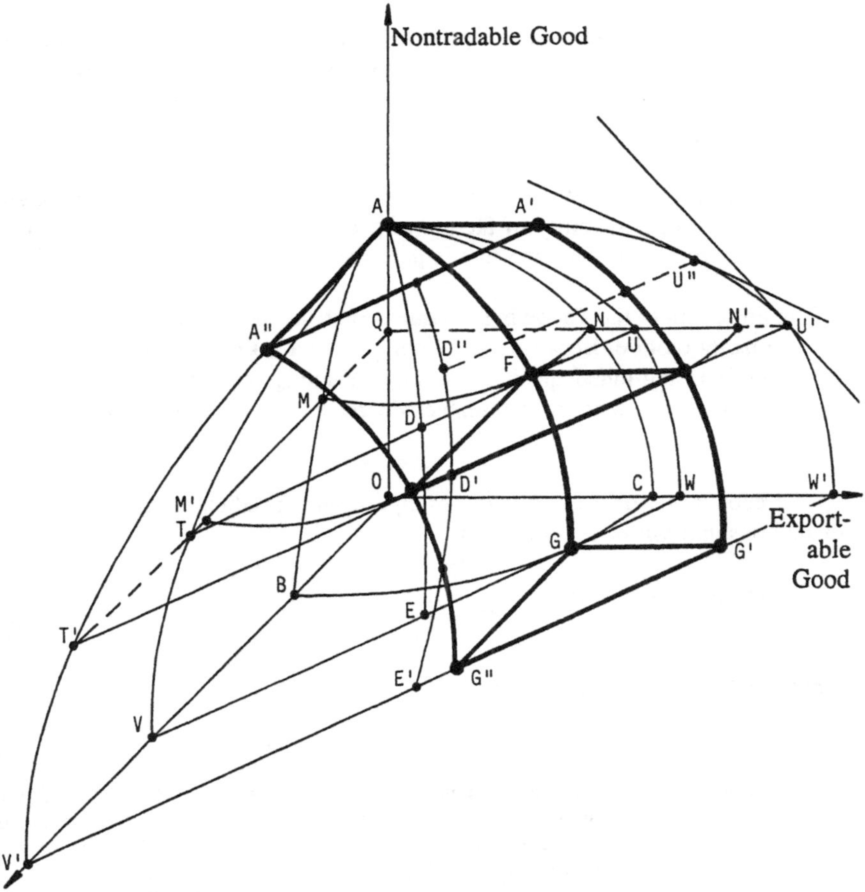

Note: explanations are provided in the text

This adds to the difficulties of the country. If the inflow of rent income fades away in later years, it has little current experience in exporting goods besides oil. However, this experience can be considered to be important for world market competitiveness. Know-how about international practices, management techniques, a cadre of regular customers and international reputation will be lost after years of almost exclusive production for the domestic market.

B.1.2. Dutch Disease in a Model with International Factor Mobility

The most serious objection against the previous model of Dutch Disease is the inappropriateness of the assumption of imperfect international mobility of factors of production. In the short run it may be plausible to consider factors of production as given and to assume a fix production possibility frontier for every country. In the medium and long run, however, many factors of production (such as real capital and labor) can be (and are!) transfered into the GCC economies from abroad.

Can there be a decrease in the production of tradable goods (T-goods) under perfect international mobility of factors of production? In a simple model with a one-stage production function this is not possible.

The intuition is the following. Assume that the factors of production are internationally mobile. Because the economy is small, the factors of production are available in unlimited quantities at the prevailing real price. Then it is not obvious that the production of tradables decreases if the price of nontradables increases.[16]

The economy works as follows. In equilibrium production of nontradables equals consumption of nontradables:

$$q_N = c_N \tag{1}$$

The trade balance is zero:

$$F + q_T = c_T \tag{2}$$

where F is the rent income from abroad.

[16] Because the analysis concentrates on the real economy, a note on the nominal figures seems to be called for. Assume that the actual nominal figures are linked through money supply to the real figures. Monetary policy has no real effect. If at all, this can only be justified by the concentration on long run effects. Formally, one can achieve this with the following model. The real consumption values c_T and c_N as well as the real exchange rate e are determined by the real model. Foreign prices (p_T^* and p_N^*) are fix. With PPP one gets $p_T = E\, p_T^*$, where E is the nominal exchange rate. By definition, $p_N = p_T / e$. With Fisher's Quantity Equation of Exchange, $c_T\, p_T + c_N\, p_N = v\, M$ is obtained, where v is the exogenous velocity of money circulation and M is the exogenous money supply. From this, E can be calculated:

$$E = \frac{v\, M}{\left(c_T + \frac{c_N}{e}\right) p_T^*}$$

Consumption:

Both tradable and nontradable goods are normal goods: an increase in income leads to higher consumption for both goods. In this model, let the aggregate utility function be the following homothetic Cobb-Douglas function:

$$u(c_T, c_N) = c_T^{\gamma_1} c_N^{\gamma_2} \qquad \text{with} \quad \gamma_1 + \gamma_2 = 1 \tag{3}$$

In general an intertemporal trade-off between today's and tomorrow's consumption takes place. However, with static expectations and equality between the discount factor and the real interest rate, it is possible to concentrate on the maximization for the current period.

In equilibrium, the marginal condition which has to hold is:

$$\frac{\partial u}{\partial c_T} + \frac{\partial u}{\partial c_N}\frac{\partial c_N}{\partial c_T} = 0 \tag{4}$$

If the left-hand side's sum is greater than zero, then aggregated utility can be increased by consuming less nontradable goods and more tradable ones.

Because $\partial c_N/\partial c_T = -e$ (due to $p_T \, \partial c_T + p_N \, \partial c_N = 0$ and $e = p_T/p_N$), one gets from equations (3) and (4):

$$\frac{c_T \, e}{c_N} = \frac{\gamma_1}{\gamma_2} \tag{5}$$

Thus, the expenditure share for each good remains constant.

Production:

$$q_T = a \, k_T^{\alpha} \qquad \text{and} \qquad q_N = a \, k_N^{\beta} \tag{6), (7}$$

where k_T and k_N are the inputs in the two sectors. Here the inputs are either capital goods or labor. It is straightforward to write down the model with more than one input; but this would not change the conclusions. If the coefficients α and β are less than 1, the production functions exhibit decreasing returns to scale. This indicates there are economic bottlenecks. Some factors are limited. Prominent candidates are environmental and infrastructural bottlenecks and institutional bottlenecks, such as property rights or public administration. The coefficient "a" represents the "economic size" or the "development level" of the economy:

- the resource endowments of the economy (including population),
- level of education, of management know-how and of technological standard of the society, and
- efficiency of production, which can be increased by regional cooperation; this point will again be considered in chapter B.2.

The equilibrium conditions are:

$$\frac{\partial q_T}{\partial k_T} = r^* \quad \text{and} \quad \frac{\partial q_N \left(\frac{1}{e}\right)}{\partial k_N} = r^* \qquad (8), (9)$$

where r* is the real price for the inputs. The asterix indicates that this price is determined by the world market.

The equilibrium condition yields for the inputs in the production of nontradables:

$$k_N = \left(\frac{a\beta}{e\ r^*}\right)^{\frac{1}{1-\beta}} \qquad (10)$$

The production of nontradables is positively influenced by a real appreciation if ß < 1:

$$\frac{\partial k_N}{\partial e} = \frac{1}{\beta - 1} \left(\frac{a\beta}{e^{2-\beta}\, r^*}\right)^{\frac{1}{1-\beta}} \qquad [< 0 \quad \text{for } \beta < 1] \qquad (11)$$

If the production function for nontradables exhibits almost constant returns to scale (i.e., if ß is close to 1), this derivative approaches $-\infty$. In this case, already a small appreciation is sufficient to induce a specific rise in the production of nontradable goods. When specifying the consumption process, it will be demonstrated that a rise in rent income from abroad increases the demand for nontradables. The larger ß, the smaller the appreciation which is needed to give rise to the additional production of these N-goods.

Result 1: There will only be a real appreciation due to an inflow of rent income from abroad if the production function of nontradables exhibits decreasing returns to scale.

In reality, at least in the short and medium run, it is likely there are factors which are not at the producers' control and which are bottlenecks. As mentioned above, an obvious candidate for such a bottleneck is public administration.

The equilibrium condition for the input in the tradables production yields:

$$k_T = \left(\frac{a\,\alpha}{r^*} \right)^{\frac{1}{1-\alpha}} \tag{12}$$

Result 2: In this simple economy with international mobility of factors of production, a change in the real exchange rate does not affect the production of tradables. Thus, even if there were a rise in the price of nontradables and in the production of nontradables, this would have no influence on the domestic production of tradables.

Note that this result only depends on the fact that neither the amount of nontradables nor its price influences the production of tradables. Otherwise, the specification of the technical production function is irrelevant.[17]

Interestingly, even though consumers initially only planned to increase consumption of tradables by a share of F, finally the consumption of tradables increases by the whole F, as can be seen from equation (12) in connection with equations (2) and (6). Consumption of nontradables does not increase by the whole e F γ_1/γ_2 to restore equilibrium because e decreases to induce the rise in production of nontradables.

There are several ways to change the economy under consideration such that Dutch Disease prevails. One has to link the production of tradables to the price of nontradables. Two ways are examined in which this can be done. First, labor

[17] There exists another problem. In the new equilibrium, the capital invested in the N-sector increases, while the investment in the T-sector does not change or (in the versions of the model to be explored immediately) decreases. There is nothing that assures that total investment is constant. Assume, for example, that total investment increases. If domestic agents would invest the differential, this would affect their consumption pattern. If foreign agents would provide the necessary capital goods, they would transfer the receipts to their home countries in future periods. The assumption of a zero trade balance would no longer hold. However, there seems to be no reason why the general conclusions (especially those concerning the production structure) should be changed by embodying specifically the investment process.

market conditions may provide such a link; second, the link may be due to a two-stage production function of tradables.

Although in the current simple model both labor and real capital are internationally mobile, there is an important difference between them. Under the assumption of transferability of gains, capitalists can employ their capital in country A, while spending the return abroad. Thus, when putting aside the question of risk, capital has to yield in every country the same real profit r* in terms of tradable goods, but this is not true for labor. Workers spend their income for the major part in the country where they work. They demand a compensation if they work in a country with higher costs of living due to higher costs of nontradable goods.

Let the only factor under control be labor, and rewrite equations (6) and (7):

$$q_T = a\, l_T^{\alpha} \quad \text{and} \quad q_N = a\, l_N^{\beta} \qquad (13), (14)$$

where l_T and l_N are the labor inputs in the two sectors.

The appropriate equilibrium conditions are then:

$$\frac{\partial q_T}{\partial l_T} = w \quad \text{and} \quad \frac{\partial q_N \left(\frac{1}{e}\right)}{\partial l_N} = w \qquad (15)$$

where w is the "producer-relevant" real wage, measured in T-goods per hour.

The foreign "producer-relevant" price index (if λ^* is constant and price changes are small) is:

$$p^* = p_T^{*(1 - \lambda^*)}\, p_N^{*\lambda^*} = p_T^* \left(\frac{1}{e^*}\right)^{\lambda^*} \qquad (16)$$

$$\text{where } \lambda^* = \frac{\dfrac{c_N^*}{e^*}}{c_T^* + \dfrac{c_N^*}{e^*}} \quad \text{(i.e., the consum. share of N-goods)}$$

The "consumer-relevant" foreign real wage w*/p* is:

$$\frac{w^*}{p^*} = w^* \frac{(e^*)^{\lambda^*}}{p_T^*} \tag{17}$$

With perfect international mobility of labor, domestic workers demand at least the same real wage; thus

$$\frac{w}{p} = w \frac{e^{\lambda}}{p_T} = w^* \frac{(e^*)^{\lambda^*}}{p_T^*} \tag{18}$$

$$\Rightarrow \quad w = \frac{w^* (e^*)^{\lambda^*}}{e^{\lambda}} \frac{p_T}{p_T^*} \tag{19}$$

Due to the various assumptions (i.e., small country, PPP for tradables, homothetic utility function) everything except e is constant. What happens if the inflow of rent income from abroad increases? Consumers will demand more nontradable goods. As was shown, a higher production of nontradables requires a real appreciation: e decreases. Thus, workers will demand a higher wage w.

Result 3: If this wage effect is present, the production of tradables will decrease even though there is no direct competition for scarce factors of production between the N- and the T-sector.

What happens to the level of real capital if it is included in the production function? With a Cobb-Douglas production function for tradables the input of capital goods diminishes if the input of labor goes down.[18] Thus, the decrease in production of tradables would be even greater.

To summarize the main result: In the simple neoclassical model the production of tradables is neither negatively nor positively influenced by a rise in rent income from abroad. This changes if the link between labor supply and costs of living is taken into account.

How realistic is this scenario for the GCC countries? First, the number of employment certificates for workers from abroad is limited, but it does not appear that this is a bottleneck for development. In the model it has been

---

[18] Essentially, this amounts to reducing "a" in equation (12).

implicitely assumed that the additional income due to the oil revenues is distributed to the consumers. Cum grano salis, this is the case in the GCC economies, especially if the specification "national" consumers is added. Furthermore, it has been assumed implicitely labor supply was only determined by the real wage, but not by wealth or income from transfer payments. This is not realistic. Wage claims are positively correlated with the level of other income.

Thus, the model does apply as long as international mobility of labor is ensured: real wages will increase and production of tradables will fall. However, employment is limited to workers from abroad. Citizens will only work in employments in which they are protected by law (e.g., government positions, counter-parts in enterprises on the management level and minimum national labor force requirements) or in high-pay positions if they are well-educated. This will be further discussed in section B.1.3. on the rentier mentality.

Another way in which the link between the price for nontradables and tradable goods production can be achieved is a two-stage production function of tradables.

As discussed earlier, the element which is necessary to achieve a real appreciation is a production of nontradables with decreasing returns to scale with respect to the inputs under consideration.

Consider the following new production function:

$$q_T = a\, k_T^{\alpha_1}\, d_N^{\alpha_2} \tag{20}$$

The element which is added now is the inclusion of nontradable goods (N-goods, d_N) as inputs in the production function of tradable goods. Such a two-stage production function seems to be a natural assumption in many cases because one can hardly imagine the production of tradables without the use of local goods (construction, transportation, consultants etc.).

In this case it is obvious that an increase in the price of nontradables increases the production costs of tradables. Thus, less tradables will be produced domestically.

Can this intuitive conclusion be changed by assuming a two-stage production function also for nontradables? No. The additional production of nontradables induces a need for more tradables as inputs. These inputs will reduce the possible consumption of tradables. This does not change the increase in the costs of inputs for the production of tradables which results in a reduction of T-goods production.

Result 4: If the production function of nontradables exhibits decreasing returns to scale and nontradables are inputs in the production of tradables, then Dutch Disease prevails.

What *implications for regional cooperation* result from the Dutch Disease models? The GCC economies are considerably open to factors of production; the previous models of Dutch Disease would not be appropriate. Because labor markets become increasingly regulated it seems adequate to investigate the implications of the model with international mobility of factors of production and two-stage production functions. The production functions for a country are:

$$q_T = a\, d_N^{\alpha_1}\, k_T^{\alpha_2} \quad \text{and} \quad q_N = a\, d_T^{\beta_1}\, k_N^{\beta_2} \qquad (21), (22)$$

In this model, two countries A and B may differ in the following ways:

a) rent income from abroad (F_A and F_B);
b) economic size (coefficients a and b in the production functions of countries A and B);
c) productivity of T-sector vs. N-sector (α_1, α_2 vs. β_1, β_2 in the production functions);
d) consumers' appraisal of T-goods vs. N-goods (γ_1, γ_2 in the aggregate utility functions).

The GCC countries differ in their rent income from abroad and in their economic importance. For simplicity, assume $\alpha_1 + \alpha_2 = \beta_1 + \beta_2$ in both countries, and the aggregated utility functions are the same in both countries.

Reference case: Cooperation of two identical economies

First, assume both economies are identical and regional cooperation has the effect of improving productivity by increasing the coefficient a (i.e., the 'economic size' of *each* economy). At first glance it may look strange that regional cooperation can improve productivity, due to the fact that all goods and factors are already mobile. One way to justify the approach is to assume nontradable goods have been restricted from trading by government intervention and these goods are tradables within the union.[19] As is shown in the next chapter (B.2.), there are several ways in which regional cooperation can improve economic efficiency in the GCC region.

In this setting, a real depreciation results due to regional cooperation if the economies are earning rent income from abroad (e.g., through oil sales); Dutch Disease is "cured" to some extent. Before giving the economic explanation for this result, it is stated mathematically. As is known from equation (5), in equilibrium:

$$\frac{1}{e}\,\frac{\gamma_1}{\gamma_2} = \frac{c_T}{c_N}$$

$$\Rightarrow \quad \frac{1}{e}\,\frac{\gamma_1}{\gamma_2} = \frac{q_T + F - d_T}{q_N - d_N} \tag{23}$$

From equations (21) and (22), in connection with the equilibrium conditions for production:

$$\frac{\partial\, q_T}{\partial\, d_N} = \frac{1}{e}\;; \quad \frac{\partial\, q_t}{\partial\, k_T} = r^*\;; \quad \frac{\partial\, q_N}{\partial\, d_T} = e\;; \quad \frac{\partial\, q_N}{\partial\, k_N} = e\, r^* \qquad \text{(24) to (27),}$$

the calculation of d_N, d_T, q_T and q_N is straightforward.

How will regional cooperation (i.e., an increase in the coefficient a) change the equilibrium condition (23)? First, concentrate on the right-hand side of equation (23). Supposing for a moment that e is fix yields

---

[19] This echoes the distinction of Balassa / Stoutjesdijk (1974) between national, regional and international goods and services. Before cooperation, only international goods and services are internationally traded. When regional cooperation takes place, regional goods and services are tradables in the cooperation region. For simplicity assume, here, that no national goods and services exist.

$$\frac{\left(\frac{\partial(q_T + F - d_T)}{\partial a}\right) / (q_T + F - d_T)}{\left(\frac{\partial(q_N - d_N)}{\partial a}\right) / (q_N - d_N)} = \tag{28}$$

$$\frac{\left(\frac{1}{1-\alpha_1-\alpha_2}\frac{q_T}{a} - \frac{1}{1-\beta_1-\beta_2}\frac{d_T}{a}\right) / (q_T + F - d_T)}{\left(\frac{1}{1-\beta_1-\beta_2}\frac{q_N}{a} - \frac{1}{1-\alpha_1-\alpha_2}\frac{d_N}{a}\right) / (q_N - d_N)} \equiv Q$$

Thus, if Q = 1, a change in the size of the economy leaves the right-hand side of the equilibrium condition (23) unchanged; the real exchange rate does not have to adjust. However, if Q < 1 (i.e., an increase in the coefficient "a" leads to a decrease in the right-hand side of equation (23)), then the real exchange rate has to increase to restore equilibrium, as can be shown with equations (21) to (27). How does the value of Q depend on the inflow of rent income? From (28) and under the earlier-mentioned assumption $\alpha_1 + \alpha_2 = \beta_1 + \beta_2$,

(i) F = 0 implies Q = 1.

(ii) F > 0 implies Q < 1. In this case, e has to increase to restore equilibrium.

Result 5: If the economies A and B are identical, the sectors "tradables" and "nontradables" are equally productive and both economies receive (the same) oil income F, then regional cooperation yields an increase in the production of tradables *and* nontradables. The real appreciation which took place in earlier periods due to the inflow of rent income from abroad is revised to some extent. The increase in production of tradables will be overproportionate, and the consumption of tradables increases overproportionately. In other words, regional cooperation can serve as a "remedy" for Dutch Disease if both economies are oil exporters. (The lessons to be learned for the GCC are stated at the end of this section.)

The economic explanation is that in a growing economy, due to the increase in "a," the oil income is relatively less important. The real appreciation is partly revised and accordingly the dominance of the service sector is partly revised.

Second case: Cooperation of an oil-exporter with an oil-importer

Suppose the two economies are still identical, except for the size of oil revenues: $F_A > 0$, $F_B = 0$. Thus, before cooperation $e_A < e_B$. Assume the effect of cooperation, besides increasing a and b, is an equalization of the real exchange rate. This may be economically justified if N-goods are "sheltered goods" (Salter 1959, p. 556), due to natural barriers and government protection. If government protection is abolished within the union, prices for these N-goods will be unified to e_C ("C" for cooperation).

There are two effects when cooperation takes place:

a) $da > 0 \Rightarrow de_A > 0$ (cf. reference case above)
$db > 0 \Rightarrow de_B = 0$ (cf. reference case above)

b) Equalization of e_A and e_B; where is the new e_C?
Consumers will buy N-goods in country B as long as $e_B > e_A$
$\Rightarrow$ e_B will decrease, e_A will increase
$\Rightarrow$ e_C will be somewhere between e_A and e_B; due to effect a) closer to e_B than to e_A.

Result 6: When countries A and B are identical (in the terms of the present model), except that A is an oil exporter while B's deposits are (almost) depleted, both countries A and B profit from cooperation in terms of overall production and income. However, cooperation helps A to reduce Dutch Disease, while it imposes this "illness" on B.

Third case: Cooperation of an economically large and an economically small country

Suppose a > b (i.e., country A is "larger" than country B).

(i) Starting from $F_A = F_B = 0$ yields $e_A = e_B$ before cooperation if $\alpha_1 + \alpha_2 = \beta_1 + \beta_2$. Thus, one is in the reference case, number (i).

(ii) Now suppose $F_A > F_B$ such that e_A just equals e_B before cooperation; then one is again in the reference case. The condition for the necessary difference in magnitude of the rent income inflows in both countries can be derived by the following procedure. Starting from $\gamma_1/(e\gamma_2)=c_T/c_N$, it is possible to calculate $\partial F/\partial e$. The result shows that for the same dF the real appreciation will be smaller in a "bigger" economy (assuming that both $a>1$ and $b>1$). In the case of $\alpha_1 + \alpha_2 = \beta_1 + \beta_2$ the following result is obtained. To induce the same increase in the real exchange rate e, F_A and F_B must differ more than a and b suggest: $F_A = (a/b)^{\sigma} F_B > (a/b) F_B$, with $\sigma \equiv 1/(1-\alpha_1-\alpha_2) > 1$. (An application for the GCC will follow immediately.)

(iii) Next suppose $F_A = F_B > 0$. This implies $e_A > e_B$ before cooperation, and a similar situation as in the second case results. Here, country B will experience a relief from Dutch Disease at the expense of country A.

What can be learned for the GCC countries? Which case is most realistic? Take the extreme case: Saudi Arabia and Bahrain. This is the third case, number (ii), with A being Saudi Arabia and B being Bahrain. It makes sense to assume that regional cooperation unifies the two N-sectors. Bahrain is closer to Riyadh than Jeddah or Abha are; if it is taken for granted that the whole non-tradables sector in Saudi Arabia can be treated as having the same price, there is no problem with making Bahrain's N-sector a part of this sector, too. Now, because F_A is much greater than F_B, e_A is smaller than e_B. Thus, the service sector prices are before cooperation lower in Bahrain than in Saudi Arabia, and it will be harder for Bahrain to industrialize after cooperation. A similar case to Bahrain would be Oman and perhaps Qatar; Kuwait and the UAE can be compared to Saudi Arabia in this model (cf. Tables 1 and 6). Note that the underlying assumption is that nontradables were protected from being traded before regional cooperation took place and that regional cooperation has the effect to eliminate protection.

B.1.3. Problems in a Rentier State

The GCC members are "rentier states." What does this mean? One can distinguish between rentier countries, rentier economies (being a subset of rentier countries) and rentier states (a subset of rentier economies).

A rentier country is a "countr[y] that receive[s] on a regular basis substantial amounts of external rent" (Mahdavy 1970, according to Abdulla 1991, p. 23).[20] A rentier economy is a special case of a rentier country, viz., "an economy in which rent plays a major role" (Beblawi / Luciani 1987, p. 11, according to Abdulla 1991, p. 24). The rentier state in turn is "a special case of the rentier economy" (Abdulla 1991, p. 25), where "the state becomes the main intermediary between the oil sector [the rent generating sector] and the rest of the economy" (Abdel-Fadil 1987, p. 83, according to Abdulla 1991, p. 24).

The GCC countries fit into the definition of the rentier economy: Rent income from oil plays a major role in the GCC economies. The service sector bias as explained by the Dutch Disease theory is the outcome of this. Furthermore, these countries are rentier states. The central government receives and distributes the oil revenues, as Figure 4 shows.[21] The figures in Figure 4 indicate shares in GCC's overall GDP. They have been calculated from the National Accounts (Appendix Table A1), the Central Governments' Budgets (Appendix Table A2) and the Balances of Payments (Appendix Table A3) for the GCC member states.

Rentier states face specific problems which are labelled as "rentier mentality" and "directly unproductive, profit-seeking (DUP) activities." These two phenomena should not be confused. While the rentier mentality creates inactivity, the profit-seekers are active, but in a resource-wasting manner.

The *rentier mentality* results if an individual receives an economic rent and has static expectations about this income. Of course, it is not necessary that the

---

[20] To be precise, Mahdavy uses the term "rentier state" for what is labeled here "rentier country." The present change of notation can be justified because the term "rentier state" was later used by other authors in a way different to Mahdavy's. Abdulla ascribes the introduction of the term "rentier state" to Mahdavy. This is not correct. Already Lenin used the phrase "Rentnerstaat" to refer to a rent-receiving society (Bhagwati 1982, p. 990, fn. 1).

[21] In the case of the United Arab Emirates, the oil revenues are actually collected and distributed by the federal government as well as by the largely independent governments of the seven emirates, mainly Abu Dhabi and Dubai.

Figure 4: Monetary Flows in a Rentier State; Shares in GCC's GDP, 1989

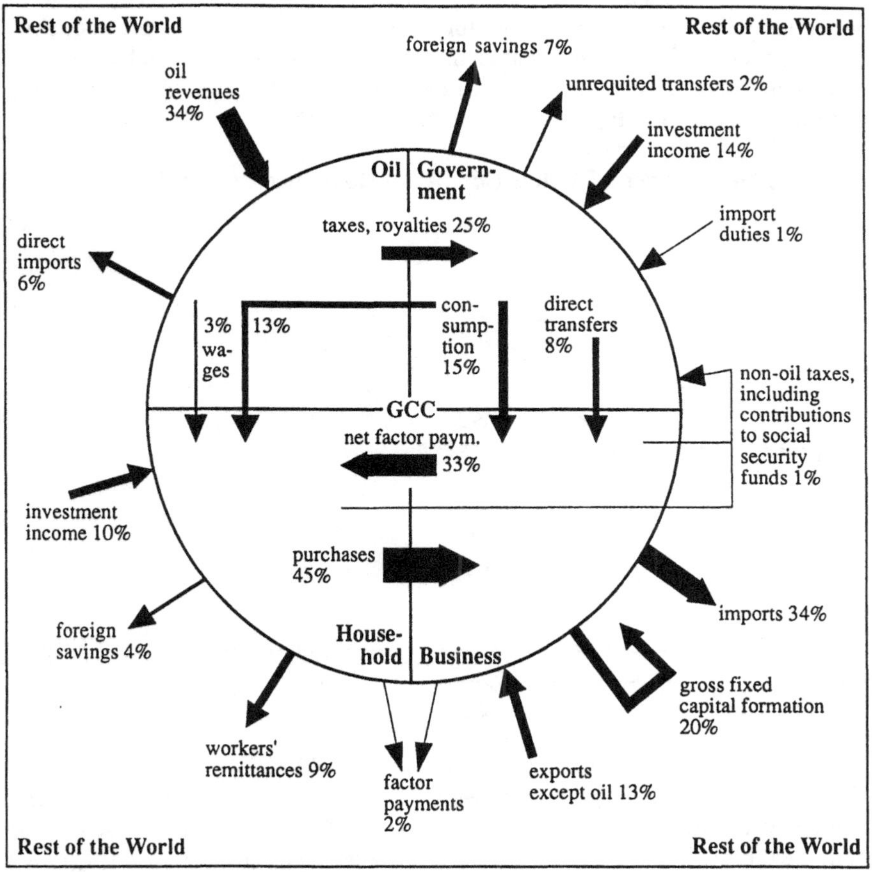

Notes: figures cover as many GCC countries as data allow for (cf. Appendix Tables A1, A2 and A3 for data limitations)

Sources: the idea for the graphical presentation has been adapted from Abdulla (1991, p. 41) who quotes Abdel-Fadi (1987, p. 87) as source; sources for figures are given in Appendix Tables A1, A2 and A3

state is the intermediary who receives and distributes the rent. However, in the eyes of an individual getting the rent from the government for a long time, it is the state that is the source of the rent, not the rest of the world. This reduces the feeling of self-responsibility and forward-looking even more. The economically important fact about the rentier mentality is its influence on labor supply. Here, labor supply is meant in a broad sense (i.e., self-employment by entrepreneurs is included). Figure 5 depicts the relationship.

Figure 5: Dependence of Labor Supply on Rent Income and Expatriates

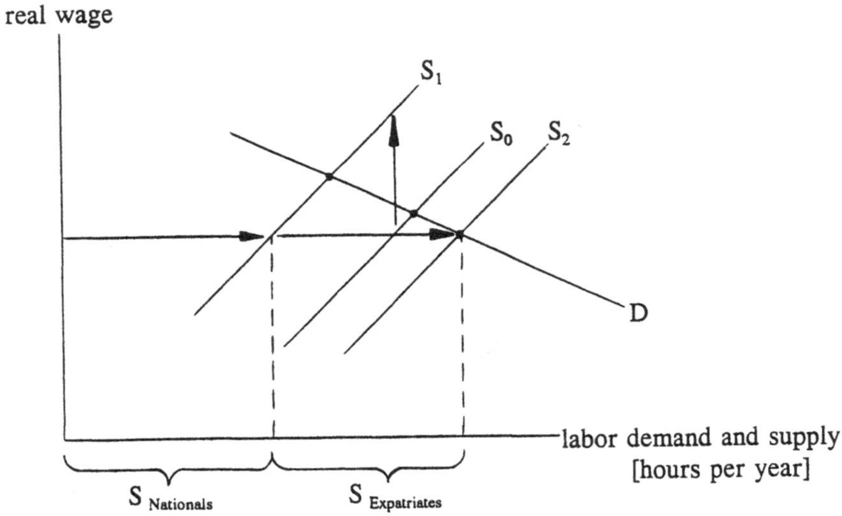

At low wage and wealth levels, labor supply will be dominated by the substitution-effect: a higher wage induces more people to work because they substitute (extra) work for leisure (positive slope of S_0). Higher non-labor income from wealth or from rent shifts the labor supply curve upward (from S_0 to S_1) due to the income-effect. People now want more leisure; their opportunity costs for additional work have increased. The result is lower employment and a higher real wage. GCC countries avoided this situation by hiring expatriate workers (resulting in a shift of the labor supply curve from S_1 to S_2), thereby reducing the job participation of nationals in the competitive sector even more.

Of course, one has to be careful in order not to exaggerate the rentier mentality. Many GCC nationals feel it is a pleasure to be creative and do socially valuable work. Nevertheless, there is much anecdotal and serious evidence of the existence of rentier mentality in GCC countries. In analyzing the GCC labor market, one of the leading Gulf economists summarized the situation as follows:

- the share of foreign workers in total employment in the six GCC states ranges between 40 to 80%;
- local labor participation in the non-governmental sector ranges from 2 to 30%, with a median of 10% only;
- there is substantial disguised unemployment in the public sector;
- recently open unemployment of nationals was envisaged by some GCC countries (Al-Fayez 1992, p. 13).

Special forms of (self-)employment, which result if expected gains are high enough, are *directly unproductive, profit-seeking (DUP) activities*. In general, they result if individuals or groups feel they can improve or protect their share of the rent sufficiently by influencing the government or secondary rent distributors in one way or another. In this case, the society does not only suffer the usual deadweight loss, but there is a tendency to transform rents into social costs.

The "full rent-dissipation hypothesis" by Posner (1975, p. 812) states all rents are wasted by DUP activities: "If 10 firms are vying for a monopoly having a present value of $1 million, and each of them has an equal chance of obtaining it and is risk neutral, each will spend $100,000 (assuming constant costs) on trying to obtain the monopoly." However, this hypothesis is not correct, neither theoretically nor empirically. The simplest theoretical model to inquire into Posner's conjecture is as follows (cf. Tullock 1980). Let there be two identical rent-seekers. They face a lottery with value V. The winning probability of player 1 is $p_1 = x_1 / (x_1 + x_2)$, where x_i is the stake of player i. The winning probability of player 2 is $p_2 = 1 - p_1$. Player 1's expected net profit is $E_1 = p_1 V - x_1$. Calculating the Nash-equilibria from the marginal conditions is straightforward and yields $x_1 = x_2 = V/4$ or 0. The only solution which is stable is the first (i.e., V/4). Total costs are V/2, but not V as Posner supposed. However, the case of N players yields $N x_i = V (N - 1) / N$, which is for N = 10 close to Posner's full rent-dissipation.

Rent-seeking can absorb more resources than rents at stake if the rent-seekers are too optimistic about their individual probabilities of winning, but this need not be the case for excessive rent-seeking. Even when being rational and well-informed, rent seekers may invest more than is actually at stake.

Tullock (1980) inquired into the following formula for the individual winning probability:

$$p_i = \frac{x_i^r}{\sum_j x_j^r}$$

where the sum is over all participants, and r is a positive coefficient. The bigger r, the flatter the cost curve (i.e., the marginal costs an individual faces when she wants to increase her winning probability by a fixed amount – given the other players' expenditures – decreases in r). The larger r, the more an additional \$ pays off. Here, the optimal total rent-seeking inputs can be greater than the total rent V. In equilibrium, $N x_i = r V (N - 1) / N$, which is stable for $r < N / (N - 2)$ and which is less than V only for $r \leq N / (N - 1)$. (For details see Tullock 1980).

Empirically, Posner's full rent-dissipation hypothesis has been discredited for the U.S. federal budget (Tullock 1988, pp. 469-478). The rent-seeking activities of the lobbyists in Washington do "not seem to be even close to the economic value of the favors dispensed by the government" (p. 469). As will be pointed out immediately, also in the context of the GCC economies, doubts about the validity of Posner's hypothesis are possible.

Krueger (1974) introduced the term "rent-seeking" for the wasteful struggle for monopoly profits resulting from the distribution of import licences by the government. Bhagwati (1982) puts rent-seeking activities in a broader framework and groups DUP activities into four all-embracing categories. Especially the possibilities to lobby for better treatment by the government are manifold. Economic agents may try to influence trade policy, government spending, the tax system, regulations, control mechanisms and penalties.

Are the GCC societies rent-seeking societies? A detailed study of the rent-opportunities in the GCC should start with the government budgets. Of course, for outsiders it is difficult to assess the various channels through which rent-seekers may gain control over the governments' decision making process. Only some distributive means which are common to all GCC countries and which may be susceptible to lobbying will be highlighted (cf. Abdulla 1991, pp. 28-32). Most or all GCC states

– buy private land at prices that are much higher than their market value;

- employ nationals even if there is no real need for them, thus, creating hidden unemployment and distracting labor from productive activities;[22]
- issue limited numbers of work permits for expatriate workers, such that demand for these permits exceeds supply;
- provide goods and services, particularly in the areas of health, education, housing and social services;
- develop infrastructure, such as highways, airports, and seaports;
- restrict to nationals the practice of many professions and trades, such as wholesale and retail trade, import and export, rental, banking, insurance. This limits the competition on some labor markets and some service markets considerably and creates the profession of "sponsor" (arabic: al-kafīl = sponsor, bail; agent). The sponsor is necessary to get an entry visa, he acts as a trade agent, service agent, distributor, employer, and partner in joint ventures (Westerich 1990, p. 467). "The influential Saudi business community consists of a few families who are continually solicited by potential [foreign] investors" and merchants (Ernst & Whinney 1989b, p. 3). Insofar as the sponsor is only necessary to get access to a profession or trade, his price or fee should be almost zero in a competitive environment. The problem in practice is that it is not possible to set up binding contracts which restrict the rights of the sponsor, and changing the sponsor is not easy.[23] An important regulation is that companies in the GCC states have to be at least 51% GCC-owned. Exceptions to the rule are Saudi Arabia, Dubai's Jebel Ali Free Zone since 1985 and Bahrain since 1991 (but most direct subsidies and incentives are restricted to companies with a GCC-majority, as will be shown in the next section). In its struggle to prepare for the post-oil period, Bahrain allows 100% foreign-owned businesses. "The decision to allow wholly-owned foreign companies will come as a shock to many of Bahrain's merchants who have traditionally enjoyed monopolies on the representation of foreign companies' goods and services" (Nicholson 1991);
- "regulate the type and size of industrial undertaking through an approval and license process" (As-Sudais 1985, p. 265). In addition, advice, technical assistance, exemptions, protection and financial aid are provided. "Refusal of an industrial license application at the present time is often based on the

---

22 Sultan Qaboos from Oman complained that the youth was rather waiting for government jobs than seeking employment in the private sector. He advised young men and women "not to waste their time waiting for vacancies in government employment different to those in which they have been trained" (Arab News 20 November 1992).

23 For example, the sponsor is responsable for the actions of foreign partners. Often he even keeps their passports and has to agree on travels abroad (Müller 1990).

grounds that a similar plant exists or that a similar license has already been issued" (As-Sudais 1985, p. 266).

Some means of GCC governments to distribute rents do not seem to exhibit opportunities for rent-seeking: states subsidize basic food, electricity, water, gas, and gasoline, and they collect almost no taxes.[24]

However, the existence of government interventions is not enough to explain the waste of resources by DUP activities. In addition, lobbyists must be convinced that they can significantly influence the distribution of rents (e.g., in the above model, a small r yields only small rent-seeking activities when compared to the total rent available). Furthermore, they have to take dynamics and asymmetry into consideration. If there is the credible threat of overbidding by a powerful competitor for the rents, then total rent-seeking activities may be quite small (Yang 1993).

Some evidence points to the existence of DUP activities in the GCC. A profit-protecting activity by importers is to hinder competition that could result from domestic or regional production. This is all the more true for the GCC countries because trade has been a major business activity for a long time, whereas manufacturing and industrial production only recently came into being. Refering to the Gulf, Hablutzel (1981, pp. 7f) concludes that "the communities of importers – represented in Chambers of Commerce, and generally constituting powerful interest groups – regarded the importation of an article as far more interesting than its domestic production and tended, in asserting their vested interests, to retard the advent of industrialization to some degree" (according to Abdulla 1991, p. 47). Therefore, it is important for new industrial investors to have an influential sponsor; and thus, one unproductive activity creates the next.[25]

---

[24] Of course, some scope for rent-seeking activities exists in the field of direct cash subsidies, but these are "limited to only a few basic products, such as poultry production, meat products, fresh milk and some vegetable oils" (Al-Fayez 1992, pp. 16f). The tendency is to replace such subsidies by tariff protection.

[25] Hence, the *directly* unproductive activity of industrialists lobbying against merchant lobbyists may be *indirectly* productive or welfare-improving. Bhagwati had such effects in mind when he added the word "directly" in the title of his study on directly unproductive, rent-seeking (DUP) activities. It is an example for his Category-2-activities (which shift an initially distorted situation to a finally distortion-free one) which may be either welfare-improving or immiserizing (Bhagwati 1982, pp. 996f, 1000). Refering to the analysis of second-best situations, Bhagwati (p. 991) notes that "when distortions exist almost anything can happen."

A related aspect is the degradation of manual work which can be primarily ascribed to its historically low valuation in society, but also to the fact that the marginal return on rent-seeking activities is higher than on productive work. The vocational trainings, which are available only to GCC nationals, do not serve in practice to train manual workers; rather, the graduates want to improve their chances of getting white collar jobs, in the government if possible.

Serious doubts can be raised about the claim that DUP activities result in waste of the same magnitude as the rent at stake in the GCC economies. First, GCC societies are not open in the sense that rents can easily be diverted from one recipient to another. This is mainly due to the tribal nature of the GCC societies.[26] Second, if the population grows at a higher rate than rent income, winning probabilities would diminish more and more in the future. Government employment would reach a satiation level and middle or high ranks would not easily be available for new entrants. The positive future expectations for GCC oil income have been outlined in section B.1.1. However, these revenues are unlikely to grow faster than GCC's population. According to World Bank estimates (World Bank 1992, pp. 268, 285) GCC's population will more than double between 1990 and 2025 (i.e., within one generation) from 22 million to 57 million.

The pressure on young GCC citizens to seek productive activities gets higher as rents per capita are reduced over time when the population increases more rapidely than government revenues and as rent-seeking becomes more and more costly when government's freedom of action is limited by vested interests. Sheikh Hisham M. Nazer, the Saudi Minister of Planning, in 1984 referred to this when he described the future of Saudi Arabia: "The only way to achieve this [Saudi Arabia's survival in the modern world] is to create an environment in which healthy, well-educated individuals can work; and thus, add to the competitiveness of the nation. ... The sooner our people learn that the only way towards a better life is hard [and productive] work, the sooner we will solve the problem of a tired youth" (Entwicklung + Zusammenarbeit 1984, p. 16; own translation).

---

[26] Tullock (1980, p. 103) pointed out that "if one is going to distribute rents, nepotism is a good thing because it reduces the number of players and, therefore, the total investment [in rent-seeking activities]. This is one of the classical arguments for hereditary monarchies." Of course, he hastens to point out that this is not costless because, by reducing the number of competitors for a specific rent (e.g., a job), "you may eliminate the best candidate or even the best two thousand candidates." One should also not miss the "if" in the pro-nepotism argument.

B.1.4. Problems with Exploiting Comparative Advantages

Because the governments in the GCC want to assist their countries' economic development by supportive and indicative planning, they have to make up their minds about which investments deserve administrative, technical and financial support. One theoretical answer would be to give identical incentives to all sectors by non-discriminatory low interest rates, equal import tariffs on all products, equal tax rates etc. However, this would require that government allows the private sector to build the necessary infrastructure and charge other users a fair price. A strategy of balanced growth with the simultaneous promotion of all sectors would only be appropriate if the governments were convinced that productivity as well as external effects were equal in all sectors.

If governments want to promote specific activities, two general lines could be pursued: supporting either the production of nontradables or the production of tradables. In both cases the long-run comparative advantages of the Gulf societies should be assessed. First and mainly the tradables production will be discussed.

The question "What are the international comparative advantages of the GCC countries?" is generally answered along the lines of the Heckscher-Ohlin Theorem of relative factor endowments. For tradable goods and international immobility of factors of production – the context of the Heckscher-Ohlin Theorem – it states that international trade leads through a shift in factor prices to a change in factor employment relations in favor of the abundant factors and to the disadvantage of the scarce factors. This implies comparative advantages for some tradable services in the GCC:

- services which exploit advantages due to experience and location (i.e., trade, banking and finance, oil-related management services, tourism).

Because Gulf planners noticed an abundance of oil, gas and financial resources, they saw two more lines of comparative advantages:[27]

- downstream production in the oil sector (i.e., petroleum refining and petrochemicals production); and
- energy- and capital-intensive production.

---

[27] To give just one example: "By international standards, all inputs (i.e., land, capital, electricity, water, energy sources and fuels) are provided at comparatively lower rates [in the GCC] *owing to the region's revealed comparative advantages*" (Al-Fayez 1992, p. 12, emphasis in original).

However, the Heckscher-Ohlin result changes if factors can be internationally traded. GCC countries do not restrict the employment of financial resources to the import of capital goods; these resources can be invested abroad without problems. Petroleum can be exported instead of using it as an input in the domestic production process or as an energy source. A different case is the use of associated gas as feedstock or energy source. This gas has high transportation costs; and thus, it can justifiably be sold at nominal cost. But, even with cheap input of energy and feedstock, it is not inevitable that the above two production lines are profitable. Important factors of production are still missing – such as technical know how, capital goods, management skills, skilled labor, organization (Looney 1989) – and transportation and marketing costs may be quite high.

To these objections, there are two theoretical answers which both take a dynamic view, but point in different directions. First, one could note that some manufactured goods have only *imperfect substitutes* on the world market (Benjamin / Devarjan / Winer 1989). Here, local producers could gain production and management experience through learning by doing. Later, when oil revenues decrease, products for the world market could be produced to earn foreign exchange for importation of production factors and consumer goods for which GCC countries have a comparative disadvantage. Looney (1989, p. 96) points in a similar direction when saying it "would be wise to shift [Saudi Arabia's] industrialization strategy away from dependence on low growth export markets, reorienting it toward higher growth domestic consumption good industries." To add an additional argument in favor of this strategy: Backward and forward linkages are higher than in oil refining or petrochemical production; producers of local consumer goods "create demand for a whole range of other related products and materials" (Gulf Economic & Financial Report November 1989, p. 3; which is also a good source for an overview over niches in the Gulf markets). This approach should not be confused with a strategy of promoting only small to medium size industries.

Second, there is Cline's approach of *Arbitrary Comparative Advantages* (Cline 1982). In a dynamic environment, factors such as government intervention may determine the development of comparative advantages. In the current context this could mean the GCC countries gain comparative advantages in the areas of refining and petrochemicals if they only push these sectors hard enough to drive other countries out of business. As industrial organization theory emphasizes, such strategies are risky because competitors' governments might retaliate; also it is not self-evident that the fruits of these efforts can be reaped as there is always the threat of re-entry.[28] After all, the fact that the establishment of an industry is possible does not mean that it is optimal to direct resources in its direction.

Governments in the GCC supported industrial activities related to downstream oil production, energy- and capital-intensive production and advantages due to experience and location by providing the appropriate complementary infrastructure, such as transportation and communication systems, education, and utilities. Examples are Saudi Arabia's Yanbu Industrial City on the Red Sea (start-up in 1982) and Jubail Industrial City on the Gulf (1982), Bahrain's banking infrastructure with its Offshore Banking Units (1975), and Dubai's Jebel Ali Free Zone (1985).

In cases of "highly capital-intensive and high-risk basic and heavy industry projects" (Industrial Strategy 1985), state-owned companies establish the businesses. The primary example is the *petroleum refining industry*. In 1989, refining made up for about 35% of total manufacturing. Its share in GDP was about 3.3%, compared to 9.4% for total manufacturing (see Appendix Table A1). The relative sizes of the refining industry in the GCC member countries are listed in Table 7.

Table 7: Relative Sizes of GCC Countries' Oil Refining and Petrochemical Industries in 1992 and 1988, respectively (%)

	Bahrain	Kuwait	Oman	Qatar	Saudi Arabia	UAE
Refining	8	26	3	2	54	7
Petrochemicals	4	13	0	13	64	6

Notes: for refining: share in crude capacity (b/d) as of 1 January 1992; for petrochemicals: share in total production capacity (tons) in 1988
Sources: see Appendix Tables A4 and A5

The dominating refining capacities are with Saudi Arabia and Kuwait. Appendix Table A4 presents details concerning the refinery industries in the GCC. Especially, it shows that the refineries in Kuwait, Oman, Qatar and the UAE are completely government owned. The Bahraini government ownes 60%

[28] To be sure, Cline had mainly *new* technologies and goods in mind where the first-comer acquires a comparative advantage (e.g., in the semiconductors technology). However, the fundamental idea (government interventions create comparative advantage) and problems (retaliation, threat of entry of competitors) can be transfered to the case of existing industries.

of Bahrain's refinery; the rest stems from an U.S. company. The Saudi government owns about 74% of the Kingdom's refining capacity, while 16% are owned by U.S. companies, 9% by a Greece company, 1% by Japanese investors and 0.2% by the Kuwaiti government. Petroleum refining industries in the GCC operate profitably. For instance, Samarec, which has been operating three Saudi refineries and was responsible for the Kingdom's marketing of refined products, reported (according to Arab News 16 June 1993) a high accumulated profit from 1988 to 1992.[29]

A similar field is the liquefaction of *gas*. The governments of Oman, Qatar and the UAE are planning to invest $15.2 billion until the year 2000 to build or expand liquefaction plants (Jordan Times 25 July 1993). The liquefied gas is mainly exported to Japan. In addition, Oman constructs a $4 billion underwater pipeline to transport gas to India (Egyptian Gazette 2 July 1993). Saudi Arabia and Kuwait have yet to exploit their huge gas reserves.

A second area for large-scale projects is the *petrochemical industry*. Governments began in 1981 to establish the necessary plants. Saudi Arabia has proceeded farthest in this sector, as it can be seen from the above Table 7. The main products are ammonia, urea and methanol; for details see Appendix Table A5.[30] The government owned Saudi Basic Industries Corporation (SABIC) is the major producer.[31] The question of international competitiveness will be treated in section C.1.4. on GCC's international bargaining position.

---

[29] Samarec, the Saudi Arabian Marketing & Refining Company, took over Petromin in 1988 and was merged itself with Saudi Aramco by a cabinet decision in June 1993. It employed 3,549 workers in the refining sector, and 4,800 in distribution. At its 60th anniversary in May 1993 Saudi Aramco had a total labor force of 47,500; of these, 73% are Saudi nationals (Arab News 29 May 1993).

[30] Gulf production of methanol represents 10.3 percent of the world's consumption of 13.3 million tons; in the case of ethylene it is 3.3 percent of the total 49.5 million tons (Saudi Gazette 25 December 1991). GCC countries produce and export almost 3 percent of the world nitrogen fertilizer demand in 1990 (Horndasch 1990, p. 157). GCC states' export of standard plastics amounted to 5 percent of world consumption in 1990 for low density polyethylene (low DPE) and linear low DPE, and 8 percent for high DPE (Horndasch 1990, p. 157).

[31] The category "chemicals" contributed in 1990 54% to SABIC's total revenues of $2.4 billion (Saudi Basic Industries Corporation 1991). Plastics, which is also grouped under the heading of petrochemicals, contributed 11%. The three other arms of SABIC are fertilizers (17%; also a petrochemical product), metals (14%) and industrial gases (4%). SABIC had in 1990 almost 9,000 employees in 15 manufacturing affiliates, 62% of which are Saudi nationals (Arab News 13 July 1993).

Two recent developments have to be noted. First, private investors are encouraged to participate in these activities. For example, in Saudi Arabia, it is envisaged that the petrochemicals sector invests $8 billion from 1991 to 1995 (thus, increasing the Saudi petrochemical industry by 50%), of which $2 billion are estimated to be in the private sector (NCB Economist April 1992, p. 4). In addition, GCC governments started partial privatization of public sector companies (in part as a result of budget pressures resulting from low oil prices). Already in 1984 SABIC sold 30% of its shares to Saudi and GCC nationals (Gulf Economic & Financial Report February 1988). The GCC-owned Gulf Investment Corporation expects a further discernible shift toward privatization of existing state-owned enterprises until the year 2000 (Al-Fayez 1992, p. 14).

Second, it is the intention of governments to cut subsidies more and more. In the early 1980s it was common belief that virtually no industrial project in the GCC could be sustained without government subsidies and loss compensation. The UAE minister of Finance and Industry is quoted by Bsaisue (1984, p. 232) as stating that "all our industrial projects in the Gulf area are operating at 10-15 percent losses" (according to As-Sudais 1985, p. 282). The share of subsidies, transfers and loans from government to private sector in Saudi Arabia's GDP increased from 0.4% in 1970 to 7.3% in 1981/82 (As-Sudais 1985, p. 136). In the second phase of Saudi Arabia's strategy on petrochemicals, which started in 1990, more complicated organic compounds were produced with the help of foreign joint venture partners. However, this phase is expected to proceed more slowly. By some this was attributed to the expectation that "the ground rules have been changed, as 'incentive cured' will no longer be offered to future joint venture partners. The second round of plants will need to be financially sound *in themselves* in order to secure foreign joint venture partner participation" (Saudi Consulting House 1988, p. 82, emphasis original). However, in the early 1990s no such decline in incentives could be detected. Nevertheless, it is increasingly difficult to find foreign partners which provide their technology. This will be discussed in the context of GCC external relations in section C.1.4., where also another specific problem of the petrochemical industry will be discussed, viz., the protection by the EU, the USA and Japan against imports of these products from the Middle East.

Finally, a third field where capital-intensive investments arise is the *metallurgical industry*. After finalizing the aluminum projects in Bahrain, Dubai (UAE), Qatar and Saudia Arabia, the GCC region will produce about 10 percent of the world's 14 million tons per year (Arab News 2 November 1992). The same countries are also planning to raise their iron and steel output, while Oman steadily increases its copper production. The relevant enterprises are for the major part government owned, such as SABIC and Aluminum Bahrain (ALBA). The bulk of the metal industries output is exported to Japan.

Private entrepreneurs produce downstream and domestic-market oriented products. Examples are goods based on petrochemical products and aluminum, durable and nondurable consumer goods (e.g., garments, textile, paper, sheet glass), electrotechnical products, products for the education and health sector, communications technology and construction sector goods.[32]

The overall importance of the manufacturing activities is 9.4% in GCC's GDP in 1989. Refining makes up for 3.3%, petrochemicals for about 1%, and other manufacturing for some 5 or 6%.[33]

The share of private manufacturing in GDP is small, but it would be even smaller if the governments did not provide attractive incentives for industrial activities. Incentives which are granted to investors in the GCC countries are listed in Table 8.

The general incentives do not vary much among countries. Governments sought to provide a modern and sophisticated infrastructure and business environment. The UAE and, to a lesser extent, Qatar differ from the other GCC countries in that they are extremely reluctant to provide special incentives such as duty exemptions on imported inputs, protective import tariffs on competing imports and tax holiday (Ernst & Young 1990b, section D.5; Jebel Ali Free Zone Authority 1992a, p. 40). This can be explained by different stages of development. The "UAE and Qatar have not yet established a tariff protection policy owing to the fact that industrial development in these countries has been

---

[32] Several business directories exist which list individual enterprises in the Gulf, grouped by business sectors. Examples are the Guide to Manufacturing Companies in the GCC by the GCC Secretariat General (1987), The Gulf Directory 1991-92 by Falcon Directory Publications [1991], The Sultanate of Oman Business Directory 1986/87 by Apex Publishing (1986), Bahrain Chamber of Commerce & Industry Directory 1990-91 [1990]. More detailed information, such as specific products, year of foundation, capital et al. are available in Bahrain's Industrial Companies Guide by the Directorate of Industry Protection & Registration (1991), in the Dubai Industrial Directory 1991-92 by Dubai Chamber of Commerce & Industry (1991) and in the Saudi Export Directory by the Saudi Export Development Center (1990). Official bulletins give details on newly established firms.

[33] Almost no disaggregated data on the manufacturing sector's contribution to GDP seems to be publicly available. From Saudi Arabian production data (NCB Economist August/September 1993, p. 3) it can be concluded that the contribution of the petrochemical sector to GDP is close to 1%. In connection with Appendix Table A1 this yields the estimate of 5 to 6% for other manufacturing.

Table 8: Incentives and Subsidies for Manufacturers in GCC Countries, 1993

	Bahrain	Kuwait	Oman	Qatar	S.A.	UAE
full capital and profit repatriation; stable, convertible currency	+	+	+	+	+	+
no taxes on salaries or wages	+	+	+	+	+	+
no taxes on self-employed	+	+	?	+	–*	+
tax rates on corporate income (%)	0	0-55†	0-50@	0-50	25-45‡	0
tax holiday on corp. income tax (years)	n.a.	10	10	5	5	n.a.
social security contr. by employer (%)	3-7	0-10	0-6¶	0	2-10	0
fees for electricity, water, fuel	low	low	low	low	low	low
communications world-wide	+	+	+	+	+	+
transportation by land, sea, air	+	+	+	+	+	+
finance assistance, cheap loans	+	+	+	+	+	+
up to 10% price prefer. in gov. bidding	+	+	+	+	+	+
duty exemption for imported inputs	+	+	+	+	+	+
free zones	+	–	–	–	–	+
industrial estates with nominal rent	+	+	+	+	+	+
protective tariffs on competitive imports	+	+	+	+	+	–
feasibility study *not* required for licensing	–	–	–	?	–	–
assistance for identif. of projects / sites	+	+	+	+	+	?
foreign cap. majority in practice possible	+	–	–♪	–§	+	–#

Notes: "n.a." means "does not apply;" * 0-45% on investment income of non-GCC nationals; † on foreign companies only; @ only on companies with foreign capital share; corporate taxes of 5 to 7.5 percent will be charged on net profits above $78,000 of Omani-owned companies starting 1994 (Arab News 12 October 1993, 1 December 1993); ‡ on non-GCC capital share only; ¶ "training levy;" ♪ in 1993, the Omani government was planning to allow foreign investors to have a 100 percent ownership in projects (Arab News 26 October 1993); § except in special projects of "public interest;" # except in Jebel Ali Free Zone

Sources: Arab Communicators [1989]; Bahrain Marketing & Promotions Office [1992]; Dubai Chamber of Commerce & Industry [1992a], [1992b]; Ernst & Whinney (1989a, 1989b); Ernst & Young (1990a, 1990b, 1990c, 1992); Jebel Ali Free Zone Authority (1992a); Murtfeld / Azzam (1990)

concentrated on large-scale export-oriented industries" and most imports in the UAE are re-exported (Gulf Economic & Financial Report February 1988, p. 5).

Impressive as the incentives may be, the constraints of the GCC economies are worth being recalled. Henry T. Azzam, one of the leading economists in the Arabian Peninsula, lists even for Saudi Arabia the following remaining "few" constraints (NCB Economist April 1992, pp. 2, 8):[34]

- lack of sufficient industrial management expertise and technical skills among the national population,[35]
- unavailability of the necessary information base,
- lack of indigenous tradition for research on technological advancement,
- lack of proper marketing for national products,
- incomprehensive industry legal code,
- high taxes once tax exemption expired, levied on total profits instead of distributed profits only,
- limited entrepreneurial vigour of the country's private sector because Saudi businessmen have in general been geared both psychologically and economically toward trade and service activities, where returns are substantial and the pay back period is rather short,
- bureaucratic constraints complicating the process of obtaining industrial licenses.

Stick for a moment with the process of obtaining industrial licenses. Economic and technical feasibility studies are required in the GCC countries to get an industrial license for subsequent company registration. In granting industrial licenses (especially when special incentives and subsidies are applied for) the governments attach importance to the market situation, technology transfer, education and training to nationals, contribution to economic development and

[34] As an additional problem he lists openness of the domestic markets to imports from all over the world. In the next chapter import protection will be criticized because it fights a domestic disturbance with an international policy instrument. Azzam himself adds that tariff protection should be granted only if local value added is high, and "[i]ndustries applying for protection should adhere to certain levels of specifications and standards and be able to compete in price and quality in the local market. Over-protection would reduce competition and lead to high prices of industrial products, thus harming the consumers and dampening future export potentials" (NCB Economist April 1992, p. 8).

[35] For instance, severe management deficiencies in small businesses in Saudi Arabia have been detected by Al Hajjar / Presley (1991). More than two thirds of the 222 small firms which filled in their questionnaire did not establish business on the basis of a feasibility study, did not keep financial records, did not have separate bank accounts for the firm or did not prepare annual budgets.

utilisation of local inputs and manpower (for Saudi Arabia cf. Saudi British Bank 1991, p. 32).

The Kuwait Institute for Scientific Research (KISR) conducted a detailed study on the subsidies for private sector investments in the GCC in 1987 at the invitation of the GCC Secretariat General. Some 30 firms from six traded goods sectors were included. The study suffered from many shortcomings, such as inadequate book-keeping in the enterprises, different accounting standards (e.g., for depreciation), and dissimilar final products. Nevertheless, the findings support the impression from Table 8. Overall, the average subsidy accounted for about 20 percent of total production costs. The main receivers in relative terms were cement producers. Subsidies reducing production costs and those increasing returns from sales contributed almost equally to the improvement of the companies' profits. The main sources in reducing costs lay in the fields of electricity, land rental and loans; labor input was not subsidized. Subsidies on revenues were mostly granted through preferential prices for sales to the government; cash subsidies played almost no role. Saudi Arabia paid the highest subsidies per cost unit, while the UAE granted almost none. Of all industries almost one half could have survived without the government subsidies.[36]

Recently, another sample of 75 industrial establishments has been surveyed in the GCC (Al-Fayez 1992, p. 16). One of the results was that 65 percent of them benefited from government procurement policies. The subsidized cost of capital ranges from 4.9 to 6.2 percent, which is judged by Al-Fayez as being quite low (Al-Fayez 1992, p. 9). Due to the industrial licenses policy, monopolies exist and they fully exploit the protection provided through tariffs (Al-Fayez 1992, p. 15).

Rasheed Al-Sharhan from the Industrial Bank of Kuwait believed that no industrial project in Kuwait would be implemented if the government would consider the short-term economic opportunity costs. The return abroad would be much higher than at home. Sophisticated infrastructural outlets, subsidies on electricity and water, medical care for foreign workers, missing multiplier effects because foreign workers send abroad large parts of their wages and salaries and most tradables are imported: all this can only be supported by the

[36] With the exception of two companies, all employed more than 50 workers; the average was 170 employees. Expatriates accounted for about 90% of total labor force. It has to be added here that small to medium industries with employment of less than 50 workers find it difficult to draw on concessionary or medium to long term loans, at least in Saudi Arabia (NCB Economist August/September 1993). This indicates a bias towards large companies.

hope for future growth effects and by pointing to the social necessities (Al-Sharhan 1992).

At first glance, it seems subsidies for service sector activities are much smaller. Most costs arise from labor costs, which seem not to be subsidized. However, this is not true. The government absorbs most of the qualified national labor at highly attractive wages. The private industrial and service sector have to compete with these wages if they want to hire GCC workers to fulfill their obligations to employ national laborers. Experts complain about "long-standing site disadvantages [in the GCC region] which have to be overcome, mainly by reducing the *too high labor costs*" (Murtfeld / Azzam 1990, p. 75, author's translation, emphasis added). The problem of Dutch Disease is not overcome because production of non-oil traded goods are not promoted enough. A recent report by the state-run Emirates Industrial Bank (EIB) of the UAE indicates that GCC states continued to depend heavily on oil revenues despite their search for other income sources. "Among the reasons it cited were the relatively low allocations for the development of non-oil [industrial] sectors and the large government subsidies to services and other [non-industrial] sectors," which lead only to redistribution of funds but not to manufacturing (Arab News 4 April 1993).

B.1.5. Conclusions

Some long-term concerns of GCC policy makers and policy options are presented in Table 9.

Table 9: Impact of GCC Development Strategies on Some Long-term Problems

Strategy / Problem	investment in foreign capital markets	oil-dependent industry: refining	oil-dependent industry: petrochemicals	downstream or oil-independent industry and services: export oriented	downstream or oil-independent industry and services: domestic market oriented
per capita income decreases due to high population growth	– *	±	±	+	–
diminishing income due to limited oil reserves	+ †	– ‡	±	+	–
volatile income due to volatile world oil market	+	+	+	+	–
social problems due to unemployment of GCC citizens	–	– ¶	±	+	+

Notes: + strategy helps to solve problem; – strategy does not help to solve problem; ±: + or – depending on further assumptions; * initial savings are large enough for sustaining a specific per capita real income after oil is depleted only if $r \geq g + x$, where r is the real interest rate on foreign capital markets, g is the population growth rate and x is the part of the initial savings which represents (if distributed among the population) an acceptable per-capita real income; † if population growth is zero; ‡ if competitiveness depends on cheap own oil input; ¶ because not labor intensive and with little spill-over effects

This analysis points to the necessity of establishing export-oriented, skill-intensive and cheap-energy-independent industries and services because they exhibit the greatest long-term potential in view of a growing native population and diminishing oil revenues. Of course, as an intermediate stage, oil-dependent industry may serve to acquire technical skills, management know-how and world-wide marketing experience. To a limited degree this is also true for a domestic market oriented production, but knowledge of foreign markets is not created.

It is important to note that population growth might be expected to stop if high income and social security levels are maintained for some time. This is the experience of other high-income regions, and family planning does not violate Islamic religious laws. But, even if population is stable, the strategy to invest funds abroad would still have the major disadvantage of creating almost no employment in the GCC region itself. In addition, a policy of investing all capital abroad "would have been socially unacceptable as this would have implied the creation of a 'coupon clipping' rentier society consisting of idle citizens living in perpetual retirement" (Stournaras 1985, pp. 24f). Thus, social antagonism was predicted.

In view of this analysis, the GCC countries have to promote manufacturing activities, especially as production of exportables is hindered by the Dutch Disease induced real appreciation and by the rentier mentality in a rentier state. Subsidies and incentives have to be linked to productive activities to further attitudes like innovation, dynamism and risk-bearing. To be sure, in an ideal world with perfect foresight and complete markets, the promotion would be unnecessary, but this is unlikely in the GCC problems' context. For example, many people can be considered to be short-sighted and to not realize that the selling of oil is an asset transformation, rather than an acquisition of genuine, sustainable income.

Starting from this chapter's analysis of the basic common characteristics and dissimilarities of the GCC economies, next the possibilities and limitations for regional cooperation to overcome economic problems in the GCC are investigated.

B.2. Possibilities and Limitations of Regional Economic Cooperation in the GCC

The Gulf Cooperation Council's basic objectives include:

"To effect coordination, integration and interconnection between member states in all fields in order to achieve unity between them" (Charter 1981).

The ways in which the GCC tried to achieve this objective in the field of economics will be pointed out in chapter B.3. Here, the meaning of and the pros and cons for economic coordination, integration and interconnection will be spelled out in the GCC context, keeping in mind the basic characteristics of the GCC economies which have been explored in chapter B.1.

First, classifications of economic cooperation efforts are provided (section B.2.1.). Next, the effects of four distinct groups of cooperation efforts are analyzed: trade liberalization (B.2.2. and B.2.3.), freeing of factor movements (B.2.4.), joint projects and incentive coordination (B.2.5.) and coordination and harmonization of economic policies on other fields (B.2.6.). The measures which have to be taken, the preconditions to achieve the desired positive effects and possible negative effects will be discussed. In each section, the general discussion is accompanied by a discussion of the specific situation of the GCC economies.

B.2.1. Classification of Economic Cooperation Efforts

One approach to understanding the meaning of the above mentioned GCC's basic objective to achieve unity through coordination, integration and interconnection is to study the Council's own interpretations.

As Abdulla Yacoub Bishara (1984, pp. 40f), the GCC's Secretary General from 1981 to 1993, notes, unity is the "final objective." According to Bishara, the concept of unity has its roots in "the dreams of the great Arab pioneers who strove for Arab unity... In the 1940s and 1950s my compatriots, the Kuwaitis, traveled down the Gulf without any need for official papers. It was that strong sense of oneness that brought the Gulf together in its present structure, the

GCC." Thus, it is clear that unity does not only mean unanimity, but also a common market, if not one state.[37]

For the former Secretary General "economic integration is not a goal in itself, but ... a vehicle for bringing about the final objective, which is the unity of the Gulf" (Bishara 1984, p. 41). Of course, the present study does not look at economic integration from this view-point. Rather, it tries to evaluate the integration efforts from an economic perspective.

What is the distinction between cooperation, coordination, integration and interconnection? It makes sense to consult Balassa (1961b, 1961a): When analyzing the forms of economic integration, Abdullah El-Kuwaiz (1984, p. 46), GCC's Assistant Secretary General for Economic Affairs since 1981, uses the classification of Balassa (cf. Figure 6).

Figure 6: Balassa's Classification of Economic Cooperation

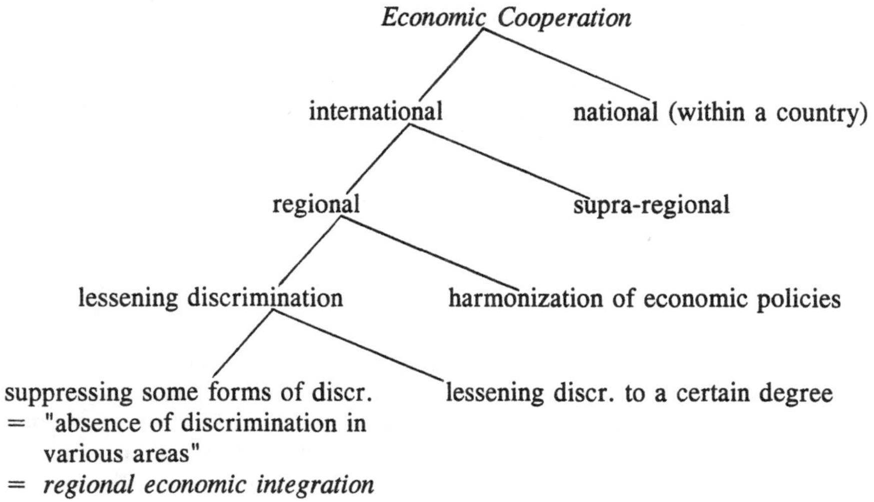

Source: Balassa (1961b, pp. 1-6)

---

[37] Because the GCC took no practical step whatsoever to enlarge its group, the reference to *Arab* unity may not be convincing. Investments in non-GCC Arab and Islamic states by GCC states are contingent on the condition that these investments "increase possibilities for the success of industries in the GCC States" (Industrial Strategy 1985).

With respect to the classification of Figure 6, the Gulf *Cooperation* Council chose to exclude no possible regional cooperation steps a priori in its Charter. It allows for the coordination of economic policies and for the partial or total suppression of various forms of discrimination against member countries' citizens. In addition, the term "interconnection" in GCC's charter stresses that cooperation is not limited to legislative measures, but that it shall also be practical in the sense of building bridges and roads.

Varying degrees of *integration* are possible (Balassa 1961a, p. 2; 1961b, pp. 5f):

1. *Free Trade Area:* suppression of discrimination in the field of commodity movements among member countries. However, as long as tariffs against non-members are not equalized, customs authorities have to distinguish between partner and foreign products according to the shares of value added in the product.
2. *Customs Union:* complete free trade of commodities within the union and a common tariff wall against non-member countries.
3. *Common Market:* customs union and abolishment of restrictions on factor movements and services. However, non-nationals such as foreign workers are excluded from free movement.
4. *Economic Union:* common market in which national economic policies are harmonized in order to remove discrimination that was due to disparities in these policies. This includes a joint industrial policy.
5. *Complete Economic Integration:* common market in which economic policies such as monetary, fiscal, social, and countercyclical policies are unified and in which a supra-national authority is set up whose decisions are binding for the member states.

El-Kuwaiz is careful to only mention the first four forms of economic integration. One could think he did not want to touch the sensible subject of national sovereignty. However, this is not the case. What he wanted to stress is that the question of national sovereignty arises at the first stages. Example: Once a common tariff wall against non-members is erected, no national authority can change this tariff without jeopardizing the whole union. "In essence, integration is a compromise on behalf of the member states, which give up their sovereignty in the making of economic decisions to the common economic authority of the GCC" (El-Kuwaiz 1984, p. 47).[38]

---

[38] In addition to giving up sovereignty to a common GCC authority in the domain of trade relations with the outside world, El-Kuwaiz (1984, pp. 47f) lists the following domains: terms of competition, investment policy, agricultural policy, development plans for under-developed regions, encouragement of infant industries, protection of investments, natural

Balassa's concept has been criticized because it is only applicable to market economies and its five steps may be in the wrong order (As-Sudais 1985, pp. 9-20). However, the GCC economies are essentially market economies and policy makers are free to change the order of steps. Balassa's order is quite useful in the context of the GCC.

It has to be noted, nevertheless, that some important objectives of GCC economic cooperation are hard to group into Balassa's classification, viz., increased negotiation power vis-à-vis the outside world, joint infrastructural and other projects, joint strategy vis-à-vis foreign workers and for manpower development.

Another classification of regional cooperation efforts groups its possible positive and negative effects: efficiency gains from taking advantage of comparative advantages and of economies of scale, reduced transaction costs, increased mobility of factors of production, international bargaining power, etc. From the point of view of certain policy makers, negative side-effects may be the dislocation of economic activity or the increased dependence on other countries. In the context of the GCC, it seems to be most appropriate to analyze the positive and negative impacts while studying the policy measures one by one. One reason is that the GCC politicians followed Balassa's schedule relatively closely, as will be pointed out in chapter B.3.

---

resources, transit, transportation, postal systems, mass media, labor forces, balance of payments, exchange rates, capital transfers, monetary policy, movement of goods and factors, development aid, oil and foreign investment.

B.2.2. Free Trade Area

Economic cooperation in the field of merchandise trade requires decisions about liberalizing intra-group trade, unifying trade policies against third countries and changing effective protection against third countries. The direct effects of each of these decisions are changes in the transaction costs of trade. These may result in immediate trade flow changes. More important, the longer-run investment, production and consumption decisions in all countries are altered.

"Transaction costs are the costs of specifying and enforcing the *contracts that underlie exchange* and therefore comprise all the costs of political and economic organization that permit economies to capture the gains from trade" (North 1984, p. 7, emphasis in original). Thus, these costs are, in general, welfare-improving and necessary in economies with a high degree of specialization. They play an important role in modern economies, as Douglass C. North (1984, p. 7) indicates: "How big a percentage of gross national product are these costs? No one has yet measured them, but even a casual examination of national income accounts suggests that today in advanced western countries they may comprise as much as 50 percent of GNP." Here, attention is limited to costs associated with international trade.

Transaction costs in international trade are the costs associated with exchanging goods.[39] Some are benefitial (e.g., collection and distribution of information), some are unavoidable (e.g., transportation costs), and some could be eliminated with efficiency-improving results (e.g., tariff and non-tariff barriers). Figure 7 provides an overview over these costs.[40]

[39] This differs in one detail from North' definition where the transportation costs could be excluded. This difficulty arises because the transaction cost approach has been developed for the manufacturing sector to be able to distinguish these costs from narrowly defined production costs.

[40] An alternative possibility is to group transaction costs in the following seven categories which follow the lines of Albach [1986, p. 115]: 1. search costs, 2. communication and information costs, 3. negotiation costs, 4. decision-taking costs, 5. capital transfer costs, 6. control and enforcement costs, 7. contract-changing costs. This would lead to almost the same result, but obviously with the same qualification as in the previous footnote.

Figure 7: Transaction Costs in International Trade

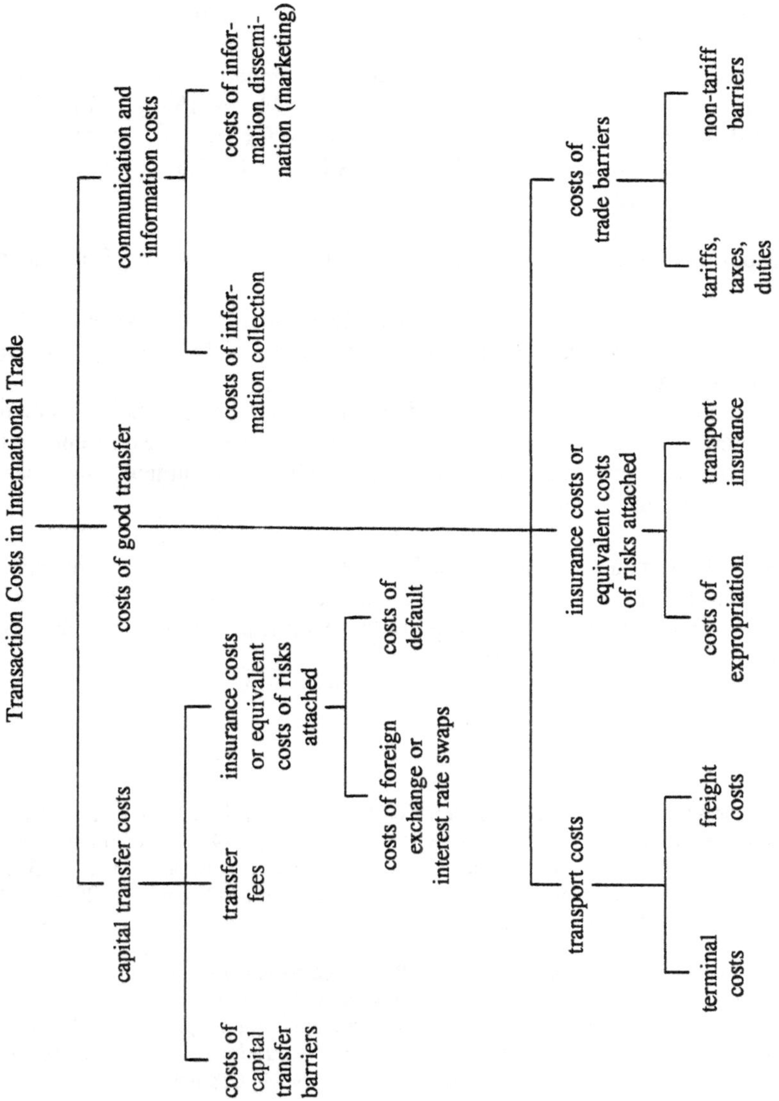

Source: Amelung (1990, p. 6)

Figure 7 shows that tariff barriers are but one obstacle to international exchange of merchandise. Other cost sources, their cost significance in the GCC and the potential influence of GCC governments are:[41]

- capital transfer barriers; does not apply because there are no exchange controls in the GCC,
- capital transfer fees; low due to a reasonably competitive banking sector,
- default risk; low among GCC trading partners (Moore 1990, p. 21),[42]
- terminal charges; minor and non-discriminatory for GCC products,
- transportation; low because GCC countries have established state of the art transportation systems,
- expropriation risk; almost nonexistent,
- transport insurance; only high in times of crises (Iraq-Iran war, Iraq-Kuwait war),
- collecting information; high due to insufficient market transparency; GCC governments could assist Chambers of Commerce & Industry by laws and networks to gather information,[43]
- information transfer; low because of sophisticated communication systems,
- marketing; medium to high because companies have little experience with marketing their products in the GCC region; GCC governments could assist with training and other facilities.

The tariff and non-tariff barriers will be dealt with extensively in this study, especially in this section, in section C.1.2. and in section C.2.1. Together with information and marketing costs these are the main transaction costs which are of concern for regional producers.

---

[41] To be sure, this is the situation in the GCC in the early 1990s, but cum grano salis it also reflects the situation before the GCC's foundation in 1981. Exemptions are the terminal charges which are nondiscriminatory due to a GCC agreement since 1983, and transportation where the bridge between Saudi Arabia and Bahrain has been built after 1981 (although the contracts had been signed before).

[42] In contrast, US exporters insist that full advance coverage of the value of exports is made by GCC importers through a regional bank; according to a study by the Council of Saudi Chambers of Commerce and Industry this is a major contract problem in the view of GCC importers (Arab News 16 April 1993). The same is true for EU exports to the GCC, as was also discovered in a field survey (Council of Saudi Chambers of Commerce & Industry 1992, p. 11).

[43] In a field study which was conducted in 1986, Saudi managers reported that accurate and disaggregated information on trade and production was not available or out-dated (Soufi / Mayer 1991, p. 52).

In the rest of this section attention will be restricted to discussing tariff barriers to trade, but the analysis can often be transfered to non-tariff barriers and other government-induced cost sources by simple change of notation.

To analyze the possible effects of trade policy on trade flows and production, *a thought experiment with three countries* is conducted: the home country A, the partner country B and the rest of the world C. Each has a non-prohibitive trade barrier against its two neighbors (Figure 8).

Figure 8: Real Trade Flows Between Three Countries with Nonprohibitive Trade Barriers

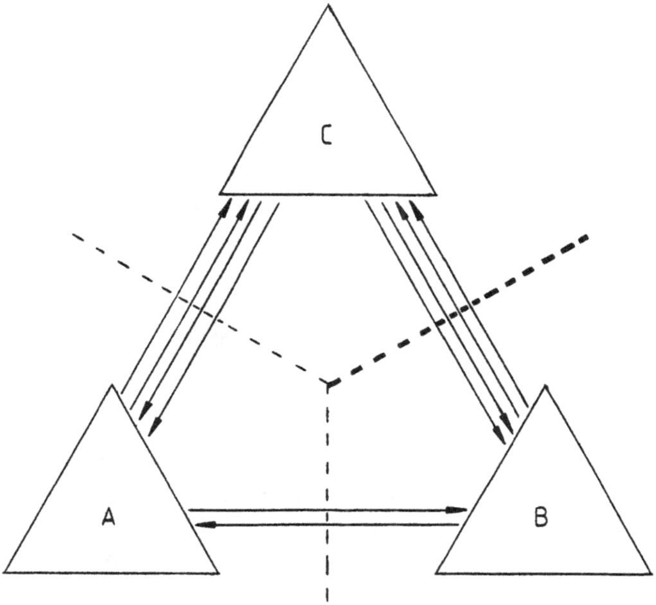

Trade restrictions between countries A and B are eliminated; they form a *Free Trade Area*. The major effects are depicted in Figure 9.

There are three immediate effects and two possible second-round effects. One immidiate effect is *intra-union trade creation:* the increase in trade between A and B due to the reduction in transaction costs between A and B. The second is *trade diversion:* A and B shift some of their imports from C to the partner country because imports from C have become relatively more expensive. A third possible immediate effect is *trade deflection:* "goods originating in nonmember countries are transshipped from the member with the lowest exter-

Figure 9: Major Real Effects of Liberalizing Trade Between A and B

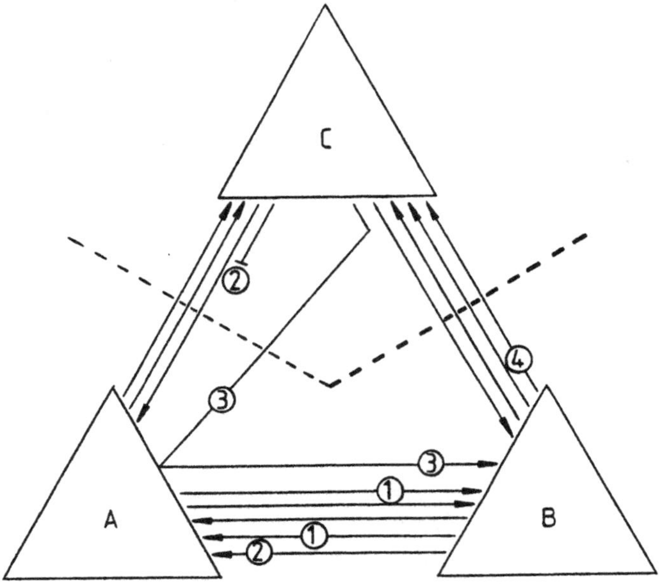

Notes: 1: intra-union trade creation; 2: trade diversion; 3: trade deflection; 4: extra-union trade creation

nal protection to members with higher levels of external protection" (Torre / Kelly 1992, p. 4). Rules of origin are imposed to eliminate such trade deflection. A second-round effect is *extra-union trade creation* resulting from more competitive firms in A and B due to higher quantities of production.

Another second-round effect may result from the restoration of overall equilibrium in the balance of payments. From taking a casual look at Figure 9 one might suspect that the trade balance equilibrium of "country" C is distorted; but this is not necessarily the case. Assume, for example, C's trade flows before creation of the A-B Free Trade Area were balanced:

$$P_X\, Q_X - E\, P_M\, Q_M = 0$$

Let the effect of the trade diversion be a 5% decrease in exports Q_X. In addition assume that the price of import goods decreases by 10% because A and B become more competitive. If this leads to extra-union trade creation of 5.6%, then C's trade balance is still in equilibrium, although export quantities decreased and import quantities increased. However, in general, equilibrium will be distorted and the capital balance, the exchange rate, prices or quantities have to adjust.

For members of a newly created free trade area, the overall welfare effect from forming the free trade area is ambiguous. Before 1950, it was believed by economists that the member countries would profit because they took a move in the right direction: they reduced welfare-diminishing trade barriers; goods were cheaper for consumers. In this setting world-wide free trade is the first-best solution. Reduced tariffs are thought to allow for static effects and for dynamic effects. *Static effects* arise for those companies which profit from trade creation and trade diversion as well as from economies of scale by moving down the cost curve. *Dynamic effects* arise from economies of scale by moving down the learning curves, from spill-over effects of know-how, from increased competition, from an improved investment climate and from a stepped-up pace of technological change (Torre / Kelly 1990, pp. 3-6).

However, even though Viner (1950, chapter IV) accepted the starting-point that world-wide free trade is first best, he noted that welfare in A and B may decrease due to trade diversion. The key to understanding this insight are the revenues from the import duties. The decrease in these revenues due to the trade diversion can be great enough to offset the positive (trade creating) effect of shifting the economies' investments towards a more efficient production structure. For details see Michaely (1976, pp. 75-79). After all, from the *theory of second best* it is known that "a change which brings about the satisfaction of *some* of the optimum conditions (in this case making some relative prices equal to some rates of transformation in production) may make things better or worse" (Lipsey 1960, p. 498, emphasis in original). Given the level of outside trade barriers, the optimal intra-group tariff level will in general be above zero (Berglas 1979); but the optimal tariff rate is hard to calculate in practice.

It has been argued that there was only very limited potential for intra-GCC trade creation in a free trade area because pre-GCC tariff levels were already minimal (e.g., As-Sudais 1985, pp. 253-255). However, a closer look at GCC members' customs duties prior to creating the GCC Free Trade Area in March 1983 (cf. Table 10) shows that this is only part of the story.

Standard rates were minimal and few products were protected by higher rates. However, care has to be taken in interpreting this. With the exception of the United Arab Emirates, all GCC countries felt that protecting (parts of) their local industries by import tariffs of 15% and more was worthwhile. Some even

Table 10: GCC Members' Customs Duties Before Creating a GCC Free Trade Area in March 1983 (%)

						United Arab Emirates			
Types of Products	Bahr.	Kuw.	Oman	Qatar	Saudi Arabia	Abu Dhabi	Dubai	Ras Al-Khaim.	Ajman
Food and Necessities	5	-	-	-	-	-	-	-	-
Nonessential Goods	10	-	-	-	-	-	-	-	-
Tobacco	30	-	-	-	-	-	-	-	-
Alcohol	70	¶	75	70	¶	25	-	-	-
Paints	-	-	20	-	-	-	-	-	-
Bananas	-	-	25	-	-	-	-	-	-
Records/Musical equipm.	-	-	-	15	-	-	-	-	-
Select. types of steel bars	-	-	-	20	-	-	-	-	-
Standard Rates	-	4*	2	2½	3†	1	3‡	2	3

Note: reprinted from *Middle East Economic Digest* 27, no. 36 (9 Sept. 1983), p. 2.
* Selective 15-25% duty to protect local producers.
† Selective 20% duty to protect local producers.
‡ 2% for products imported by air and 3% for products imported by sea.

Source: Ramazani (1988, p. 204); additional note: ¶ in Kuwait and Saudi Arabia the importation of alcohol is forbidden for religious reasons

tried to attract foreign investors with the promise to erect import barriers once they begin producing for the domestic market. Thus, the fear for future increases in protection was all but too real. An effective free trade area could have eliminated this fear for GCC producers. In addition, the concept of *effective protection* states that the nominal tariff rates of 15 or 20% can be misleading. The effective protection for domestic factors of production can be several times the tariff rate. Tariff escalation will be higher, the higher the share of imported inputs and the lower the nominal tariff rate for these imported inputs. This is important for GCC producers which have, in general, to import most of the raw materials. The potential for increases in intra-GCC trade also depends on the external tariff imposed in the case of creating a customs union.

B.2.3. Customs Union

Continuing the thought experiment, next, a *Customs Union* is formed. Transaction costs are reduced substantially. Above all, tariff collecting costs at intra-group borders are eliminated by definition. Domestic value added (which has to exceed a specific amount for goods to be eligible for intra-group free trade in a free trade area) is not controlled any longer. The distinction between tariff-exempted and non-exempted goods ceases.[44] Accompanying paper work in the factories becomes superfluous. By the same token, the unproductive search for ways to achieve trade deflection, despite border controls, is stopped.

Estimates of cost from local contents requirements for the free trade agreements between individual EFTA countries and the EU are available.[45] "[I]t is quite clear that documentation and the administration of origin rules impose heavy costs on exporters and could cause delays and discourage trade, and it is not an overestimate if these costs are assumed to equal some 3 per cent of the value of the goods traded" (Herin 1986, p. 8). By also taking efficiency losses of industry into account, "the total *costs of the economy of rules of origin are in the range of some 3 to 5 per cent of the value of the goods* involved (if a fairly conservative estimate is applied)" (Herin 1986, p. 11, emphasis in original). If this was also a good estimate for the GCC, the following estimate would be obtained. The GCC, Secretariat General (1991, pp. 129-134) reports that total trade of "products of national origin" was $3,052 million (taking export figures) or $1,515 million (taking import figures). Products of national origin are those which are eligible to intra-GCC free trade (i.e., their value added in the GCC is not less than 40% and GCC citizens own not less than 51% of the producing plant). In section B.3.2. this will be explained in more detail. Four percent of the average trade figure amount to some $100 million, which is about 0.07% of GCC's GDP. It could be argued that the control costs for EFTA-EU free trade are higher than those for intra-GCC free trade because the rules of origin are more complicated. They stipulate that the traded product has to be (according to the 4-digit CCCN classification [46]) different from its third-country inputs if the sum of these inputs exceeds a certain limit (Herin 1986, pp. 2f). Thus, producers have to keep track of the origin, value and clas-

---

[44] Here it is assumed that free trade within a GCC customs union is also granted to products from enterprises which have less than 51% GCC ownership.

[45] EFTA: European Free Trade Association; full members have been in the relevant year 1984 seven countries, viz., Austria, Finland, Iceland, Norway, Portugal, Sweden, Switzerland.

[46] CCCN: Customs Co-operation Council Nomenclature

sification of their own and their sub-contractors' inputs. It will be pointed out later that the GCC countries were also quite ingenious in imposing administrative burdens on producers, traders and authorities.

A possible positive effect from high external barriers has to be mentioned. Investments from outside the GCC market may be higher if external trade barriers are high. This effect is reduced by the subsequent transfer of gains, by probable retaliatory measures from foreign countries, and by the resistance of this newly-established local industry to the lowering of the barriers after some time. In the GCC where capital is abundant, it is more important to get access to foreign know-how. This can be achieved by high external barriers. As will be shown, a better strategy is the introduction of domestic subsidies if positive external effects from production are present.

Not considering the reduction in transaction costs from elimination of intra-group border controls and the increase in foreign investment, the situation worsens if import restrictions against the rest of the world are increased; cf. Figure 10.

Figure 10: Major Real Effects of Forming a Customs Union

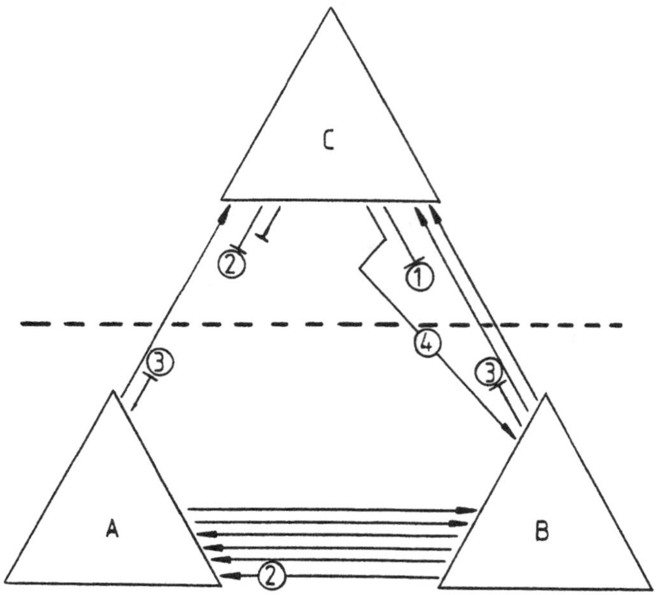

Notes: 1: trade suppression; 2: trade diversion; 3: retaliatory trade suppression; 4: reduction of trade deflection

Trade suppression is a first-round effect: the trade flows from C to the union diminish because some trade is no longer profitable. To the degree that the partner country's producers become competitive, *trade diversion* takes place. To the extent that trade deflection was not already forestalled by imposition and control of local content requirements, *trade deflection is reduced* further. Some foreign firms may still prefer to ship their goods to only one country and sell it from there to other GCC countries. If this is seen as a problem, then it seems to be a good solution to distribute total collected import duties according to an agreed-upon scheme among all GCC members. The second-round effect may be *suppression* of imports into C. This decrease of trade from A and B to C is likely. As a reaction of the rest of the world to the immediate elevation of import barriers by the customs union, the outside world probably takes actions of *retaliation*. Producers in the customs union experience a *cost push for inputs* which may in theory be outweighed by a cost reduction due to increasing economies of scale.

At a minimum, consumers in the customs union with a "fortress mentality" (i.e., with increased import restrictions), are bound to lose. Final goods become more expensive. Some producers may profit from the trade diversion, but others will lose due to retaliation and cost push effects.

The conclusion so far is that the GCC is likely to gain from creating an outward-oriented customs union (i.e., a customs union with low external tariffs). But shouldn't the GCC abolish trade restrictions altogether? Doesn't the same reasoning as above hold for any import barrier? Or, alternatively, if there are good reasons for import restrictions, why shouldn't tariff walls against the outside world be enlarged in a customs union? The discussion of tariffs will, therefore, be summarized.

Digression: Import Tariffs versus Production Subsidies

In a world without externalities and market imperfections, free trade would be the first-best solution. One version of the infant-industry argument states that due to market imperfections investors are not willing or are unable to invest in projects which are associated with large deficits in the first years, even though they are profitable. Tariff-protection is advocated. It is well-known that (supposing the government knows which is the "right" production structure) the state should not protect the industry by tariffs, but it should either eliminate the market failure or it should provide subsidies financed by lump-sum taxes. The production effect and the negative real-income effect during the first phase remain, but the substitution effect due to the price distortion does not take place (Adebahr / Maennig 1987, pp. 190-193; the discussion of Figure 11 below provides details). Another reasoning for a protectionist trade policy for infant industries is based on externalities. The 'market imperfections' argument as well as the 'externalities' argument and there applicability to the GCC will be dicussed in more detail immediately when inquiring in the applicability of the so-called "new trade theories."

The "best-known traditional argument against free trade" is the terms-of-trade argument (cf. Baldwin 1992, pp. 807-812). Assume that a country has international market power with respect to a certain product. By restricting exports the country can achieve higher prices and a higher welfare level. For the GCC this would only apply to oil. A short-cut can be taken on this subject because, for the time being, the GCC countries accept that OPEC is the body which decides on oil-price policy. Moreover, domestic production decisions for oil need not be influenced by the adoption of import duties or export tariffs because the GCC governments have direct control over production quantities.

"New trade theory" or "the industrial organization (I-O) approach to trade theory" stresses the usefulness of trade restrictions under imperfectly competitive conditions (cf. Baldwin 1992, pp. 812-828). Internal economies of scale and external economies in the context of the GCC will be examined.

If unit costs fall for a firm over a wide range of output, then it may be appropriate to protect the domestic industry until it achieves a high level of production and is internationally competitive. Sources of internal scale economies can be large initial outlays on equipment or on research and development, and learning-by-doing effects.[47] New trade theorists point to market imperfections such as the adverse selection problem on credit markets, which render it difficult to grant subsidies (e.g., interest rate subsidies). Import tariffs may yield better results. For the GCC markets this strategy is, however, for most products inappropriate. It does not make sense to adopt import protection as an export-promoting policy if the GCC market is too small for achieving the necessary level of production anyway or where domestic production already exceeds the domestic market's demand. This is the case in the petroleum refining and petrochemical industries. Most other products are either non-tradables or they do not exhibit increasing returns to scale over a significant range or output quantity.

External economies are stressed as another reason for the need of import restrictions. This is not new, because consistent stories in favor of the infant-

---

[47] Proponents of the infant-industry argument one century ago pointed out that learning-by-doing effects will eventually lead to international competitiveness.

industry argument were based on positive externalities such as knowledge spill-overs from high-technology industries. Export subsidies could be thought of to promote the production of socially favorable items. The optimal solution would not be achieved, however, because the domestic prices are still distorted. Therefore, what is called for is a subsidy for the whole production, not only for the exported part. Baldwin (1992, p. 821f; emphasis added) takes this as an example for a general policy lesson: "The policy message of the *domestic distortions literature* that has developed in the last 25 years is to deal with a domestic distortion by introducing another domestic distortion that just offsets the initial distortion. An international distortion will not do this and may or may not increase the country's potential welfare... International policies are proper only when an international distortion exists, such as in the terms-of-trade case."

Some leading GCC economists are aware of this fact. For example, Khaled Al-Fayez (1992, p. 8), Chief Executive Officer of the Gulf Investment Corporation, stressed in an address to the Second GCC-EC Industrial Conference in 1992 that "cost incentives ... had in fact served the economies of the region well, for as compared to tariffs, subsidies do not create price distortions nor do they reduce consumer welfare."[48]

To illustrate this general point, take the case that an import tariff is imposed on a certain product to protect domestic production. This is a frequent case in some GCC countries. To take just one example, as part of the incentive structure for small and medium size industries for domestic market production, Saudi Arabia grants protective import tariffs of 20% to certain domestic producers; for a complete overview cf. sections B.1.4. and C.2.1. Let there be two tradable goods. The production sector is characterized by a production possibility frontier and profit maximization.[49] Consumers maximize their aggregated utility function. Figure 11 depicts this situation.

Initial production of goods 1 and 2 is represented by point A, initial consumption by B. Good 1 is exported. Suppose that an increased production (not consumption!) of good 2 is socially favorable because positive externalities, such as spill-overs to other producers, are associated with its production. For

---

[48] As is illustrated in Figure 11, consumer welfare will in most cases be reduced by the introduction of subsidies, at least initially, when compared to the ex ante situation. Probably, Al-Fayez meant that consumer welfare is improved when compared to the tariff solution.

[49] The introduction of nontradables would not change the general conclusion of the superiority of subsidies over trade barriers as long as only specific goods are protected. International mobility of factors of production is excluded in this illustration. The general result extends to this if decreasing returns to scale are assumed.

Figure 11: Import Tariffs vs. Production Subsidies to Correct for a Domestic Production Distortion

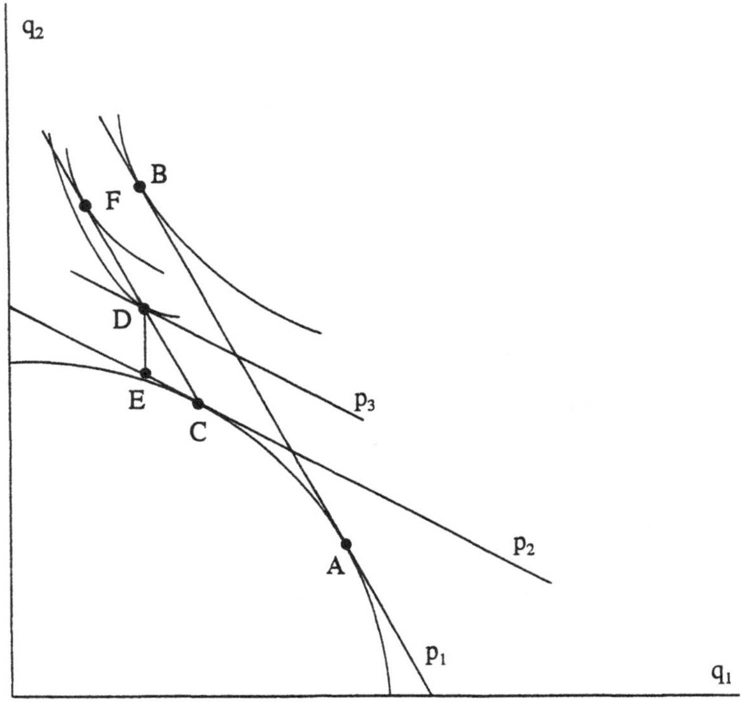

Note: explanations are provided in the text
Source: adapted from Adebahr / Maennig (1987, p. 191) and Baldwin (1992, p. 806)

example, to reach a higher growth path in the next period, production should be at point C today. A social planner who knew the shape of the production possibility curve, the aggregated indifference curves and the optimal point C could determine the appropriate import tariff. Domestic relative prices are determined by the slope of the line p_2.[50] Consumption takes place at D, assu-

[50] If the money supply is fixed, velocity is constant in Fisher's quantity equation and real income does not depend on the price level, then absolute prices are different at p_2 and p_3. The same is true for the exchange rate. Therefore, the planner has to know D from the indifference curves to be able to calculate the correct import tariff in domestic currency. If

ming the nondistortionary distribution of import duties DE to the domestic consumers. Note that the country's terms of trade (slope of p_1) are different from consumers' marginal rate of substitution.

Alternatively, a subsidy on the production of good 2 is introduced which is financed by a tax on the production of good 1. Again, production takes place at point C, but consumption is at point F which is prefered by consumers to point D.[51] Thus, the domestic production distortion should be cured by a subsidy-tax-combination on domestic production.

Besides these theoretical difficulties, practical difficulties arise when a specific import tariff shall be implemented. Even if one has chosen some level of effective tariff protection which shall be granted, it is not easy to calculate the appropriate actual tariff on this specific import commodity. As has been stated in section B.2.2., the concept of *effective protection* states that nominal tariff rates can be misleading. The effective protection to domestic factors of production can be several times the tariff rate. Tariff escalation will be higher, the higher the share of imported inputs and the lower the nominal tariff rate for these imported inputs. Thus, "a uniform tariff covering all imported goods – final products as well as inputs – has the unique property of providing equal effective protection to all import-substituting activities" (Harberger 1993, p. 10). Such a uniform tariff is preferable to subsidies if it is introduced for revenue purposes (which has not been necessary in the GCC states yet and which is problematic for theoretical reasons) or if a government cannot group the industrial activities according to their positive externalities.

From this digression on tariff theory it follows for the GCC so far that domestic subsidies are preferable to trade impediments. It should be kept in mind that this measure is not without problems, too. The proper level of subsidies is not easy to determine, reduction of subsidies in later years is often heavily opposed and trading partners might feel that the interests of their industries are affected and they may retaliate (e.g., by subsidizing their own industries).

For the GCC, two arguments remain in favor of trade barriers. First, the importation of some goods may be unwelcome for religious, cultural, medical

---

the tariff was paid in foreign currency, the knowledge of the production possibility frontier and C would suffice.

[51] In the monetary model of the previous footnote the planner does not have to know the aggregated indifference curves because C and F correspond to the same absolute prices; the knowledge of F is not necessary to the planner.

or safety reasons. Second, in international bargaining situations it may be a threat. For example, Kuwait's oil minister Ali Ahmad Al-Baghli used the threat of imposing import taxes on goods from those members of the European Union which introduce an energy/carbon dioxide tax and thereby raise the price of oil in their countries (Arab News 15 March 1993).

Thus, the abolition of trade restrictions within the GCC and against the rest of the world cannot be expected to have negative consequences if measures are taken to promote the appropriate industries by domestic incentives. Could one expect large positive effects on intra-regional trade from the GCC's introduction of a free trade area or a customs union with low external tariffs? This leads to the old debate of *competitive versus complementary economic structures*. If economic production structures are competitive (i.e., similar) before the free trade area is established, it is often believed that no gains can be achieved. "They all produce the basics – canning facilities, plastic bags, dairy products – that is why intra-Gulf trade has been minimal" (Ziad El-Taki according to Moore 1990, p. 21). True, the structures in the GCC were similar during the early 1980s, in the sense that they relied heavily on exports of oil, produced mainly non-tradables and had a small industrial base. The amount of intra-regional trade was minimal. But it is wrong to understand complementarity as a static phenomenon. "Complementarity grows in line with international specialization engendered by trade. It should be the objective rather than the precondition of trade liberalization" (Rieger 1991, p. 229).

There is another strong theoretical reply to the argument that complementary production structures are necessary for free trade to be welfare improving. From the theory of customs unions it is known that the trade diversion effect may be welfare reducing (see above). Thus, a partner country which imported goods from a low-cost source before the free trade area was established may lose if imports shift to the high-cost partner – despite the complementarity of production. Conversely, two competitive economies will in general spezialize their productions after trade restrictions are lifted and will reach welfare improvements (Lipsey 1960, pp. 489f). "The central issue is the cost structures of the prospective members, relative to the costs of *outside* countries. Complementarity is desirable *if* the countries are close to (or below) world cost levels. Then the gains per unit of trade creation will be large, and the costs per unit of trade diversion small" (Wonnacott / Lutz 1989, p. 70, emphasis in original).[52]

---

[52] Similar production structures before trade liberalization may point to similar and strongly convex consumer tasts rather than to similar production costs. Of course, this would only be the case for goods which are nontradables because of natural or artificial trade barriers.

The World Bank estimated that sub-Saharan Africa could tremble intra-regional trade to 18 percent already with its existing know-how. Torre / Kelly (1992, p. 39, emphasis in original) conclude that "[a]lthough subject to qualification, this result could be seen as evidence of the possibility of efficient trade switching, provided that countries are willing to remove barriers to trade on a fairly comprehensive basis... The thrust of this argument would apply *a forteriori* to regional trading arrangements among middle-income developing countries." Implicitely, Torre / Kelly associate middle-income countries with a medium stage of product diversification. This is not the case in the GCC, and the GCC area has not the historically founded segmentation of markets as sub-Saharan Africa. However, there is certainly scope for broader regional exchange once protectionist attitudes are further reduced.

The GCC members may very well specialize in different economic activities and exchange goods and services. To give just a few examples: Bahrain may be a financial center, produce aluminum and repair ships; Dubai may be a commercial center and active in entrepôt trade; Kuwait may be a center of the refining industry as well as a financial center; several areas may become recreational centers; Saudi Arabia could specialize in downstream manufacturing of petroleum. Product and process specialization (e.g., in the petrochemicals or fertilizer industry), could lead to intra-industry trade. Of course, the market forces should decide about the allocations, but they can only work if they get a chance to work. This not only comprises the commitment to coordinate incentives and the creation of a free trade area or customs union as long as there is minimal trade; but it means above all that the free trade is not restricted by non-tariff barriers as soon as competitors from partner countries start outbidding domestic producers. Intra-industry trade enhances competition, efficiency and, thus, international competitiveness.

Even though the question of welfare improvement is ambiguous when creating a free trade area, one result is evident: If there is a minimal degree of tradables production, intra-union trade increases when preferential trade arrangements are established. In the case that this minimal degree has not been achieved yet, it may come about after the preferential trade arrangements are implemented. This result is transferred to the customs union case if restrictions to outside trade are not reduced by too much.

The creation of a customs union has advantages to foreign competitors who want to serve more than just one market in the union. If there are net gains to foreign competitors from the reduced market segmentation, then international bargaining power of the union members increases by creating a customs union. For instance, the European Union made reduction of tariffs on petrochemical products from the GCC dependent on the establishment of a GCC customs union. However, even with zero intra-union tariff rates and quotas, *customs formalities are not automatically eliminated*. They may still exist due to different health or safety standards.[53] Thus, two forms of customs unions can be distinguished: type I, in which only tariffs and quotas are zero; and type II, in which intra-union customs procedures are eliminated altogether.[54] Still, even in a customs union of type II market segmentation is not zero from the point of view of a foreign supplier. Even in the UAE, which has no internal border controls whatsoever, the business of foreign suppliers "must be registered with the municipality of each Emirate in which activities of the business are conducted" (Ernst & Young 1990, pp. 15, 17). This increases set-up costs and operating expenses.

One result from the analysis of Dutch Disease has to be repeated here. If regional cooperation merges the six nontradables sectors of the GCC countries into one sector with uniform prices, then Bahrain, Oman and probably Qatar, would experience a real appreciation which makes industrialization more expensive (cf. section B.1.2.).[55] This is not to say that Bahrain, Oman and Qatar will lose from the customs union in absolute terms, but as workers in the tradables sector demand higher wages and as the input of nontradables becomes more costly, industrialization depends more than before on government subsidies. On the other hand, Saudi Arabia, Kuwait and probably Abu Dhabi and Dubai, will face a real depreciation; thus, making industrialization less expensive.

---

[53] In the European Union, still another reason is differential rates of value added taxes (VAT). As the VAT had to be paid in the country of destination and was reimbursed by the country of origin, customs declarations were necessary in the beginning. Even in the Single European Market, since 1993, red tape exists: declarations have to be submitted to the local authorities and these national authorities are linked to detect tax evaders. Starting in 1997 all formalities will be abandonned and VAT has to be paid only in the country of origin for products originating in the EU. Similar tax problems do not yet exist in the GCC.

[54] Type II implicitely requires mutual recognition of national rules and regulations for tradable commodities. This type II is one important element of the 'EU Single Market' which was realized for the major part until 1993. "By targeting national frontiers the Single Market directly challenged national sovereignty" (Schaub 1992, p. 4). Non-tariff barriers are reduced as red tape at the borders is eliminated.

[55] Note that this result is special to the GCC insofar as it is only a small step from considering the Saudi Arabian nontradables production as one sector to considering the whole GCC nontradables production as one sector in a customs union.

In a free trade area or a customs union transitional adjustment costs arise from the reallocation of resources; these costs are higher if reallocation is sluggish. Labor and capital mobility reduce these costs (Torre / Kelly 1992, p. 4). If (contrary to the recommendations of the domestic distortions literature) high external tariffs are adopted, openness to foreign investments seems to be advisable. This allows foreign producers to supply the market by producing within the union. The welfare increasing effect is not obvious. The reasoning follows the line of the possible welfare decreasing effects of trade diversion. If foreign investments reduce import requirements, then the positive effect from increased domestic production may be offset by the reduction in collected import duties (Feenstra 1992, p. 170). The situation worsens even more if the prices of domestic factors of production increase due to increased competition because of the new investment.

Even under complete regional freedom of commodity movement there are transaction costs for this trade because it requires the aid of services and factor movements (e.g., transportation and financing). The reduction of these costs is but one merrit of a common market, as will be demonstrated now.

B.2.4. Freeing of Factor Movements in a Common Market

A common market allows for free and equally treated flows of commodities, services and capital, free movement of workers and freedom of establishment for self-employed and corporations.

Thus, *factors of production are mobile* in a common market. This mobility allows for a better allocation of resources because it furthers equalization of real factor prices. The Heckscher-Ohlin theorem states that free trade results in a tendency towards factor price equalization even without factor mobility (cf. section B.1.4. and Balassa 1961a, pp. 80-83). Samuelson (1948) demonstrated complete factor price equalization under restrictive assumptions. These assumptions include equal production functions and preferences, zero transportation costs, homogeneous production factors, no dynamic effects (the same productivity growth in all regions; tomorrow's factor supply does not depend on today's factor price), typical factor-intensity for the production of every good regardless of relative factor prices (Adebahr / Maennig 1987, pp. 56-69, 110-114).

Given the unlikeliness that the restrictive conditions of the Heckscher-Ohlin-Samuelson model are fulfilled, factor mobility will help to move in the direction of factor price equalization. Efficiency is improved. Of course, not everybody will profit from this; especially high-paid scarce factors may experience an income loss which is not compensated by the reduction in prices of consumer goods.

A negative real shock to one country of the common market may have negative spill-over effects for the other members (e.g., because of higher costs for imports from this country). One possibility to avoid the adverse effects on partner countries is factor mobility. Other possibilities are exchange rate and price adjustments. Factor mobility is especially useful if the shock strikes only a specific sector (thus, rendering exchange rate adjustments problematic) or if the common market is embedded in a currency union with sluggish wage adjustment. Real extraregional shocks which hit mainly one GCC country are hard to imagine, but they do occur, as Iraq's invasion in Kuwait demonstrates.

Internal shocks to one economy may arise from a fiscal policy which decreases the possibility for productive employment of factors. In these cases, the owners of factors in the GCC shock country will profit most from regional factor mobility. They can avoid the adverse effects to a certain extent. Other members will profit less from factor mobility if they are dependent on the supply from this member. At the moment such dependence is rare.[56] Another fiscal shock may be transfered to partner economies through increases in the real interest rate when one member's government runs a budget deficit. In the GCC this risk is not high because all members are relatively small and the GCC countries are integrated in international capital markets.[57]

One major argument in favor of free trade and factor mobility is dynamic gains in an "economy now experiencing a 'virtuous circle' of higher growth, higher confidence and higher investment combined with lower unemployment, lower wage pressures and lower needs for public support" (Schaub 1992, p. 2).

For the GCC, several *objections* can be raised against the conjecture that factor mobility will significantly increase economic efficiency and the welfare of all participating countries. A practical objection is that a common market, in general, only frees national factors of production. However, many workers and a large share of the know-how are from abroad. Thus, the effect of introducing a common market may be negligible if free factor movement applies only to national factors.

The basic requirement for a liberal intraregional trade regime to be efficient is outward orientation. Outward orientation is also a requirement for freeing of factor movements to be more efficient. This is especially true in the case of the GCC, which depends on foreign workers and technology; however, GCC politicians feel that economic efficiency conflicts with the important social goal of increasing national participation in the labor force. As was shown in the discussion of the rentier mentality and the socio-cultural background of the Arabian peninsula societies (section B.1.3.), low-paid blue-collar jobs are inacceptable to most GCC citizens. Linking subsidies for individuals to their employment in the productive sector could be one element of a solution strategy. In essence, this would be a wage-subsidy for national workers.

---

[56] One example may be GCC tourists to Bahrain, but Bahrain's supply of tourist attractions is almost immobile and can hardly respond to internal shocks by simply moving to another country.

[57] For instance, three-months interest rates on Interbank Saudi Riyal Deposits were almost equal to three-months Eurodollar interest rates. For the years 1988 to 1991 the average relative interest rate difference between the Dollar and the Riyal was -0.7% of the Dollar interest rate; the relative differences ranged from -3.9% to +3.6% (NCB Economist December 1991, p. 4). This demonstrates not only the credibility of the Saudi Riyal's link to the US Dollar, but also the absence of a "political" or "country" premium, i.e., of "substantial transaction costs, information costs, capital controls, risk of future capital controls and default risk" (Frankel / MacArthur 1987, p. 7).

More theoretical objections infer that some GCC countries will lose from factor mobility in the GCC. "Producers in the developed country may consider the less developed partner an unfair competitor because of its low wages" (Wonnacott / Lutz 1989, pp. 70f). Workers in the developed region may fear the shift of investment from their region into the less developed low-wage region. On the other hand, the less developed regions may point to agglomeration effects. The center or "rich" region may attract qualified labor from the periphery or "poor" region. Such movement of labor may result in an absolute deterioration in the "poor" area if there exist regional economies of scale. These scale economies can be explained by "social and economic overhead and other forms of agglomeration economies [which] contribute to higher factor returns" (Balassa 1961a, p. 85). It is also argued that if "integration entails ... capital movements, the polarisation of industrial activities is likely to be even more marked," because the "larger and more advanced member countries" will supply industrial goods to its agricultural neighbors (Nienhaus 1987, p. 44). However, as has been shown when discussing the industrial structure in the GCC economies, every country has more advanced and more backward regions. The problem exists more on national levels than on a GCC level. Moreover, even though the richer countries were able to provide more subsidies, they had also a greater disadvantage from Dutch Disease. However, the problem of asymetric gains in terms of industrialization from a common market cannot be discarded altogether for the GCC.

Due to a small industrial base, Oman faced an industrial goods trade deficit vis-à-vis the rest of the GCC during the 1980s (cf. the statistics in section C.1.2.). Given that all GCC countries view non-industrialization as a problem and assuming there exists a tendency towards centralization of industries as rich countries pay much higher subsidies: How can the GCC compensate the losers? *Financial transfers* are complicated to calculate and to agree upon. Also, they have been discarded because they present no "real" substitute for lost industrial output (Nienhaus 1987, p. 45). Balassa proposed the *package approach* (Balassa / Stoutjesdijk 1974, pp. 28-32). Each country gets at least one additional industrial project. This might facilitate reaching an agreement on integration projects and it might enhance stability of the agreement if withdrawing means losing access to the regional market. The risks could be spread out by joint financing of all projects. As will be shown, the GCC adopted this approach to some extent; but such planned industrial specialization faces problems of practicability, sustainability and efficiency. A third option would be *asymetric barriers* to trade within the common market. Oman could be allowed to protect its industries. Nienhaus (1987, pp. 46-48) proposes to review the establishment of "custom-drawback unions" which were first proposed by Elkan in the 1960s. This amounts to allowing industrial trade deficit countries, such as Oman, to maintain tariffs against nondeficit countries. This bears severe theoretic problems (Shouldn't the overall industrial output be relevant? Long-term planning of enterpreneurs is problematic when a country with a close-to-zero balance swings back and forth with its tariffs), increases measurement and control costs, and may save inefficient industries from healthy competition. But, at least it leaves some room for competition and is often acceptable as a pragmatic solution. The GCC accepted several exceptions from free trade when establishing its free trade area in 1983 (cf. section C.3.2).

Trade of invisibles or services is an important element for the GCC to increase economic efficiency: If trade or across-investment is to be increased, it is necessary that marketing efforts, credit, insurance and communications can flexibly adopt to new situations.[58] Dornbusch suggests there are also direct gains from scale economies and competition to be reaped (Dornbusch 1992, p. 83). This is not only the case in financial services, such as banking, underwriting and insurance, but also in "accounting, consulting, legal services, construction planning, design, telecommunications and others." In the GCC, in the past most of these services were provided by foreign firms; but as GCC citizens become increasingly educated, there is ample scope for their future participation. This point is not different from the possibilities of increasing trade in commodities. In addition, some services are already provided by GCC firms (e.g., airtravel, banking, health care, consulting and education). For an in-depth investigation see Kassem / Habib (1989).

[58] There exists anecdotal evidence that services in these areas have not been optimal in the beginning of the GCC. As-Sudais (1985, p. 259) reports that Saudi Arabia continued to import a large portion of its cement from the Far East, even though the UAE was facing greater cement surplus.

B.2.5. Incentive Coordination and Joint Projects

Even if a common market is established, optimal resource allocation is not guaranteed. National economic policies can impose considerable uncertainty as well as considerable discrimination to foreign companies which want to compete in the domestic market. Now, such effects will be analyzed for the case where the source of sub-optimality is a direct intervention into the cost structure or even into the production structure through incentives for producers and through joint projects of the countries of the common market.

How can incentives or subsidies be grouped? As in the present context incentives indirectly impose trade restrictions, the General Agreement on Tariffs and Trade (GATT) negotiations focus on these subsidies. The GATT Uruguay Round which started in September 1986 attempted to specify different groups of subsidies in its draft Agreement on Subsidies and Countervailing Measures (General Agreement on Tariffs and Trade 1992, pp. 26f.). Only "specific subsidies" can be subject to remedies. A specific subsidy is, "for the most part, a subsidy available only to certain enterprises or within a specific geographical region" (General Agreement on Tariffs and Trade 1992, pp. 26f).

Thus, a major source of unequal competition is already left out by the GATT draft agreement: exceptionally low levels of taxes or costs for utilities economy-wide. A *fiscal-externality problem* may arise. If the tax base is very mobile, a country may gain from imposing a low tax, but it imposes a negative external effect on other countries. In such a nonzero-sum game it would be best for all players (i.e., governments) to cooperate and agree on binding pre-play commitments. Even if the players are not able to make binding commitments, the cost of retaliation in the next rounds may prevent actors from deviating in infinitely repeated games. A practical reason for leaving such general incentives out of the GATT negotiations is that monitoring is very costly, if not impossible. It is not enough to just compare the overall tax burden because self-selection of enterprises may result in very different economic structures. Comparisons of incentives have to be industry-specific and have to take into account taxes, subsidies, cost-effective regulations, and hidden or secret arrangements. Even more important, a mutual understanding would have to be reached about the "best" tax burden. GATT, with its diversity of members, is for the time being not the appropriate panel to find a solution. The GCC with its relatively homogeneous economies may very well decide upon avoiding the fiscal-externality problem.

The draft GATT agreement establishes three categories of *specific subsidies*. 'Prohibited subsidies' are those paid contingent either upon export performance or upon the use of domestic, rather than imported goods. The complaining signatory is eventually allowed to take countermeasures. 'Actionable subsidies' injure the industry of another signatory, nullify or impair the GATT benefits of other signatories, or pose serious prejudice to the interests of another signatory. Countermeasures may be allowed by the Subsidies Committee. 'Non-actionable subsidies' include, subject to conditions, assistance for research and assistance to disadvantaged regions. Countermeasures can only be taken if such subsidies result in serious adverse effects to the industry of another signatory.

To the extent that subsidies are granted to exports only, they advance dumping on foreign markets. In the draft GATT agreement, dumping is a spatial price-discremination by firms. The so-called currency dumping is not considered as dumping because it is not spatial discrimination. The same is true for the so-called social and environmental dumping. In a regional grouping, currency dumping can be eliminated by forming a monetary union; in the next section, the question of a GCC monetary union will be discussed. Unequal producer costs due to soft social and environmental requirements can be avoided in the GCC by similar legislation. This legislation has to cover industries which (actually or potentially) engage in intra-GCC trade and which produce goods used as inputs in the production of intraregionally traded goods.

What if the size of the GCC market and increasing economies of scale point to a natural monopoly for the production of a specific nontradable good?[59] Examples may be the production of petrochemicals, steel or aluminum for further downstream processing. If entry costs are low, tax competition between regions and the threat of entry results in a socially optimal production and price level. However, low entry costs are unlikely under increasing economies of scale. In this case, the establishment of joint companies is the best solution for the GCC countries if they are unable to open their markets for the goods in question to foreign competitors. In addition, such joint companies provide the possibility to gain specific technical and managerial experience for workers from all participating countries.

Another reason for joint projects occurs if a project can only be realized if all parties commit themselves to the project. This is especially the case for infrastructural projects which link the GCC countries (e.g., electrical power grids, roads, pipelines, bridges, airports, railroads). It is also the case when regional economies of scale call for joint efforts in the areas of education and research. Especially for the small GCC countries, "[r]egional universities, and

---

[59] In a customs union, a prohibitive import tariff provides a natural explanation for such nontraded goods.

technical colleges, and research into area-specific problems, jointly financed and managed by the participating countries" (Balassa / Stoutjesdijk 1974, p. 20) are advisable.

Indispensible for exploiting the advantages of an increased market by large-scale industries is the unification of standards.

Because costs and benefits from joint companies and projects are often tangible and pecuniary, such cooperation is "susceptible to conflicts about a 'fair' and 'equal' distribution of benefits and costs, as well as about management and locational issues" (Langhammer / Hiemenz 1990, p. 8). Such conflicts pose a threat to the whole regional cooperation effort in cases where a subset of members can implement the project. The countries left out may feel a weaker obligation to stick to their obligations and to remain members.

One question still needs to be answered: If domestic subsidies are better than import restrictions, why shouldn't a country protect its infant industry by domestic subsidies which are even higher than those in the partner countries? It makes a difference whether partner countries' prices are expected to be low for a long time or only as long as the domestic industry exists. In the former case, the domestic economy can profit from the permanent improvement in terms of trade. The question remains also under permanent foreign subsidies: Don't positive external effects from industrialization point to the necessity of high domestic subsidies? Yes, but the correct subsidy level is likely to be over-estimated, and coordination of subsidies would still be preferable to the fiscal externality problem.

If support to domestic industries is provided, competition between enterprises may nevertheless occur if two conditions are met. An enterprise's own subsidies and the subsidies provided to competitors and contractors should be specified in advance for a considerable long time in the future. Access to governmental support should be free to all enterprises. Low planning risk and equal treatment are as relevant to entrepreneurs as the absolute level of subsidies.

It is sometimes argued that it "would seem contradictory that governments provide substantial assistance and protection while at the same time welcoming competition" (As-Sudais 1985, p. 265). But, this is not true. Competition leads to increased efforts, and subsidies compensate for positive external effects. Subsidies allow for the implementation of socially desirable projects which are not profitable for private producers, although they deliver their best efforts. To prevent pro-forma activities from collecting windfall profits, subsidies should only be granted as a specified percentage of private investment. Other assistance, especially avoidance of competition by tariff protection or not granting additional business licenses, should be denied.

B.2.6. Coordination of Economic Policies in Other Fields

Important as the abolition of trade barriers, the unification of external tarrifs and the freeing of factors of production are, an efficient allocation of factors of production may still be hindered by uncoordinated policies in other fields. Fiscal policies (viz., the coordination of direct production subsidies and incentives) have just been discussed. Policies which can also distort competitive relationships are countercyclical, social and monetary policies. As Balassa (1961b, p. 12) puts it: "Given [a high] scope of governmental economic policies, an optimal allocation of resources would not come about in a regime of free trade, because divergences in monetary, fiscal and, partly, social policies would distort competitive cost relationships. Thus, a certain degree of harmonization in economic policies becomes necessary." Countercyclical, social and monetary policies will be treated one by one. With regard to the coordination of *international economic policy* let the reader be reminded that it was pointed out before that the GCC should try to achieve free-trade agreements with major trading partners and that its possibilities to influence their terms of trade are limited to crude petroleum.

Since the mid-1980s, GCC countries have been faced with low oil prices, which had a significant impact on *fiscal policies*; and subsequently, oil income and government revenues have diminished. This led to reduced expenditures and substantial budget deficits. If only one country runs a deficit and if income elasticity for imports from GCC partners are high, then the partner countries profit from the deficit, too. At the moment, intra-GCC trade is low and positive spill-over effects are very limited. Does this render the whole issue unimportant to the GCC? No. A main source of subsidies to the producing sector is preferential treatment in government purchases. There is always the tendency to grant preferential treatment only to domestic producers. In the next chapter it will be shown that the GCC allows for a discriminatory policy in this field, although producers from GCC partner countries are granted preferential treatment with regard to third country competitors. Governments will make little use of discrimination if demand for domestic producers' products is high and if partner countries do not discriminate either. In a recession, however, the temptation is high to limit special treatment to domestic suppliers. GCC governments can resist this temptation if they jointly agree to run specific deficits and to keep their purchasing policies open.

As to *social policies*, these are characterized by low-cost or even cost-free provision of housing, medical care, unemployment pay and old-age pension. The coordinated reduction of these consumer subsidies in the Gulf Cooperation Council countries can have positive effects on economic efficiency. One reason is that the government has more means left to raise incentives for productive activities. More important, rentier mentality can be avoided or reduced. The coordinated reduction of consumer subsidies can reduce public pressure which refers to high subsidies in neighboring countries as reference cases.[60]

The question of coordination of monetary policies will now be treated in some more detail. Of course, monetary coordination has many facets; the one which is discussed most controversily in the GCC is the question of a common GCC currency which might be labeled *"Gulf Dinar" or "Gulf Riyal"*. Those which want to introduce the Gulf Dinar immediately argue along the lines of the foundation-stone theory, their critics believe in the correctness of the culmination theory (Kloten / Grosch 1993, pp. 162f). The foundation-stone theory stipulates that "monetary integration [in the GCC] could create favourable conditions which might hasten the process of economic integration ... with regard to [member countries'] economic conditions and policies," as Tahir / Paul / Al Mahmeed (1987, p. 1) and also Zaidi (1990, pp. 764, 766) believe. Complete monetary integration is only possible if GCC states give up national sovereignty to a joint GCC Central Bank.[61] In general, possible advantages from fixed exchange rates and a common GCC currency are the elimination of exchange rate uncertainties and the reduction of transaction costs. This may improve conditions for intra-GCC trade. Countries which have a relatively high inflation rate due to an extensive fiscal policy will face a real appreciation, lose international competitiveness and are forced to change their policy.

Opponents of this optimistic view argue with the culmination theory, which states that a "single [GCC] currency could only be introduced at the end of a drawn-out process involving several stages of economic integration;" this is the position of the Central Bank of Oman (Tehran Times 14 January 1992) and of Hitiris / Hoyle (1986). Several *criteria for an optimum currency area* have been established. Some of these criteria for the GCC are reviewed now to see which steps the GCC would have to take in the view of these culmination theorists.

- Capital markets should be integrated because this facilitates the financing of temporary current-account imbalances; in the GCC, capital markets are sufficiently integrated.

---

[60] Fear of emmigration into neighboring countries might be another reason for coordinating consumer subsidies, especially in the presence of a common market and non-discrimination in the payment of these subsidies.

[61] This necessity, plus the GCC governments' unwillingness to surrender political and economic sovereignty, led Tahir / Paul / Al Mahmeed (1987, p. 91) to draw the conclusion that a common currency was not feasible in 1987.

- Member countries' production should be diversified or the countries should depend on the exportation of the same product because real shocks should not be country-specific; this is especially problematic in the GCC when (and if) 10 or 20 years from now oil price shocks will play a much greater role in Saudi Arabia, Kuwait and the UAE than in Bahrain, Oman and Qatar.
- Factor mobility is required to make real adjustments possible if real shocks occur (Mundell 1961); the necessity for the GCC to increase this mobility has been discussed, and in the next chapter it is shown which steps the GCC took in this regard.
- Member countries should be open in the sense that intra-regional trade flows are high relative to GDP, because this leads to high gains for producers from reduced exchange rate risk and reduced transaction costs; for the time being intra-GCC trade is low.
- Smallness of potential member states would point to the profitability of a currency union because after unification the larger nontradables sector provides a nominal anchor for domestic prices in the case of an overly devaluation (Aghevli / Khan / Montiel 1991, p. 10). Another reason is that the greater domestic currency base might allow to de-link from the US Dollar because the process of saving and capital accumulation is hampered unless a suitable numéraire and store of value exists. However, the GCC countries are not attempting to overly devalue, and experts believe that the GCC currency is still relatively unimportant with regard to its use as "reserve or ... international trading currency" (Tahir / Paul / Al Mahmeed 1987, p. 3). They recommend the linkage of a Gulf Dinar to an appropriate basket of currencies from major trading and investment partners.
- Coordinated fiscal and industry-promotion policies are required as a precondition for forming a currency union to minimize negative spill-over effects (e.g., resulting from a country running a high budget deficit and absorbing scarce financial means, thus exporting high real interest rates to partner countries); although the GCC countries are currently all facing budget deficits, fiscal policies are not coordinated.

Thus, several conditions are not met. Some might insist that a common GCC currency is nevertheless not a problem as most GCC exchange rates are linked to the US Dollar. Graph 4 proofs this to be right since 1987 for all GCC currencies except the Kuwaiti Dinar. However, as GCC economies become increasingly diversified, the link to the US Dollar is more and more questioned; and as intra-GCC trade flows increase, the transfer of external shocks will eventually pose problems.

Although the creation of the Gulf Dinar would not have remarkable immediate real effects, it would indicate that the GCC countries are willing to sur-

Graph 4: Nominal Exchange Rates of GCC Currencies Against the US Dollar, 1973-1992

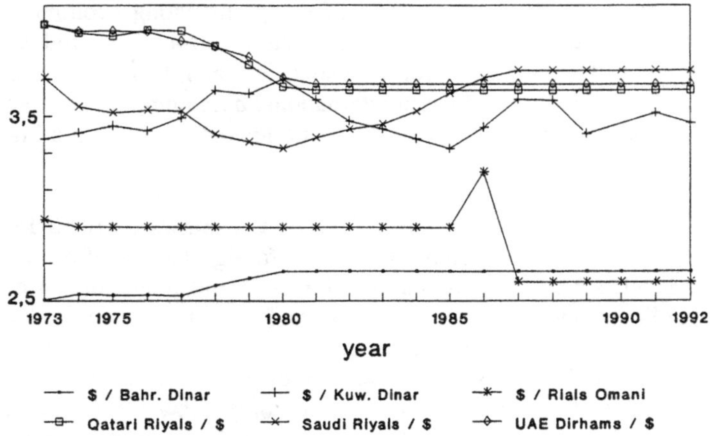

Note: values for 1992 are from end of June
Sources: International Monetary Fund (1992b, 1992c)

render national sovereignty, make further steps to integrate their economies, and coordinate fiscal and other economic policies. Still, problems with different impacts of oil price shocks would persist.

B.2.7. Conclusions

Regional economic cooperation can have positive and negative overall effects for factor allocation and welfare of the participating economies. The positive effects are the creation of a larger market through the reduction of transaction costs (which allows for specialization and taking advantage of economies of scale) and the increased international bargaining power. Negative effects may result due to trade diversion from a low-cost source to a high-cost source.

The negative effects can be reduced if the GCC is outward oriented (i.e., if it has low barriers to extraregional trade and to foreign factors of production). On the one hand, a free trade area allows for unilateral reductions in external tariffs by the liberal members. On the other hand, a customs union reduces the transaction costs by eliminating control of domestic origin requirements. The best combination is a customs union with low external tariffs. One should not overlook the fact that a free trade area does not only allow for unilateral tariff reductions but also for unilateral tariff increases. As Odysseus could escape the threat from the Syrenes' singing by being bound at the mast, individual GCC members could escape the threat from giving in to industrial cries for protection by being bound to a customs union.

Given the determination of GCC governments to push the industrial sector, GCC governments should treat small and large companies differently. For large companies which still have to gain experience on the world market, it may be appropriate to avoid duplication of efforts, at least in the beginning. Later, other enterprises can be established which profit from the first-runners' experience. Even if reduced by subsidies, competition from international competitors is essential.

For small companies which concentrate on the GCC market, the best policy is to create a GCC Common Market and fix incentives. The creation of a GCC Common Market not only increases efficiency by regional competition, but it also allows for the exploitation of economies of scale. If the clientele of a product is small and transaction costs to other regions are high (e.g., due to high transportation costs, different consumer tastes and artificial trade barriers), then the individual GCC markets may be too small for some producers in that they cannot take advantage of increasing economies of scale.

As-Sudais (1985) expected the gains from introducing a GCC Free Trade Area or a GCC Customs Union to be very small. Static effects were expected to be small due to:

- low pre-union tariff levels,
- little variation of production costs among members,
- narrow industrial bases in each country, and
- the domination of inefficient small-scale industrial firms in the private industrial sectors.

Dynamic effects were expected to be small because:

- competition was unwelcome to GCC members (evidence: they highly subsidized existing firms and were ready to protect many potential businesses),
- new investments would need more support than mere widening of the market by elimination of trade barriers (viz., clarity and stability of regional industrial policy; increased industrial opportunities as a result of downstream industrial integration in public sector industries such as petrochemicals, steel products, aluminum etc.; industrial orientation and experience of the people), and
- economies of scale could be expected for few industries only.

Even though an increase in intra-GCC trade after the *effective* trade liberalization in the GCC is expected for many theoretical and practical reasons, As-Sudais' general conclusion is valid: The coordination of industrial plans, industrial policies and industrial regulations is an important additional element to improve economic efficiency. If the governments are not willing to allow for long-run dynamic effects, then the economic gains from a cooperation council will be small.

In the GCC, countries with relatively low oil income will demand compensation when entering a free trade area because their competitors receive higher subsidies in terms of direct support, better public education for workers, lower costs for inputs, etc. Countries with high oil revenues will point to the fact they are constantly facing the problems of Dutch Disease, which still exists in a preferential trade area if there are still nontradables, and of rentier mentality. They point to lower wages as a competitive advantage in the "poor" country. Compensation mechanisms are not easy to agree upon. They may consist of direct financial transfers (e.g., when distributing revenues from import duties in a customs union), package solutions for the establishment of industrial enterprises, allowing some partners to erect protective tariff barriers against member countries' products and the establishment of joint ventures.

In reviewing experience with regional integration groupings, Torre / Kelly (1992, p. 39) draw the general conclusion that gains are maximized if the grouping maintains an outward-orientation and decides on an across-the-board liberalization of policies with automatic time tabeling. Which decisions did the GCC take to effect coordination, integration and interconnection?

B.3. Economic Decisions of the GCC

In this chapter, the official decisions of the GCC will be analysed. Evaluation of the decisions, as well as analysis of the factual implementation of the important decisions, are deferred to part C, although in some cases hints will be given.

B.3.1. Overview Over Economic Decisions and Decision Making in the GCC

Table 11 provides a chronological overview of the GCC agreements and the abbreviations which are used throughout this study and in the list of references.

Table 11: Chronology of GCC's Economic Agreements and Documents: *Abbreviation*, Title, Date of Coming into Effect

Riyadh Communiqué (1981), Foreign Ministers' Statement on the Founding of the Gulf Cooperation Council, 4 February

Decision to Establish (1981), Decision to Establish the Gulf Cooperation Council, 14 February

Final Communiqué (several years), Final Communiqués of the Annual Meetings of the Supreme Council, for exact dates see part E. References

Charter (1981), Charter of the Cooperation Council for the Arab States of the Gulf, 25 May

Rules Supreme Council (1981), Rules of Procedures of the Supreme Council, 25 May

Rules Ministerial Council (1981), Rules of Procedures of the Ministerial Council, 25 May

Rules Disputes (1981), Rules of Procedures of the Commission for the Settlement of Disputes, 25 May

Working Paper (1981), GCC Working Paper, 26 May

Economic Agreement (1982), Unified Economic Agreement of the Cooperation Council for the Arab States of the Gulf, 1 November; signed by Supreme Council 11 November 1981 (only intentions; specific measures to actually put the Unified Economic Agreement's provisions into effect were taken later)[62]

---

[62] It is a *unified* economic agreement because it replaced prevailing bilateral agreements (Working Paper 1981). For instance, a series of bilateral agreements on trade, protection and joint ventures "were signed in December 1978 between Kuwait and each of Bahrain, Qatar, the UAE and Oman" (Al-Yousuf 1986, p. 29). Bahrain and Saudi Arabia agreed at 28

Firms (1983), Permission to Establish Firms and to Work Therein in the Fields of Industry, Agriculture, Animal and Fish Resources and Contracting, 1 March
Free Trade (1983), Exemption of Products of National Origin from Customs Tariffs and Charges Having Equivalent Effects, 1 March
Professions (1983), Permission to Engage in the Professions of Medicine, Law, Accounting, Engineering and Consulting, 1 March
Transit Goods (1983), Rules and Regulations Governing Transit Goods in the GCC, 1 March
Uniform Tariff Range (1983), Establishment of a Minimum External Customs Tariff of 4 Percent and a Maximum Tariff of 20 Percent, 1 September
Firms (1984), Permission to Establish Firms and to Work Therein in the Fields of Gastronomy, Hotel Industry and Maintenance, 1 March
Professions (1984), Permission to Engage in Pharmacy and other Professions, 1 March
Land Ownership (1985), Right of Ownership of Landed Property, 1 March
Development Plans (1985), Common Objectives and Policies of the Development Plans and Programs in the GCC, 17-19 March
Agricultural Policy (1985), Joint Agricultural Policy for the GCC, 3-6 November
Education (1985), Role of Education in the Integration of the States of the GCC, 3-6 November
Environment (1985), General Policies and Principles for Protecting the Environment in the GCC, 3-6 November
Industrial Strategy (1985), Uniform Strategy for the Industrial Development of the GCC States, 3-6 November
Local Agent (1986), Permission to Export National Products Which Have Been Produced in Another Member State to Any Member State Without Appointing a Local Agent, 1 March
Students and Certificates (1986), Equal Treatment of Students and Acceptance of Study Certificates, 1 March
Government Purchasing (1987), Unified Regulations Granting Priority in Government Purchasing to National Products and Products of National Origin, 1 March
Loans (1987), Equal Treatment in Obtaining Loans from Banks and Industrial Development Funds, 1 March
Retail Commerce (1987), Permission to Engage in Retail Commerce, 1 March
Economic Declaration (1987), Economic Declaration of the Riyadh Summit of the Supreme Council, 29 December

---

February 1981 not to impose duty on imports from each other on locally manufactured goods (International Monetary Fund 1982, p. 71).

EEC-GCC Cooperation Agreement (1989), signed 15 June 1988, into effect end of 1989

Guide Foreign Investment (1989), Unified GCC Foreign Capital Investment Regulations. Guide Law, 5-7 March

Wholesale Commerce (1990), Permission to Engage in Wholesale Commerce, 1 March

Sources: official publications from the GCC Secretariat General; Ramazani (1988; Riyadh Communiqué, Decision to Establish, Rules Ministerial Council, Rules Disputes, Working Paper); Arab News (Final Communiqués since 1988); EEC-GCC Cooperation Agreement (1989; by Europäische Gemeinschaften; in German)

The main organizations of the Cooperation Council for the Arab States of the Gulf are the Supreme Council, the Ministerial Council and the Secretariat General. The *GCC Secretariat General* fulfills secretarial tasks in a very broad sense. It prepares studies, reports, meetings, draft resolutions and the GCC's budget, organizes conferences and publishes GCC documents.

The GCC was established on 25 May 1981 by the six heads of state's signing of the GCC Charter. The heads of state meet in the *Supreme Council* every November or December for three days. "Matters of interest to the member states" are reviewed by the Supreme Council (Charter 1981). "[R]ecommendations, reports, studies and common projects" of other GCC bodies have to be submitted for approval to the Supreme Council. It defines the "higher policy" for the GCC and the areas of interest. This includes the definition of areas which are of no interest and shall not be dealt with by other bodies either. Experience shows that the Supreme Council is the real center of power in the GCC and its importance for the decision making on economic cooperation can hardly be exaggerated, especially because its six members can in fact take sovereign decisions on behalf of their countries. For instance, of the GCC agreements and documents in Table 11, only very few have not officially been endorsed by the Supreme Council: Riyadh Communiqué, Decision to Establish, Uniform Tariff Range, Guide Foreign Investment.

Regardless of their economic differences, the GCC members have equal voting power (including the right to veto on "substantive matters"), contribute equally to the budget of the Secretariat General and alternate the hosting of meetings of the Supreme Council. One could suspect that the economic power is reflected in the choice of locations and representatives. In fact, some important decisions were taken in favor of the economically dominating Saudi Arabia; whereby the Supreme Council decided:

- to locate the Secretariat General in Riyadh,
- to nominate Dr. Abdullah El-Kuwaiz from Saudi Arabia as Assistant Secretary General for Economic Affairs,
- to appoint the Saudi Ambassodor to the EC, Mamoun Kurdi, as the GCC's Foreign Relations Coordinator, especially for the EC-GCC relations (Arab News 24 February 1990),
- to ask the Saudi Arabian citizen Dr. Khaled Al-Fayez to be the Chief Executive Officer of the Gulf Investment Corportation (GIC, see section B.3.5.), and
- to base the GCC Standards and Metrology Organization (SMO-GCC, see section B.3.2.) in Riyadh and appoint the Saudi Dr. Khaled Y. Al-Khalaf as Secretary General.

Other nations were not left out:

- the Kuwaiti Dr. Abdullah Yacoub Bishara has been Secretary General from May 1981 to March 1993;
- the Omani Ibrahim Subhi became the first Assistant Secretary General for Political Affairs in 1981; later his compatriot Saif bin Hashil Al-Maskery was appointed to the position;
- Musthaq Abdullah from Oman was selected in 1992 as the GCC Ambassador to the EC in Brussels (Bishara 1992);
- Sheikh Fahim Ibn Sultan Al-Qassimi from the UAE is Secretary General since April 1993;
- the Gulf Investment Corporation (GIC, see section B.3.5.) is located in Kuwait;
- the Technical Office for Communications of the GCC (an arm of the Secretariat General; see section B.3.4.) has been set up in Bahrain; and
- the Gulf University (see section B.3.6.) teaches students in Bahrain.

Agreements have to be transformed separately into law by each member country. No GCC Supreme Court exists. In case of "[d]isputes between member states" or in the case of "[d]ifferences of opinion as to the interpretation or execution of the Cooperation Council Charter" the Supreme Council can form a *Commission for the Settlement of Disputes* (Rules Disputes 1981). Thus, this commission cannot be asked for help by the business sector or peoples, and not even by individual states. Moreover, it has no decision power: the commission submits its "recommendations or opinion ... to the Supreme Council for appropriate action" (Charter 1981). According to information by the Secretariat General in October 1992, this body "has not been formed yet."

The *Ministerial Council* consists of the foreign ministers of the GCC member states. The Ministerial Council assists the Supreme Council in proposing policies and preparing recommendations, studies and projects (Charter 1981).

In addition, it serves as a link between various GCC committees and the Supreme Council. The Ministerial Council holds regular sessions four times a year; several additional emergency sessions have been performed to discuss security questions.

Other ministers or specialists gather in *committees* or sub-committees which can be launched by the Supreme Council as well as by the Ministerial Council itself (Charter 1981; for details see Rules Supreme Council 1981, and Rules Minsterial Council 1981). "In practice [Gulf Cooperation] Council activities have rapidly expanded with scores of ministerial and sub-cabinet-level meetings on a range of subjects, not only in the economic and social areas but also in the defence and internal security arenas" (Twinam 1992, p. 5).

Five committees were formed by the Supreme Council at its first meeting (Working Paper 1981). The Supreme Council specified in detail the tasks of these bodies, and the members of the Supreme Council remained in control of the decision making at every stage. The composition and lables of some of the five committees have been changed [63] and additional bodies have been established. Table 12 lists details of the economically most important GCC committees.

Table 12: ***Economically Important GCC Committees*****; Members; Important Agreements Drafted; Minimum Number of Meetings During First Five Years of GCC**

Financial and Economic Cooperation Committee; ministers of finance and economy; Unified Economic Agreement (1982) drafted in 1981, Transit Goods (1983) drafted in 1982, Guide Foreign Investment (1989); 11
Industrial Cooperation Committee; ministers of industry; Industrial Strategy (1985); 4
Commercial Cooperation Committee; ministers of commerce and industry; 5
Administrative Council for Standards and Measures; ministers of commerce and industry; 4
Ministers of trade; several meetings

[63] The following committees were stipulated in the Working Paper (1981): the Committee for Economic and Social Planning, the Committee for Industrial Cooperation, and the Committee for Social and Cultural Services. Instead of the Committee for Financial, Economic and Trade Cooperation, the Committee for Financial and Economic Cooperation has been formed. The tasks of the envisaged Oil Committee (which should have been formed by ministers of foreign affairs, oil ministers and finance ministers) were performed by several other groups, especially the meetings of the ministers of petroleum.

Ministers of petroleum; Petroleum Security Plan, signed in 1982; 10
Economic and Social Planning Committee; ministers of planning; Development Plans (1985); 3
Permanent Ministerial Committee for Communications; ministers of communications and ministers of port, telegraph and telephone; Internal Rules of the Technical Office for Communications of the GCC; 2
Agricultural Cooperation Committee; ministers of agriculture; Agricultural Policy (1985); 3
Ministers of electricity and water resources; 2
Social and Cultural Service Committee; labor and social affairs ministers; 3
Environment Cooperation Committee; 1

Note: For the exact titles of ministries in the GCC states see Appendix Table A6.
Sources: Alkazaz (1990, p. 29); GCC, Secretariat General (1988); Peterson (1988, pp. 225-227); Ramazani (1988, pp. 205-228); Working Paper (1981)

Besides the Supreme Council, the Ministerial Council and the Secretariat General, the most important body for the GCC's economic development is the Financial and Economic Cooperation Committee, which is in charge of implementing the Unified Economic Agreement. It was entrusted by the Supreme Council with the task of studying ways to achieve financial and monetary cooperation, freedom of factor movements, liberalization of trade exchange, and cooperation in the transport and communications spheres (Working Paper 1981).

In addition to the afore mentioned, several other groups met at least once to discuss economic cooperation and to take specific measures. To mention just a few: ministers of transportation and communications; port officials; oil industry officials, and several other petroleum expert groups; ministers of education; ministers of housing; immigration and passport authorities; environmental experts; development fund, basic industries and marketing officials; governors of central banks.

Experts also met in several conferences and seminars, for example:
- conference on development, in the UAE, March 1983, sponsored by GCC Secretariat General;
- conference on industrial development, in Bahrain, May 1984, sponsored by GCC Secr. Gen. and Gulf Organization for Industrial Consulting (GOIC);
- petroleum seminar, in Kuwait, December 1984, sponsored by the GCC Secretariat General and Kuwait Petroleum Corporation;

- symposium on establishing an Agricultural Research Network for the GCC countries, in Kuwait, 17-19 October 1988, organized by Kuwait Institute for Scientific Research, Arab Fund for Economic and Social Development, Kuwait Foundation for the Advancement of Sciences and GCC Secretariat General;
- trade seminar, March 1985, sponsored by GCC Secretariat General and General Agreement on Tariffs and Trade (GATT);
- conference on the globalization of financial markets, in Kuwait, October 1989;
- roundtable on the cooperation of fiscal policies in the GCC countries, in Abu Dhabi, September 1991, organized by the Arab Monetary Fund in co-operation with the GCC Secretariat General;
- conference for marketing petrochemicals, 3rd annual meeting in Jubail (Saudi Arabia) in April 1992.

B.3.2. Creation of the GCC Free Trade Area

One of the first and main achievements of the GCC was the GCC Free Trade Area beginning 1 March 1983.

The Unified Economic Agreement which was drafted 8 June 1981 calls in Article 2 for the free trade area:

> Article 2: "1. All agricultural, animal, industrial and natural resource products that are of national origin shall be exempted from customs duties and other charges having equivalent effect" (Economic Agreement 1982).

The expression *"product of national origin"* refers to a product which satisfies two conditions: "at least 40 percent of the final value of the product has been added to it in the production phase, which took place in one of the Member States, and ... the percentage of ownership of the producing installation by citizens of the States of the Council is not less than 51 percent as per the Certificate of Origin" (Government Purchasing 1987). The Certificates of Origin which have to accompany each item enjoying tariff exemption are authenticated by the concerned national government agency on a Uniform GCC Certificate of Origin Form (Economic Agreement 1982).[64]

Moreover, it is explicitely noted in Article 1 of the Unified Economic Agreement that products of national origin are permitted to be imported and exported into every member state and should receive the same treatment as national products. What is a *national product*? "Each product which has been produced in one of the Member States is considered to be a national product [in that state] according to the law of the State" (Government Purchasing 1987).

The GCC Free Trade Area came into effect 1 March 1983, less than two years after the foundation of the GCC (Free Trade 1983). However, several qualifications already have been made in the agreements. The exemption of agricultural, animal, industrial and natural resource products from tariffs seems to comprise all products of the primary and secondary sector. However, the

---

[64] These agencies are the Ministry of Finance and National Economy in Bahrain, the Ministry of Finance, External Department, in Kuwait, the Ministry of Commerce and Industry in Oman, the Qatar Chamber of Commerce, the Ministry of Commerce in Saudi Arabia and the Ministry of Economy and Commerce in the UAE (GCC, Secretariat General, 1988, p. 32). In practice, however, before the Certificate of Origin is published to the border authorities, a GCC committee has to confirm the decision that specific products of a specific firm are duty-free in the GCC. In the case of dispute, a delegation studies the firm in question (Al Bassam 1992).

inclusion of handicrafts and art is open to interpretation. Fish resource products are excluded.[65]

Kuwait implicitely excluded and Oman explicitely excluded additional products from free trade. Kuwait excludes natural resource products from free trade: these goods are not exempted from duties in the Ministerial Decree No. 52 for 1982 by the Ministry of Industry and in the Customs Directives No. 5 for 1983 by the Directorate General of Customs (GCC, Secretariat General, 1988, pp. 29-32). Oman does not exempt the following products from import tariffs: cement and its derivatives; asbestos products; plastic and polysterene products; paints; vegetable oils and hydrogenated oils; industrial cleaning agents; automobile batteries; and electric lamp bulbs (GCC, Secretariat General, 1988, p. 21).

Article 24 of the Unified Economic Agreement allows for such exceptions if "differences in the level of development" or "temporary local situations" call for them. However, it must have been decided upon by the Supreme Council, and should only be for a specified period.

As was shown in chapter B.1.4., *government purchases* play a dominant role in GCC countries. If national products are granted priority in government purchases, this creates a nontariff barrier to trade. From 1 March 1987 priority in government purchasing was granted to national products (i.e., products from the country itself) and to products of national origin (i.e., products from member countries with 40% local value-added and 51% GCC-ownership) (Government Purchasing 1987). Actually, GCC countries had already granted priority in government purchasing to national products if they were comparable to foreign products with respect to price, quality and the time of delivery. In some countries products from other GCC members were granted priority if no national products were available (GCC, Secretariat General, 1988, pp. 84-91). Now the condition that the price should be competitive was dropped. National products had to be given a price preference of at least 10 percent over foreign products and of at least 5 percent over products of national origin. This is a violation of the Unified Economic Agreement which stipulates in Article 1:

> "2. All agricultural, animal, industrial and natural resource products that are of national origin shall receive the same treatment as national products" (Economic Agreement 1982).

---

[65] Fish resource products are not a sub-group of animal products. This becomes clear from the explicite distinction in the document Firms (1983).

Although in clear contrast to this article of the Unified Economic Agreement, a country is allowed by the just-mentioned regulations on government purchasing to grant a 30% price privilege to its national manufacturers and a 0% price privilege to producers from GCC partners. In practice, "[a]ll across the GCC, a 10% price preference is given to locally produced goods vis-à-vis their foreign equivalents and a 5% margin vis-à-vis GCC-produced equivalents" (Al-Fayez 1992, p. 15).

There are, however, special privileges to GCC producers which only compete with foreign companies. "In the event that there is no national product available, products of national origin will be given a price preference of 10 percent over similar products" (Government Purchasing 1987). In addition, the CIF price of foreign imports is enlarged by relevant customs duties, even if the foreign product in question is actually exempted from the customs duty for one reason or another (cf. section C.2.1. for the actual tariff rates in GCC countries and possible exemptions). As in the case of the GCC Free Trade Area, it is again Oman which explicitely makes exemptions, viz., "contracts and projects for defense and security units" (GCC, Secretariat General, 1988, p. 102).

One practical element of intra-regional free trade is the permittance of free transit for goods which are traded among nonadjacent countries. This is especially important for transit through Saudi Arabia. The Unified Economic Agreement called in Article 5 on member states to "grant all facilities for the transit of any member state's goods to other member states, exempting them from any duties and taxes, whatsoever" (Economic Agreement 1982). Fees for specific services which are also levied on domestic products are not considered as duties and taxes (Economic Agreement 1982, Article 2,2). In putting these arrangements into effect, beginning 1 March 1983 free transit was granted in the GCC region (Transit Goods 1983). Several technical conditions apply (e.g., storage of goods for transshipment is allowed in duty free areas for six months). A problematic condition results from Article 6 of the Unified Economic Agreement: "Transit shall be denied to any goods that are barred from entry into the territory of a member state by its local regulations." This opens the door to intensive checks of contents, as well as to the denial of transit rights to specific goods in an arbitrary and sudden way.

One element of free trade is the mutual recognition of *technical standards* to overcome this nontariff barrier to trade and to allow for integrated production processes. The GCC established the "Standardization and Metrology Organization for G.C.C. Countries" (SMO-GCC) to set up common standards. It has far-reaching means to achieve its most important task, the "harmonization between the standards and measurements" in the GCC, but also to promote quality control (Al-Khalaf 1992, p. 2; GCC, Secretariat General, 1988, pp. 184f). In 1982, the Supreme Council decreed the conversion of the Saudi Arabian Standards Organization (SASO) into the SMO-GCC; its Basic Statute was approved in June 1985 (GCC, Secretariat General, 1988, pp. 182f). However, SASO was not dissolved; rather, its Secretary General also became SMO-GCC's Secretary General and SASO concluded an agreement of standards with the USA in April 1993 on its own (Arab News 9 April 1993). SASO's technical standards are generally adopted by SMO-GCC. Before 1985 the number of standards ranged from about 460 in Saudi Arabia to some 50 in Bahrain, Qatar and the UAE (Peterson 1988, p. 153). By mid-1988, 99 Gulf standards had been approved (Middle East and North Africa 1991, 1990, p. 234). In practice, international standards have a great influence on GCC producers because the latter want to compete with imported products, export to the world market and use world-market production technology. Besides adopting US standards, the SMO-GCC strives for close cooperation with the European Union's standardization organizations, especially since the EEC-GCC Cooperation Agreement was signed in 1988 (Al-Khalaf 1992; EEC-GCC Cooperation Agreement 1989). The Agreement stipulates in Article 3 the promotion of "cooperation in the field of standards and metrology;" in Article 11 it calls for "overcoming trade barriers."

B.3.3. Steps Toward a GCC Customs Union

A common uniform customs tariff for the GCC has not been established yet.

Article 4 of the Uniform Economic Agreement states "[m]ember states shall establish a uniform minimum customs tariff applicable to the products of the third countries." The "protection of national products from foreign competition" was explicitely mentioned as "one of the objectives of the uniform [minimum] customs tariff." Thus, a customs union is not envisaged by the Unified Economic Agreement. However, in 1987 the Supreme Council decided to "rapidly complete the necessary arrangements to set up *the Gulf Common Market*, [which] will be accomplished through the unification of the types and levels of customs duties applicable to goods coming from foreign countries in an effort to protect national products which are in competition with these foreign products" (Economic Declaration 1987, emphasis added).

The first practical step to reach a GCC Customs Union has been the implementation of the uniform tariff range as of 1 September 1983, more than four years earlier than stipulated in the Unified Economic Agreement (Uniform Tariff Range 1983; Economic Agreement 1982). Each GCC member had to charge tariffs between 4% and 20% on the CIF value of imports from non-members. The UAE, Saudi Arabia, Oman and Qatar had to raise their standard rates to 4%, while Bahrain's and Kuwait's tariffs could remain unchanged. It was also agreed upon that a minimum import tariff of 30% had to be imposed on tobacco and its derivatives.

In the spring of 1989 GCC ministers of industry were reported to have suggested high common external import tariffs to protect local industries (Middle East and North Africa 1991, 1990, p. 234). The source adds that "[m]inisters of finance, meeting in the following month, agreed to divide imports into four categories for tariff purposes, but were reported to have failed to reach agreement on exact levels of tariffs." According to another source, the GCC ministers decided in the spring of 1989 to "levy 25% customs duties on foreign goods competing with local manufacture," but it has not enforced this tariff yet (Ernst & Young 1990b, section D.7).

According to the Arab News (23 November 1992), the Financial and Economic Cooperation Committee agreed in May 1992 "on a seven-year timetable to establish a common market and to unify their customs tariffs on foreign commodities." The common external tariff was seen as the basis for forming a GCC Common Market and for international negotiations, especially with the US, the

EU and Japan. The EU insists the GCC Customs Union is a precondition for a free trade agreement.

The Supreme Council was expected to discuss the introduction of a common uniform external tariff at its 14th meeting in Saudi Arabia in December 1993. Specifically, it was assumed that the Supreme Council reviews "the proposals of a uniform customs tariff on foreign imports of eight to 10 percent" (Arab News 16 June 1993). However, at its October 1993 meeting, the Financial and Economic Cooperation Committee has "not reached any recommendation to unify customs duties" (Egyptian Gazette 28 October 1993). In addition, newspaper reports on the Supreme Council's December 1993 meeting and its final communiqué did not mention any decision on a GCC Customs Union or the seven-year time table (e.g., Arab News 23 December 1993).

B.3.4. Freeing of Factor Movements to Achieve a GCC Common Market

In 1983 GCC Secretary General Bishara first expressed the vision of reaching a GCC Common Market by 1990: "Our goal is that by the end of the 1980s, the Gulf will be one common market, with all the obligations and privileges which that step entails" (Bishara 1984, p. 41). This goal was confirmed in December 1987 by the Supreme Council (Final Communiqué 1987). The Customs Union had still a (long?) way to go in 1993. But what about freedom of movements of the production factors labor and capital?

The long-term goal of achieving freedom of factor movements was already written down and itemized in the Unified Economic Agreement:

> Article 8: "The member states shall agree on the executive rules which would ensure that each member state shall grant the citizens of all other member states the same treatment granted to its own citizens without any discrimination or differentiation in the following fields:
> 1. Freedom of movement, work and residence.
> 2. Right of ownership, inheritance and bequest.
> 3. Freedom of exercising economic activity.
> 4. Free movement of capital" (Economic Agreement 1982).

With respect to the freeing of factor movements and services to achieve a GCC Common Market, several steps have been taken. GCC nationals are now allowed throughout the GCC to engage in a wide range of businesses if they obtain the necessary licensing and registration.

By gradually applying Paragraphs 1 and 3 of Article 8 of the Unified Economic Agreement, GCC nationals were permitted to *establish firms and work therein* in the fields of industry, agriculture, animal and fish resources, and contracting (Firms 1983) as of 1 March 1983. The only qualification applies to Oman where fishing itself is prohibited to non-Omanis (GCC, Secretariat General, 1988, p. 21). One year later the same freedom has been allowed in the fields of gastronomy, hotel industry and maintenance (Firms 1984). Of course, GCC citizens have to go through the same licensing and registration procedures as nationals; in particular, this includes an economic and technical feasibility study (explicitely for the UAE see GCC, Secretariat General, 1988, p. 8).

By applying Paragraph 1 of Article 8, GCC nationals were allowed in all member countries to *practice the professions* of a) medicine, b) law, c) accounting, d) engineering, and e) administrative, economic, technical, agricultural, fisheries and industrial consulting as of 1 March 1983 (Professions 1983). At least two major exemptions have been reported to the GCC Secretariat General. Bahrain excludes the consulting professions (GCC, Secretariat General, 1988, p. 16). The United Arab Emirates placed high hurdles: they required a licensee to be a UAE resident; an applicant for licensing is not allowed to practice any other profession; a non-UAE lawyer is not allowed to employ non-GCC citizens in his office; and a non-UAE lawyer applying for licensing is not allowed to hold a GCC government job at the time he submits his application (GCC, Secretariat General, 1988, p. 10). As of 1 March 1984, additional professions have been liberalized: pharmacy and other professions (Professions 1984). General conditions are that the professional has the necessary qualification, licensing and registration, be an actual practitioner of the profession, and that he is a resident in the place where he practices the profession. In addition, pharmacists had to import medicines through a national authorized agent until general GCC agreements on engaging in wholesale and retail commerce where reached. A draft of Unified Regulations for the Practise of Accountant was set up in the early 1990s (GCC, Secretariat General, [1992]).

In a clarifying decree from November 1983, the Supreme Council allowed the above firms to receive all necessary services and public utilities, to obtain entry visas for their necessary staff and to sell the final products; similarly, the professionals were allowed to obtain services, utilities and visas (GCC, Secretariat General, 1988, pp. 38f). As of 1 March 1986, firms were also allowed to export their products of national origin to any GCC member state without appointing a local agent in the country of destiny for this pupose (Local Agent 1986). These were the first steps to allow for wholesale and retail commerce. Similarly, the GCC Supreme Council decided in December 1993 to allow Gulf air carriers (i.e., Saudia, Gulf Air, Kuwait Airways, Emirates Air; cf. section B.3.5.) to operate in the member states without the need for a sponsor (Arab News 23 December 1993).

The permission to engage in *retail sale* was granted to all GCC nationals in every GCC member country on 1 March 1987 (Retail Commerce 1987). The permission to engage in *wholesale commerce* was granted on 1 March 1990 (Wholesale Commerce 1990). Qualifications for a native-born GCC citizen are that he himself is engaged in the trading, is a resident of the state and restricts himself to one activity in one place. Naturalized GCC citizens may open branches, but may be required by the host country that its citizens participate in the ownership of the company in an amount not to exceed 50 percent. In 1992, the draft of a Unified Law on Commercial Registration in the GCC countries was circulated in the GCC (Gulf News 18 June 1992). Traders would have to register within two months of opening a commercial activity with the Ministry of Commerce and Trade. The registration number would have to be included on any publication.

An obstacle to across-investment is the granting of preferential treatment to domestic competitors. It was a major step to encourage GCC across-investment when the Supreme Council decided to grant *equal treatment in obtaining loans* from banks and industrial development funds to all native-born and naturalized GCC citizens on 1 March 1987 (Loans 1987). A loan can only be obtained if it is put to use in the state granting the loan. In the case of industrial loans the investor must of course obtain the necessary industrial license that is required of nationals. For industrial loans, the relevant organizations are the Bahrain Development Bank (since 1992), the Industrial Bank of Kuwait (1973), the Oman Development Bank (1976), the Saudi Industrial Development Fund (1974), and the Emirates Industrial Bank (1982); in Qatar, the Minister of Finance and Petroleum may grant loans at concessional terms.

By gradually applying the above-cited Article 8, Paragraph 2, of the Unified Economic Agreement, the right of *ownership of landed property* was granted to all GCC nationals starting 1 March 1985 (Land Ownership 1985). However, several qualifications apply. Ownership or inheritance is restricted to personal residence and to an area not exceeding 3,000 square meters. To conduct the above-mentioned economic activities GCC nationals are only allowed to rent land. In December 1993, the Supreme Council decided to let Gulf nationals own property in the member states also for commercial purposes (Arab News 23 December 1993).

Article 8 of the Unified Economic Agreement, which was quoted above, calls inter alia for nondiscrimination regarding freedom to engage in economic activity and freedom to transfer capital. This was interpreted by Saudi Arabia as stating that income *tax rates* and corporate tax rates should not distinguish between Saudi and GCC nationals. Thus, since 1985, Saudi Arabia requires that GCC citizens pay zakat duties (zakat is a religous wealth tax which is calculated by complex rules) instead of income tax duties (GCC, Secretariat General, 1988, pp. 152-156). Zakat duties are lower than income tax duties. Similar rules have been adopted by Oman and Qatar (Ernst & Young 1992), and Bahrain and the UAE central government are not imposing taxes anyway.

Visa requirements for GCC nationals were dropped in August 1987 (Peterson 1988, p. 227). Later, Oman and the UAE only required each other's identity card and in 1993, Kuwait allowed all GCC citizens to enter only with their identity cards; this is of more psychological than practical importance.

GCC citizens are allowed in some cases to buy and sell shares of companies from other GCC countries. This was first the case for the stocks of SABIC (Saudi Basic Industries Corporation), which have been floated by the Saudi government. In 1986, Bahrain allowed GCC citizens to sell and buy *shares of joint-stock companies* to an extent not exceeding 25 percent of total capital of the company (GCC, Secretariat General, 1988, pp. 157-164). Later, it was decided to "allow GCC nationals to appropriate shares of joint stock companies and to transfer them" (El-Kuwaiz 1990, p. 192). Until October 1993, only Bahrain and Oman have abided by the GCC agreement, but Oman restricted stock ownership by non-Omanis to 49% or less (Arab News 26 October 1993).

Because an efficient *communications network* is essential for exchange of goods, services and factors of production, the GCC established the "GCC Technical Office for Communications" as an arm of the GCC Secretariat General on 16 September 1985 (GCC, Secretariat General, 1988, pp. 191-199). Its headquarters is in Manama, and it is concerned with wireless and cable communications in the GCC. An urgent task was the elimination of existing interference between wireless frequencies. The Technical Office works toward unifying operating services, it represents the GCC members in international organizations, it undertakes studies, it proposes new laws and standard specifications and it prepares and attends conferences and symposia. Recently Bahrain, Kuwait and the UAE have agreed to set up a $50 million marine cable link to improve telephone, data communication and TV transmission systems (Arab News 18 January 1993).

B.3.5. Incentive Coordination and Joint Companies and Projects

The GCC took no specific measures to coordinate member countries' incentive structures. However, general efforts were made in the fields of development plans, industrial strategy, foreign capital attraction and environmental protection. In addition to the Technical Office for Communications of the GCC and the Standardization and Metrology Organization of the GCC (SMO-GCC), which have already been dealt with in sections B.3.2. and B.3.4., respectively, the GCC established or took over three institutions to serve its integration efforts: the Gulf Investment Corporation (GIC), the Gulf International Bank (GIB) and the Gulf Organization for Industrial Consulting (GOIC). Several joint GCC projects have been studied (e.g., a GCC railroad, a GCC gas pipeline, a GCC export oil refinery, a GCC crude oil pipeline, a GCC electricity grid). As of 1992, only the electricity grid was still under consideration. The promotion of private sector Gulf joint ventures is one of the principle objectives of the Federation of GCC Chambers (FGCCC).

> Article 21 of the Unified Economic Agreement stipulates that the GCC "member states shall seek to unify laws and regulations pertaining to investment with the object of attaining a common investment policy that will channel its internal and external investments towards what will serve the interests and aspirations of its people in development and progress" (Economic Agreement 1982; as cited in Guide Foreign Investment 1989).

Internal investment can be made by domestic, GCC or foreign investors. Complete regional economic integration requires that all economic agents are granted the same privileges when investing in a specific member country. In addition, it is required for *complete* integration that all countries impose the same privileges and obstacles to investors – but such congruency of rules is not desirable. Each region has its own environment and needs its own regulations. Nevertheless, by coordinating certain investment policies, regional integration can reduce the imposition of negative externalities on neighbors.

Medium-term *development plans* are important tools, especially in Kuwait, Oman and Saudi Arabia, for achieving economic development by guiding production, consumption and redistribution.[66] Therefore, it has been an important

---

[66] *Kuwait:* after establishing a formal planning framework the First Five Year Plan has been launched for 1985/86-1989/90, but already before less elaborate five year plans existed (e.g., during the 1976-81 plan period industrial zones were set up in Shuaiba, Shuwaik and Ahmadi); *Oman:* First Five Year Plan 1976-80, Second 1981-85, Third 1986-90, Fourth 1991-1995; *Saudi Arabia:* First Five Year Plan 1970/71-1974/75, Second 1975/76-1979/80,

achievement for the GCC to form common objectives and policies of the development plans and programs in the member countries (Development Plans 1985). The need "to achieve coordination and harmony among their respective development plans with a view to achieving economic integration between them" was already stressed by the Unified Economic Agreement (1982, Article 10). For the *industrial sector*, the GCC elaborates the objectives, which have already been mentioned in the document on development plans, in an additional document (Industrial Strategy 1985). As both agreements form a unit, they will be discussed simultaneously herein. The general comment is that the GCC countries view industrialization as important for their long-term development. Starting from this, four observations are made: a) the GCC outlines specific industries which deserve support; b) member countries are allowed and urged to support their domestic industries; c) some incentives are listed which should be reduced; d) the member countries are essentially granted freedom to implement whatever policies they want.

ad a) In specifying which industries shall receive specific assistance by the GCC governments, the comparative advantages are emphasized. In addition, industries must be capital-intensive, utilize locally available energy and other raw materials and exhibit upstream and downstream linkages to the already existing iron and steel, aluminum, copper, refining, petrochemicals and cement industries (Industrial Strategy 1985).

ad b) Private sector firms and cooperatives which invest in such industrial projects should be "encouraged and induced" (Development Plans 1985). This sounds like subsidies and other incentives. Possible incentives, which could be provided to projects on a selective basis, "include the following: Technical aid, ... provision of utilities, ... tax exemptions, ... credit on easy terms, ... granting priority by government purchasing agencies, ... export promotion centers,

---

Third 1980/81-1984/85, Fourth 1985/86-1989/90, Fifth 1990/91-1994/95. Efforts to draw up comprehensive development plans in the other GCC states were insignificant. *Bahrain* drew up a Six Year Plan for 1982-87. The first plan was written in the *UAE* for 1981-85, but it was not approved and implemented. Now, the UAE Ministry of Planning compiles data on planned investments from the individual Emirates and prepares three year investment plans. Abu Dhabi had a loose development plan for 1977-79. In *Qatar* a Supreme Council for Planning was formed in May 1989, but it did not implement any several-year plan. In the 1980s the implementation of the plans has suffered from falling oil prices and some plans had to be revised. After Iraq's invasion in Kuwait, the recently finished plan for Kuwait was rendered useless and had to be replaced by a new plan in the following years. The GCC countries' planning can be characterized as indicative, supportive and active (cf. Koppers 1991, pp. 42-46, which provides also a classification of development plans).

... training national manpower, ... establishing industrial cities and zones" (Industrial Strategy 1985).

ad c) "Direct and indirect subsidies on many goods and services" shall be rationalized; especially the cost of producing public services and utilities should be reduced by "rationalizing their use" (Development Plans 1985). This calls for lower subsidies for water, electricity and other goods. Industrial incentives should be gradually unified, licensing procedures should be unified and minimum requirements for new industrial plants should be agreed upon (Industrial Strategy 1985). In addition, GCC states are encouraged to coordinate between them "wage scales, benefits, incentives and employment contract conditions in the industrial sectors" (Industrial Strategy 1985).

ad d) The document on development plans calls on the one hand for "selecting growth centers" and on the other hand for "giving more attention to ... local projects" (Development Plans 1985). If there is any project which a GCC government wants to support, it is most probably possible to group the project into one of these two categories. If not, it may refer to the general clause which states that it "was agreed that each member state would adopt priorities which are suitable to its needs and abilities" (Development Plans 1985). The Economic Agreement (1982, Article 24) already assured the member countries that in implementing the Agreement "consideration shall be given to ... the local development priorities of each."

The guide law for dealing with foreign investors does not achieve the goal stipulated in the above-cited Article 21 of the Economic Agreement. The attraction of *foreign investment* is a major goal of the GCC countries to get access to sophisticated technologies, management techniques and other know-how. In the guide law for unified GCC foreign capital investment regulations from 1989, the GCC emphasized that it wanted to achieve "fair and integrated distribution of [foreign] investment" (Guide Foreign Investment 1989). "[D]iscrepancies of incentives, concessions and exemptions granted to foreign investors" shall be lessened, and the allocation of foreign investments shall be coordinated. However, the reader who hopes that the guide law fixes specific upper limits for incentives is disappointed, and the reader who fears that a GCC office is established which plans investment allocations to avoid competition and 'duplication' is alleviated. Despite its lofty ambitions which are laid down in its preamble, the guide law only requires from the individual GCC members to specify some obligations and incentives which a non-GCC investor faces, such as fields in which foreign capital investments are permitted, maximum foreign capital participation, licensing procedures etc. The guide law does not limit the freedom or flexibility of the GCC members in dealing with foreign investors to any noteworthy degree, although its strict application could somewhat increase the transparency of incentives and regulations.

Among the regulations and institutional arrangements which were still under consideration in 1990 are (El-Kuwaiz 1990, p. 193):

- a patent office to protect industrial patents,
- an arbitration center to handle disputes that may arise from investment activities,
- guidelines for commercial agencies and trademarks,
- a system for investment of foreign capital,
- a system to protect industrial products of national origin,
- rules for coordinating and encouraging the establishment of industrial projects,
- general principles of a consolidated industrial system.

In order to discuss ways of effectively improving laws to attract foreign investment the GCC technical committee for investment policies met in January 1993 (Arab News 18 January 1993). A study prepared by the GCC Secretariat General and the Gulf Organization for Industrial Consulting was reviewed. According to the Arab News, a major obstacle is the requirement that nationals have at least a 51 percent ownership in any company.[67]

One field where possibly harmful incentive competition may arise is *environmental protection*. A country may be tempted to impose low environmental standards to attract additional investors, especially if the country is small and the negative externality can be transfered to other countries. In 1985 the Supreme Council adopted general policies and principles for protecting the environment in the GCC (Environment 1985). No specific measures have been taken, but it becomes clear from the text that the heads of state attach high importance to this topic. With regard to the question of incentive coordination, they call for joint action and common standards in all relevant fields (e.g., they wish to "develop the regulations, legislation and measurements necessary for protection of the environment [and] to work toward their unification"). Negative external effects imposed on GCC partners shall be prevented: it is intended to "coordinate the efforts being made by the Member States for preventing negative effects arising from development and industrial projects in one state from affecting the environment in the neighboring states."

---

[67] As discussed prior, Bahrain dropped this requirement in 1991, and it is also not applied in the Jebel Ali Free Zone (UAE). In Saudi Arabia it is enforced in most cases, sometimes with the carrot of incentives which are linked to domestic capital majority, or sometimes with the stick of not granting a license otherwise.

While the coordination of incentives is an indirect intervention into the production process, the promotion and establishment of *joint projects and companies* is a direct one. What did the GCC achieve in this respect? Neither the document on coordination of GCC development plans nor the one on a unified GCC industrial policy is a regional industrial master plan for the GCC region. Such a master plan has not yet been written and probably never will be, but several joint projects have been evaluated and some have been realized.

One specific goal of GCC economic cooperation was the preparation of "studies of investment opportunities and economic feasibility of projects in the production sector" and their coordination with member states; specifically the need for linking of infrastructural projects in member states and for setting up industrial joint ventures among some or all member states was emphasized (Development Plans 1985). In particular, two institutions assist the GCC in achieving these goals: the Gulf Investment Corporation and the Gulf Organization for Industrial Consulting. These institutions also assist the GCC in promoting private sector joint-ventures; Articles 9 and 13 of the Unified Economic Agreement called for this promotion "to link their citizens' economic interests in the various spheres," and "to achieve economic integration, productive interface, and common development on sound economic basis."[68]

The *Gulf Investment Corporation GSC (GIC)* is an investment company which is registered in Kuwait as a Gulf Shareholding Company (GSC) (Gulf Investment Corporation 1990; 1991; 1992). The six GCC governments subscribed in equal amounts to the $2,100 million capital, of which $540 million is paid-up. Business activities commenced in November 1983. GIC has "to invest its own funds and those which are deposited therewith in various investment activities *inside and outside* the shareholding states and to contribute towards furthering and developing the economic and financial resources of the shareholding states" (Gulf Investment Corporation 1982a; emphasis added). From this, from GIC's Articles of Association and from the internal division of GIC in a finance group and a projects group, it is clear that the contribution to the economic development, integration and diversification of the GCC states by promoting and financing investment projects is only one goal of the Corporation (Gulf Investment Corporation 1982b; 1992). Even this activity has to yield an acceptable return: GIC shall carry out "promotion of projects and investing therein with the *purpose of realizing profits*, particularly such joint ventures which may serve the aims of cooperation amongst the shareholding countries with a view to developing their economies and achieving integration between

---

[68] Besides stressing economic viability, the GCC often insist that "harmful competition" has to be avoided. These contradictory positions will be discussed in section C.2.2.

them" (Gulf Investment Corporation 1982b; emphasis added). It is part of GIC's corporate mission to "provide a commercially acceptable return" (Gulf Investment Corporation 1991). Thus, the GIC should not be misunderstood as being a classical development fund.

In 1991 the GIC took over the *Gulf International Bank (GIB)*, one of the five largest banks in the GCC with respect to total assets (Institute of Banking Studies 1989, p. 18). GIB was established by the governments of the GCC countries and Iraq in 1975 and it was facing severe financial difficulties in 1989 and 1990.[69] GIB is an international merchant and wholesale commercial bank headquartered in Bahrain (Gulf International Bank 1990; 1991). "In the future GIB will operate mainly as a wholesale commercial bank, while the Corporation will function primarily as an investment bank" (Gulf Investment Corporation 1992). GIC and GIB will again be discussed in section C.1.3.

To realize regional cooperation and coordination in the Gulf industrial sector, a specialized organization has been set up. The *Gulf Organization for Industrial Consulting (GOIC)* is a nonprofit organization with an annual budget of some $5 million, headquartered in Doha (Gulf Organization for Industrial Consulting 1991). GOIC was originally established by the governments of the GCC countries and of Iraq. In January 1991, during Iraq's occupation of Kuwait, the membership was revised to only include the GCC countries.[70] It has the objective to realize cooperation and coordination amongst its member states in the industrial sector. Among its various tasks is the identification, evaluation and promotion of industrial joint venture projects, the studying of ways to improve GCC's industrial policies and the provision of industrial consulting services to both private and public institutions, as well as to the GCC Secretariat General. The GOIC itself, in contrast to the GIC, does not invest in projects: in 1990, 89% of its assets of $6.3 million were bank depos-

---

[69] While shareholders' equity was $726 million at the end of 1988, in 1989 a special charge of $725 million had to be taken against troubled LDC exposures and in 1990 provisions of $465 million had to be made against exposure to counterparties affected by the Gulf crisis. In 1989 shareholders had to pay a further call of $359 million, resulting in $1,001 million of paid-up capital. To allow for a ratio of shareholders' equity to total assets of 6.4% (as against -0.5% otherwise), GIC invested $450 million in GIB's capital on 31 December 1990. In April 1992 the capital of GIB was restructured by reducing the paid up capital by the accumulated loss, retroactive to the beginning of 1991.

[70] In 1989, Iraq was relieved from the payment of its total outstanding contributions of $7.7 million, its obligations of at least seven years. From this and from the fact that Iraq's theoretical share was only 17%, it is safe to conclude that the GCC countries were dominant in GOIC even before January 1991.

its. It is quite interesting to study GOIC's achievements in some detail, especially its bad luck in promoting regional joint ventures (cf. section C.1.3.).

The GCC Secretariat General studies a number of joint projects on its own. Three are carried out, viz., "a company to produce pure breeds of fowl, a company for the production and marketing of seeds and seedlings, and a re-insurance company" (El-Kuwaiz 1990, p. 192). In addition, "[a]rrangements for establishing a company for manufacturing poultry and dairy equipment in the United Arab Emirates" was under way in 1989.

Besides GIC, GOIC and the GCC Secretariat General, the *Industrial Co-operation Committee* of ministers of industry plays a major role in promoting joint industrial projects. In its first meeting, October 1981, it decided to pursue this goal and to form a technical committee specializing in industrial questions (Ramazani 1988, p. 205). In 1992, the Saudi Minister for Industry and Electricity said this technical committee comprises officials in charge of issuing industrial licenses (Arab News 10 February 1992). They meet periodically to review and evaluate the progress of joint projects and make recommendations to the Industrial Cooperation Committee. While this cooperation does not limit the decision making rights of GCC member countries, it leads at least to an exchange of information. Moreover, it is most probable that joint venture companies face less red tape when selling their products in the GCC region.

The Unified Economic Agreement calls for joint efforts in the area of transportation, including *joint infrastructure projects:*

> Article 19: "1. The member states shall cooperate in the fields of land and sea transportation, and communications. They shall also coordinate and establish infrastructure projects such as seaports, airports, water and power stations, roads with a view to realising common economic development and linking their economic activities with each other.
>
> 2. The contracting states shall coordinate aviation and air transport policies among them and promote all spheres of joint activities at various levels" (Economic Agreement 1982).

The most important joint project was not a GCC project, but rather, a Saudi-Bahraini project: the King Fahd Causeway between Saudi Arabia and Bahrain, named after the Saudi King Fahd. It was wholly financed by Saudi Arabia and opened in November 1986. Almost three million vehicles crossed in 1990 (Saudi Economic Survey 12 February 1992, p. 7). The bridge was not a GCC project, especially because the contract had been awarded one year before the GCC was founded, but it makes the GCC concept more viable because all GCC countries are now linked by road, ship and air.

In contrast, the GCC project of a Trans-Gulf Railroad (which could have been an attractive mean for transportation of goods and travelers and could have been connected with Saudi Arabia's railroad from Riyadh to Dammam and to Iraq's existing railway to Europe) was "postponed." The Supreme Council agreed in 1983 to conduct a feasibility study. This study came to the conclusion that the costs of $4 billion were too high (Middle East and North Africa 1991, 1990, p. 234).

As for the coordination of aviation and air transport policies, the GCC has had rather limited success. First, although three Gulf carriers already existed, a fourth was founded in 1985. Saudia was founded in 1945 and is owned by the Saudi government. It is by far the largest Arab carrier and one of the world's major airlines. Gulf Air, founded in 1950, and Kuwait Airways, founded in 1954, are only one fifth of Saudia's size (Kassem 1989). Kuwait Airways is owned by the Kuwaiti government, while Gulf Air is jointly owned by the governments of Bahrain, Oman, Qatar and Abu Dhabi. When Gulf Air drastically reduced the number of flights to and from Dubai, Dubai felt that this was a penalty for issuing temporary operating permits to non-Arab carriers and "retaliated by starting its own carrier," Emirates Air (Kassem 1989, pp. 42f). Second, at a 1993 expert meeting, the GCC postponed the following issues: allowing the four carriers to operate from any point within the Gulf states, opening the aviation companies to private investors and allowing endorsement of air tickets purchased from other Gulf airlines (Arab News 27 April 1993). However, it was agreed in principle to establish a GCC air transport company to better achieve cooperation among the Gulf carriers. Later, in December 1993, the Supreme Council decided to allow Gulf air carriers to operate in the member states without the use of a sponsor (Arab News 23 December 1993). The GCC's airline companies did establish "a mutual company for supplying aircraft from their companies at London's Heathrow Airport" (El-Kuwaiz 1990, p. 192).

Besides the Trans-Gulf Railroad, *joint projects*, which have been studied but not implemented due to economic and technical reasons, were a GCC gas pipeline network, a GCC export oil refinery on the Indian Ocean in Oman and a GCC crude oil pipeline to a terminal on the Indian Ocean in Oman. A project which has been studied for about a decade, but was still under consideration in 1992, is a GCC electrical interconnect grid intended to reduce generating reserves. Further details on some of the projects are given in the paragraphs on oil policy coordination in the next section.

Lastly, but certainly not least, the *Federation of GCC Chambers (FGCCC)* with its 1993 Secretary General Mohammed Abdulla Al-Mulla, needs to be mentioned. Located in Dammam, it was founded in 1979 by the GCC states and Iraq, but Iraq's membership was later dissolved (Falcon Directory Publications [1991], pp. 11f). Among its objectives is the promotion of private sector Gulf economic joint ventures, free trade, free movement of production factors and a common GCC currency.

B.3.6. Other Efforts of Policy Coordination

The GCC is well aware of the *problems in rentier states* (cf. section B.1.3.) and has incorporated in its agreements several goals and possible measures to counteract. To list just two:

- Anything above a certain minimum standard of living "will be a right which the individual earns through his own efforts and accomplishments" (Development Plans 1985).[71]
- In principle, GCC governments should aim at "making the beneficiaries from public services share in bearing the expenses of producing them" (Development Plans 1985).

In addition, GCC countries want to take action to overcome the negative attitude of its citizens towards blue-collar jobs and technical jobs:

- A sufficient proportion of students shall be "guided towards technical and vocational education" (Development Plans 1985).
- The public shall be made "aware, through the media, of the importance of work as a religious and social value, with a view to change attitudes towards certain occupations which at present are not acceptable to some people" (Development Plans 1985).

The GCC was eager to stress the importance of cooperation in the fields of *reseach & development, education and training*. Article 14 of the Unified Economic Agreement urges the GCC member states to cooperate in building a genuine basis for research and development in the applied sciences, while Article 16 demands that coordinated programs for technical, vocational and professional training are implemented. The documents Development Plans (1985), Industrial Strategy (1985) and Education (1985), emphasize the importance of these goals and spell out further details (e.g., the necessity to interlink GCC research institutes). In all these agreements the invaluable relevance of science and of pro-industrial thinking was outlined.

One concrete project was implemented by the GCC states in cooperation with Iraq was the *Arabian Gulf University* in Bahrain (Arabian Gulf University [1991]; Bauer / Oehme 1989, pp. 46f; Middle East and North Africa 1991, 1990, p. 328; Tehran Times 7 January 1992). Because of Iraq's invasion of Kuwait, the GCC states discontinued Iraq's participation in 1990. The Arabian Gulf University was initiated by the Arab Bureau of Education for the Gulf States (ABEGS) in 1980. The ABEGS, which was founded by the GCC coun-

---

[71] Other possibilities to get wealthy, which are allowed for in the GCC, are inheritance (Economic Agreement 1982) and luck.

tries and Iraq in 1975, set up a sophisticated new campus for up to 5,000 students in 1988. The concept was to serve the Gulf Arabs with specialized research and training. The Gulf University has three colleges: the College for Medicine & Medical Sciences, the College of Applied Sciences and the College of Education. It provides for undergraduate and postgraduate courses. Only 20 percent of the students may come from countries other than the GCC. The sad part of the story is that only Saudi Arabia, Kuwait and Bahrain contributed their share to the contracting firms who built the University. Consequently, the complete new campus is used by Bahrain University and the Gulf University is limited to the buildings of the Medical School, where about 500 students are taking courses in all three colleges.

In the field of *monetary cooperation*, the GCC not only decided to study or to merely consider the establishment of a unified currency, it also decided to make an endeavour to achieve this goal:

> "The member states shall seek to coordinate their financial, monetary and banking policies and enhance cooperation between monetary agencies and central banks, including an endeavour to establish a common currency in order to further their desired economic integration" (Economic Agreement 1982, Article 22).

In February 1987, the central bank governors agreed in principle to coordinate their exchange rates (Middle East and North Africa 1991, 1990, p. 234). In December, the Supreme Council "praised the steps taken toward authorizing a common index for the [GCC] currencies" (Economic Declaration 1987). Explicitely, they view this as an important step toward "the achievement of the Gulf Common Market" in line with the foundation-stone theory (cf. section B.2.6.).

In 1987, the Institute of Banking Studies in Kuwait prepared a study which came to the conclusion that the GCC exchange rates should be coordinated, ideally by pegging them to a well-defined basket of currencies from major trading and investment partners and allowing for margins of $\pm$ 5 percent around the central rate (Tahir / Paul / Al Mahmeed 1987, pp. 87f, 91-93).

In fact, since 1987, all GCC countries held their exchange rates fix against the US Dollar, with the exception of the Kuwaiti Dinar which experienced minor variations (cf. Graph 4). In spite of this de facto monetary coordination, formal agreements have not been reached, and GCC finance ministers and central bank governors still held talks in 1993 on tieing their currencies to a common basket of foreign currencies. However, the Central Banks of Kuwait and of Oman pointed out that the creation of a Gulf Dinar or Gulf Riyal was "dependent on overall moves to unify Gulf markets" (Arab News 28 March 1993; Tehran Times 14 January 1992). El-Kuwaiz, the GCC Assistant Secretary General for Economic Affairs, came to the same conclusion, especially because national governments are currently not willing to make the "political sacrifices resulting from monetary integration" (i.e., the reduction in national sovereignty over monetary policy) (El-Kuwaiz 1988, pp. 227, 231).

As it was just quoted, Article 22 of the Unified Economic Agreement also calls for financial and banking cooperation. *Fiscal policy coordination* was the theme of the conference "Roundtable on the Co-ordination of Fiscal Policies in the GCC Countries" in Abu Dhabi, September 1991. Amongst others, experts from the Arab Monetary Fund, the International Monetary Fund and the GCC Secretariat General discussed revenue and expenditure policies. Participants noted the differences in national policies, the importance of coordinated (if not unified) and stable investment incentives policies in a broad sense and the virtual absence of fiscal policy coordination on a GCC level.

In the area of *banking and financial markets* there are still major targets to be achieved. Banks are not allowed to open branches in other GCC countries (Arab News 7 September 1992), accounting and reporting standards are not unified and stocks can only be traded at their own national stock market.[72] Al-Marzook (1988) eloquently points out that the development and integration of Gulf markets for short-term money, loans, stocks, bonds and foreign exchange would exhibit economies of scale and hasten economic integration.

In the field of *agriculture*, cooperation ambitions are high. The framework is the agreement on the joint GCC agricultural policy (Agricultural Policy 1985); whereby it spells out the GCC's aims in agriculture: jointly projecting future demand and external supply, jointly planning future production, studying possibilities to coordinate production policies, joint production of all sorts of inputs, common programs to preserve the natural resources and joining efforts in research and development. It was agreed upon that a study should be prepared to show ways to execute these aims. Because the agricultural cooperation will not be evaluated in part C, some remarks are made here. In the light of the ambitions of joint GCC agricultural policy, relatively little has been achieved. In 1990, five years after the endorsement of the document on a joint GCC agricultural policy by the Supreme Council, in "Middle East and North Africa

---

[72] For the permission to buy and sell stocks cf. section B.3.4. Of the GCC members, only Qatar has not yet established a stock market; for details see NCB Economist (October 1993).

1991" (1990, p. 234) the cooperation is summarized as follows: "Between 1983 and 1987 ministers [of agriculture] approved proposals for harmonizing legislation relating to water conservation, veterinary vaccines, insecticides, fertilizers, fisheries and seeds. Studies on the establishment of two joint veterinary laboratories (for diagnosis of virus diseases and for production of vaccines), and on agricultural and veterinary quarantine, have also been undertaken. In 1987 two Saudi Arabian companies were designated as official GCC producers of seed and poultry."

The Unified Economic Agreement calls for endeavours to coordinate the GCC countries' *oil industry policies* and their price policies in the OPEC.

> Article 11: "1. The member states shall endeavour to coordinate their policies with regard to all aspects of the oil industry including extraction, refining, marketing, processing, pricing, exploitation of natural gas, and development of energy sources.
>
> 2. The member states shall endeavour to formulate unified oil policies and adopt common positions vis-a-vis the outside world, and in the international and specialised organisations."

During the first years, the impetus for coordination in the oil sector was high. Oil ministers met twice a year and other oil experts discussed ambituous plans, too. These meetings allowed Oman and Bahrain to have at least an indirect influence on OPEC decision making; the same holds for Oman and OAPEC decisions (cf. section C.3.1.). However, every country fought for its own best interests in OPEC meetings. In 1982, oil ministers "adopted a petroleum security plan to safeguard individual members against a halt in their production, to form a stockpile of petroleum products, and to organize a boycott of any non-member country when appropriate. A unified policy on the acquisition of technology was also approved... In December 1987 the Supreme Council adopted a plan whereby a member state whose petroleum production was disrupted could 'borrow' petroleum from other members, in order to fulfil its export obligations" (Middle East and North Africa 1991, 1990, p. 234). Among the concrete plans which emerged in 1982 and 1983 were the construction of a large 250,000 barrel per day GCC refinery in Oman's Salalah, the laying of a 1,700 kilometer GCC oil pipeline to link the GCC states with Oman's Indian Ocean coast, the integration of the member states' electricity networks and the integration of Kuwait and Qatar into Saudi Arabia's extensive gas grid. The former two plans were dropped later for financial and technical reasons, but the electricity network was still under consideration in 1992 (Gulf

Investment Corporation 1992, p. 8; Middle East and North Africa 1991, 1990, pp. 234f; Ramazani 1988, pp. 97-99).

The GCC countries coordinated their *development aid* in the Arab Fund for Economic and Social Development, which is located in Kuwait and in which the GCC members have a 52% share (Koppers 1992, p. 45). However, after Iraq had been forced out of Kuwait in February 1991, the GCC set up a special fund to support the economic development of their Arab allies, especially Egypt and Syria, which is scheduled to distribute $6 billion over 10 years (Arab News 29 March 1993).

The joint stance in the field of development aid is already one aspect of the important field of *external economic relations*. The interests of the GCC in this area are reflected in its agreements. The GCC wants to unify "the stands of the Member States vis-à-vis the external world in all fields whenever possible" (Development Plans 1985). The condition refers to the fact that the Supreme Council as the GCC's decision making body can only decide if consensus is reached.

Tariffs on extra-regional imports have already been discussed extensively. Article 7 of the Unified Economic Agreement deals with other aspects of external commercial policies:

> "Member states shall coordinate their commercial policies and relations with other states and economic groupings and blocs with a view toward creating balanced trade relations and favourable circumstances and terms of trade therewith. To achieve this goal, the member states shall make the following arrangements:
> 1. Coordinate import/export policies and regulations.
> 2. Coordinate policies for building up strategic food stocks.
> 3. Conclude economic agreements collectively when and if the common benefit of the member states is realised.
> 4. Work for the creation of a collective negotiating force to strengthen their negotiating position vis-à-vis foreign parties in the field of importation of basic needs and exportation of major products" (Economic Agreement 1982).

The GCC did form a collective negotiating force in the field of imports to a limited extent. Alkazaz (1990, p. 27) reports that "large amounts of specific basic foodstuffs such as rice, wheat and sugar have been procured jointly."[73] In addition, the GCC, Secretariat General, has suggested a "system for joint purchase of consumer goods by cooperative societies" or even a "Cooperative Union" (Gulf News 14 June 1992).

The need for forming a collective negotiating force arose especially with respect to petrochemical products (for details see section C.1.4.). Although negotiations have taken place to conclude free trade agreements with the EEC since 1984, with the USA since 1985 (Peterson 1988, p. 227) and also with Japan, no such agreements have yet been reached.

Parallel to these ineffective efforts, the GCC negotiated with the same blocs about improvements in other areas of common concern, especially technology transfer. The GCC's objectives are mainly stated in Article 15 of the Unified Economic Agreement:

> "Member states shall set rules, make arrangements and lay down terms for the transfer of technology, selecting the most suitable or introducing such changes thereto as would serve their various needs. Member states shall also, whenever feasible, conclude uniform agreements with foreign governments and scientific or commercial firms to achieve these objectives" (Economic Agreement 1982).

The only such agreement was reached in June 1988 with the European Economic Community (EEC-GCC Cooperation Agreement 1989).[74] In addition to aiming for cooperation in science, technology and investment, the agreement creates the framework for cooperation in the fields of energy, industry, trade and services, agriculture, fishery and environmental protection. The parties will endeavour to promote and facilitate concrete measures and the exchange of information. Article 11 stipulates that further talks will be conducted to achieve a trade agreement. A joint declaration, which has been attached to the agreement, notes several preconditions for a trade agreement. One is that the refining and petrochemical industry in the EEC is sustained to a certain extent for reasons of protecting "basic interests of the EEC" (i.e., jobs)

---

[73] In the case of wheat Saudi Arabia became a net exporter to the other GCC countries in 1986 (Grain Silos & Flour Mills Organization 1989).

[74] Strictly speaking, the agreement was concluded between the European Economic Community on the one hand and the contracting parties of the Charta of the GCC. Thus, although the acting president of the GCC Ministrial Council and the GCC Secretary General signed the agreement, it came only into force after it was ratified by each GCC country. In contrast, the European Council was able to endorse the agreement on its own.

and its "supply security." Another is that appropriate measures are taken to protect GCC's sensitive economic sectors, especially its young industries.

A Joint Council to meet quarterly has been installed in Articles 12 to 14. Since March 1990, the Joint Council of EU and GCC foreign ministers or their representatives meets annually.[75] Two months later, official negotiations between the two groups about a free trade agreement began in Brussels. The Saudi Ambassodor to the EC, Mamoun Kurdi, was at that time GCC's Foreign Relations Coordinator, especially for the EC-GCC relations (Arab News 24 February 1990). In 1992, Musthaq Abdullah was appointed as GCC Ambassador to the EC (Bishara 1992, pp. 4f).

Talks with US and Japanese officials about similar agreements have failed to produce concrete results (Arab News 18 July 1993). In a rare attack, El-Kuwaiz, the GCC Assistant Secretary General for Economic Affairs, blamed Japan for the failure of talks in Tokyo in June 1993 on economic and investment cooperation, in spite of the fact that "Japan is the biggest single economic partner of the GCC, with their two-way trade peaking at $35 billion in 1992."

Nevertheless, and perhaps more importantly, businessmen from both sides meet frequently. In February 1990, the First EC-GCC Industrial Conference was held in Grenada; in October 1992, the Second EC-GCC Industrial Conference was conducted in Doha with some 400 representatives from business and politics. In April 1993, about 170 European companies attended a trade fair in Abu Dhabi (Arab News 23 April 1993). Also in April 1993, more than 40 Saudi businessmen discussed in Washington, D.C., business relationships between GCC and USA (Arab News 16 April 1993). In December 1993, "[h]undreds of businessmen and industrialists from Japan and the GCC are due to discuss joint projects when they meet in Manama" (Arab News 18 July 1993).

---

[75] Meetings have taken place on 17 March 1990 in Muscat (Oman), 11 May 1991 in Luxemburg and 16 May 1992 in Kuwait. Three working groups have been formed for industry, energy and environment (MEED 1992, pp. 4f).

B.3.7. Conclusions

The decision making process can be stated in brief as follows. The Supreme Council of the heads of states "disposes" if consensus is reached, the Ministerial Council of the foreign ministers "proposes" (Twinam 1992, p. 4), and the Secretariat General exposes. In addition, several specialized committees make recommendations.

The GCC decided (mainly in its Unified Economic Agreement from 1981) to follow the route described by Balassa's five steps of economic integration: Free Trade Area, Customs Union, Common Market, Economic Union, Complete Economic Integration. The GCC Free Trade Area has been established in principle in March 1983. A uniform external tariff range of 4 to 20 percent was introduced six months later. Until December 1993, the GCC was not able to completely unify the third-country import tariff; and therefore, not eliminate intra-regional tariffs nor intra-border controls. Although the GCC Customs Union is not yet established, several important measures with regard to a GCC Common Market have been adopted. GCC nationals have been granted equal treatment all over the GCC in operating firms in a wide range of fields (i.e., industry, agriculture, animal and fish resources, contracting, gastronomy, hotel business, maintenance, retail and wholesale trade). Additionally, GCC nationals may engage in the professions of medicine, law, accounting, engineering, consulting, pharmacy and other professions. However, most agreements are subject to qualifications.

In the direction of a GCC Economic Union some rather vague documents have been signed on common policies in the areas of development plans, industrial strategy, foreign investment attraction, agricultural policy and environment. More concrete results have been attained by the Gulf Investment Corporation (GIC), the Gulf Organization for Industrial Consulting (GOIC), the GCC's Technical Office for Communications and the GCC Standards and Metrology Organization (SMO-GCC). With the exception of SMO-GCC, the GCC has not yet set up neither a supranational body which can make and implement decisions, nor a compensation fund or payments arrangements, nor free trade agreements with other regions.

The next part of this study is devoted to further inquiry into the practical and theoretical significance and explanations of the observed pattern of decisions on economic integration.

C. Economic Evaluation of the GCC

Major contractual achievements of the GCC are its Free Trade Area, its freeing of factor movements, and its common bargaining position vis-à-vis the EU, the USA and Japan. What are the real consequences of the GCC's efforts in these fields? How do economists and decision makers in the GCC view the prospects during the GCC's first decade? Chapter C.1. will answer these questions.

Are there built-in mechanisms in the GCC which hinder faster progress in decision making and implementation? Chapter C.2. investigates in these mechanisms. As fast progress is not an end in itself, the measures which have been taken need to be judged, as well as those which have not been taken, in the light of the previous analysis of the GCC's main economic problems (B.1.) and GCC's possibilities and limitations of regional economic cooperation (B.2.).

Mechanisms which slow down progress did not come out of the blue, but were conscious decisions taken by the Gulf leaders and the powers which influence them. Thus, the final Chapter C.3. asks if there are fundamental economic, polical or social reasons which pose obstacles to fast and far-reaching economic integration. Again, the knowledge of the GCC economies from chapters B.1. and B.2. will partly help in finding these answers.

C.1. Economic Performance of the GCC

C.1.1. Opinion Surveys and Interviews

Due to their education and their day-to-day experiences, economists in the GCC region are among the best experts on the question of GCC economic integration. Therefore, it is worthwhile to conduct opinion surveys and ask for the experiences and views of GCC economists. The author is aware of the following publications which describe opinion surveys conducted to study the opinions of different groups towards GCC integration: Arikat (1986), Nakhleh (1982, pp. 50-54), Nakhleh (1986, pp. 87-97). The most important differences to the present study are: they have been conducted when the GCC had just been established or even before; with the exception of Arikat (1986), they asked more about political, social, cultural and security issues than about economic issues; only a minority of the respondents were economists, and their opinions were not reported separately. Thus, interesting as these studies are for other purposes, they are of little relevance when assessing the economic dimension of the GCC in the 1980s and 1990s.

Therefore, in order to find out what economic experts in the Middle East think about the GCC, in 1992 roughly 40 independent interviews were conducted in the GCC countries. In addition, a one-page questionnaire was completed by 29 respondents (cf. Appendix Table A7). Appendix Table A8 provides details about the approached enterprises, scientific or governmental institutions, and banks or financial institutions, as well as response rates.

The 28 responses from organizations other than the GCC, Secretariat General, will be analyzed on the following pages. The GCC questionnaire will be dealt with later in this section.

The first question of the questionnaire aimed at finding out to what degree GCC economists perceived the GCC region as being a natural center for manufacturing or services. The answers were as follows:

Question 1: The international comparative advantages of the GCC lie in the following area:[76]

Service: 8 Manufacturing: 15 ("None": 1 both: 4 no answer: 8)

---

[76] The primary sector was not included. Nevertheless, one respondent noted that there exist possibilities to earn income from fishing.

Thus, of the 28 respondents, 20 answered this question; 75 percent of these believed that the GCC region has an international comparative advantage in manufacturing. In their comments, they pointed to the advantages of "energy intensive and oil and gas based" industries such as in the fields of "refining, gas, petrochemicals and aluminum." These advantages are due to the "availability of abundant hydrocarbon resources and capital." Taking costs of transportation and knowledge of regional habits into account, two respondents pointed to the possibility that GCC industrialists might be competitive in the GCC market with its high purchasing power and growing population. Most interview partners stressed the need for industrialization since it "supports development and helps [to] transfer ... technology."

40 percent of those who answered question 1 saw comparative advantages of the GCC in the field of services. One comment saw the service sector as being "more important for [the] GCC than manufacturing." Another comment indicated that Bahrain and the UAE could serve as centers for banking, tourism and insurance, while Oman and Saudi Arabia were good in manufacturing. Still another comment emphasized that it "requires changes and modifications in policies, laws, regulations, ... etc." before the GCC would be a good location for finance and banking.

One respondent felt that "international comparative advantages do not exist, the only cheap production factor is energy." This is not compatible with Ricardo's theory of comparative advantages where everyone has by definition comparative advantages. However, in the real world with nonzero transportation costs and unemployed production factors, it may very well be the case that the only tradable good in which the GCC region is competitive on the world market is crude oil. Some of those eight respondents who marked neither "manufacturing" nor "services" may also have believed that the GCC could profitably export only petroleum.

To summarize, the interview partners were convinced that the GCC had potential international comparative advantages in manufacturing. Thus, although the nontradables (i.e., mainly service) sector in the GCC region profited from the increase in oil revenues since 1973, economic experts did not feel that these experiences in the production of nontradable services had a great spill-over effect on the production of tradable services. The next questions aimed at finding out whether the GCC as a body helped to improve the GCC region's economic perspectives.

When studying the GCC's first decade in chapter B.3., it has been seen that the GCC Supreme Council worked towards guaranteeing intra-GCC free trade, capital and labor mobility. In addition, the transportation infrastructure was improved, and GCC heads of state hoped to support industrialization by multiple efforts. The GCC Secretary General, Abdulla Yacoub Bishara, said in May 1992: "The GCC has achieved freedom of capital, goods and personnel and is working on the common tariff" (New Arabia 28 May 1992). The interviews do not support this, as the answers to question 2 show.

Question 2: Degree to which the following targets have been reached in the GCC:

	100%		80%		60%		40%		20%		0%	$\bar{x}$	SD
a) Free trade within GCC	4	1	4	1	10	1	5		2		o	63.2	22.4
b) Transportation infrastructure within GCC	6	1	11		6		2		1		o	75.2	20.2
c) Right of movement of capital within GCC	14		6		4	1	2		1		o	81.1	23.0
d) Freedom for econ. activities in whole GCC	6		3	1	9	1	8		o		o	63.7	21.3
e) Right of ownership in whole GCC	5		9	1	7		3		3		o	67.5	24.0
f) Support of GCC by its bus. community	2		4		8		12		2		o	54.3	20.6
g) Firms' participation in GCC decision making	o		3	1	7		5		6	1	4	39.3	26.0
TOTAL	**36**	**2**	**40**	**4**	**51**	**3**	**37**		**15**	**1**	**4**	**63.5**	**25.9**

Notes: entries below percentages are numbers of responses; $\bar{x}$ = mean; SD = standard deviation

Before studying the answers one by one, it is interesting to note that the standard deviation is high. Answers ranged from 20 to 100 percent for almost every question. As comparisons to the answers of three well-known experts later in this section and other theoretical and practical considerations show, the average responses are highly reliable.

In general, even those interview partners which began with oral statements like "there is not much to be said about the GCC because it did talk but not act" or "the only functioning cooperation area was the Gulf Soccer Cup," found the GCC having been effective in certain economic areas. The highest marks were given in the fields 'freedom of capital movement' and 'transportation infrastructure.' The economic experts gave medium marks to 'intra-GCC free trade,' 'right of ownership in the whole GCC' and 'freedom to engage in economic activities in the whole GCC.' The ratings for 'support of the GCC by its business community' as well as 'firms' participation in GCC decision making' were below average.

ad 'free trade within GCC:' In March 1983 the GCC Free Trade Area was introduced. However, nine years later the interview partners still saw major obstacles to intra-GCC free trade. Instead of 100%, they rated it as being achieved to a 63% degree. In part, this is due to the concept of a free trade area itself. Only goods with at least 40 percent regional value added are granted free trade. In addition, in the GCC, goods are only freed from customs duties when the manufacturing units are owned by GCC nationals to at least 51 percent. Even after a GCC company has obtained the necessary Certificate of Origin, the importing partner country can raise objections. It might suspect that the company in question has set up a small production unit only to get cheap access to the partner country's market for its output from the large repacking unit. Such complaints have especially been raised against UAE companies. Case studies proved that firms indeed exist which purchase raw materials or final products for the purpose of reselling them as domestically produced.[77] In cases where doubts exist, a control team is sent to the company to check its capability and capacity. According to the findings and political decisions, unilateral action is taken to not exempt the products of the factory in question from customs tariffs. Example: In December 1992 Saudi Arabia decided to not exempt the products of seven UAE factories from customs duties (Arab News 30 December 1992). Such unilateral action is not in accordance with the agreement that the necessary Certificates of Origin are issued by the exporting state's concerned government office (see GCC, Secretariat General, 1988, for Saudi Arabia p. 19).

The relative failure of GCC free trade is also due to specific red tape in the GCC, mainly enforced by Saudi Arabia. Complaints by interview partners indicate the type of problems which occur:
- procedural delays (e.g. by frequently changed forms, packing requirements or the like),[78]
- doubts concerning the 40 percent local value added and disputes about the correct way to calculate it (e.g., should local raw material input be included? Should those wages and salaries to foreign workers which are sent home as remittances be included?) and to control it,
- rejection of certain items, although the producer has obtained a certificate of origin, because the certificate of origin has only been issued for similar items, but not for the sort in question,
- quantitative quotas on agricultural product imports from other GCC countries and

---

[77] The UAE government itself detected six UAE textile factories which engaged in label switching of Asian clothing to be sold to the USA. These firms were banned from exporting to the United States for six to twelve months (Arab News 20 June 1993).

[78] This is especially 'helpful' in the case of perishable goods, such as dairy products.

– high-handed decisions to block certain items from importation by arbitrary arguments.

Of course, GCC officials know about the problems of the GCC Free Trade Area. When analyzing the fact that intra-GCC trade accounts for only seven percent of total GCC trade of $123 billion, El-Kuwaiz said that it "was low because of similar non-oil industries and *border bureaucracy*" (Arab News 16 June 1993, emphasis added).

ad 'transportation infrastructure within GCC:' Although respondents agreed that GCC transportation facilities deserve high scores, they do not grant it more than 75 percent on average. As has been indicated in Table 8, the individual GCC countries have established sophisticated transportation and communication facilities. Transportation by sea, air and land is no problem in the GCC countries. However, the GCC itself was less effective in improving regional transportation systems. True, the GCC facilitated transit of goods and movement of people. But, it was not yet able to coordinate their four airlines, the project of building a GCC railway was rejected and non-GCC drivers of GCC trucks have to get entry visa for every single border-crossing.

ad 'right of movement of capital whithin GCC:' Most respondents felt that this area is the most unproblematic. Capital transfer controls are minor.

ad 'freedom for economic activities in whole GCC:' It is impressive to note the difference between GCC decisions and experts' evaluations in this field. On the one hand, it seems the GCC has eliminated obstacles to GCC professionals who want to engage in various economic activities in other GCC countries; cf. section B.3.4. On the other hand, this issue did not score more than 64 percent on average. One explanation lies in the GCC agreements themselves. For example, a closer look into the document 'Wholesale Commerce (1990)' reveals that native GCC nationals are only in principle allowed to engage in wholesale commerce all over the GCC. In practice, they have to engage in the trading themselves, must be residents of the state where they sell their goods and have to restrict themselves to one activity in one place.[79] More important, professionals have to obtain licensing and registration from national authorities. Thus, the permission to engage in economic activities is effectively not mandatory but optional to national authorities.

---

[79] For example, the UAE restricts ownership of supermarkets by other GCC nationals to one or two.

ad 'right of ownership in whole GCC:' This right is not optimal in the eyes of GCC economists, as they gave it only a value of 67 percent. The ownership of landed property is restricted to personal residence and to an area not exceeding 3,000 square meters. Nationals from GCC partner countries are only allowed to rent land for business purposes. The ownership of real capital and stocks is observed by national authorities, and ownership restrictions apply to nationals from other GCC countries; cf. section B.3.4.

ad 'support of the GCC by its business community:' The experts rate the support of the GCC by its business community only slightly above 50 percent. Interestingly, the subgroup of those experts working for the governmental sector are not more optimistic than the average of all respondents. From an economic perspective, the reluctance of the business community to fully support the GCC venture might pose a problem to regional integration. However, one should not misinterpret the answers. They indicate that the business community does not support the current GCC economic policy, but they do not indicate that business people dislike the idea of economic cooperation and integration in the GCC area. On the contrary, the personal interviews have shown that at least GCC industrialists support the idea of a GCC Common Market.

ad 'firms' participation in GCC decision making:' Respondents agree that the GCC business sector has only very little influence on GCC decision making. As has been seen in section B.3.1., the direct participation is indead nonexistent. The indirect influence is also minimal, as will be demonstrated in chapter C.3. As the interviews suggest, Chambers of Commerce and Industry in the GCC play no great role in making decisions at the top GCC level. This is not in accordance with the Supreme Council's view that the chambers should serve industrialization by providing data, determining industrial investment opportunities, promoting industrial projects at GCC level and assisting plants to overcome difficulties they might face (Industrial Strategy 1985). If plants face difficulties resulting from red tape, discriminatory laws, insufficiently trained manpower or lack of information, they should be heard by the Supreme Council. For Saudi Arabia, an empirical study from the 1980s shows that the government and the business sector disagree about the just-mentioned issues (Soufi / Mayer 1991, pp. 70-77). The study concludes that the "generally sharp discrepancies in the views of the government and the business sector reflected, primarily, a *severe lack of communication* between the two institutions" (p. 82, emphasis added). Of course, not all wishes of the business community should be fulfilled by the governments. For example, there are influential groups in the Chambers of Commerce and Industry which do not advocate competition in the GCC.

The answers to Question 2 have shown that economists in the GCC region did not only look at the labels of the GCC Supreme Council decisions, but at their real content and at their implementation. Their opinions are not in contrast to other findings of this study. According to these experts, which decisions should the GCC heads of state take in the future? Question 3 asked to name the three most important GCC activities.

Question 3: Among the GCC activities which should receive highest priority in the 1990s are:

a)
b)
c)

84 answers were given by the 28 respondents (i.e., exactly three answers per respondent). Only few did name less than three issues or more. Only 21 times, wordings from Questions 1, 2 and 4 were repeated. These two facts together indicate that the respondents carefully thought about the future necessities of the GCC.

Following Balassa's five steps towards regional economic integration (cf. section B.2.1.), the answers can be grouped into six categories, depending on the step to which they refer:
1. free trade area (10 answers),
2. customs union (10 answers),
3. common market (8 answers),
4. economic union (17 answers),
5. complete economic integration (8 anwers), and
6. other (31 anwers).

These answers show that the majority of experts strongly supports much deeper GCC economic cooperation in the future. Looking at the answers in more detail confirms this general impression.

ad 'free trade area:' One third of the respondents saw the introduction of "free trade within GCC" as being an important issue for the future, and one respondent called for a better "transportation infrastructure within the GCC" to further trade exchange in practice. Thus, although it is known to the GCC public that the GCC Free Trade Area was introduced in 1983, still many economists believe that the reality does not fully deserve this label. In connection with Question 2.a), reasons for this have just been listed. Further investigation follows in section C.1.2.

ad 'customs union:' Although only one answer was "customs union," six others amounted to almost the same: "toward the unified common external tariff," "unifying tariff systems on imports," "uniform tariff," "unified external tariff," "common external tariff" and perhaps "harmonization of trade policies." Three respondents seem to demand intra-union customs procedures to be eliminated altogether:[80] "knock down borders between the GCC [countries]," "free transportation between GCC countries" and "free passage (documents, passports)." Indead, it would be a major achievement for the GCC to introduce an effective GCC Customs Union.

ad 'common market:' One respondent demanded "integration of a common market" for the GCC, another one referred to the movement of capital in demanding "right of ownership in whole GCC." The other six answers in this category were about the abolishment of restrictions on labor and services when asking for "movement of labor" and "freedom of economic activities."

ad 'economic union:' The emphasis of the harmonization of national economic policies in an economic union lies on the *removal of discrimination* that resulted from disparities in these policies. The following questionnaire answers fit more or less well under this heading: "harmonizing fiscal policies," "harmonizing monetary policies," "science sector," "financial activities," "information coordination," "public service" and "removing red tape." In addition, the six answers concerning industrial policy may be viewed as being aspects of an economic union: "industrial cooperation," "industry," "manufacturing and industrialization," "common industrial strategy," "uniform strategy for industrial development" and "industrial activities." Of course, one might argue that some of these issues require a supra-national authority and, thus, belong to the next group.

ad 'complete economic integration:' A direct reference to the supra-national economic authority with far-reaching power which is associated to Balassa's notion of complete economic integration seems to be the entry "organizational development." Two respondents want the "unified economic agreement" to be implemented, which would amount to almost complete economic integration. For example, the Economic Agreement (1982) calls for "an endeavour to establish a common [GCC] currency." Indead, five times a common currency was named as one of the GCC activities which should receive highest priority in the 1990s.

---

[80] This has been labeled "customs union of type II" in section B.2.3.; in type I, only tariffs and quotas are zero.

ad 'other:' (i) From parts of the literature and rhetorics of GCC officials one might expect that economic cooperation with other Arab countries is one of the important issues in the future. However, only few responses dealt with foreign relations, none of which explicitely mentioned GCC-Arab cooperation: "free trade agreement [with] EEC and USA," "deal with other people (countries)," "economic relations arrangements" and "development funds."[81]

(ii) Of much greater interest was the question of internal and external security: "safety and security in the region," "unite the army," "security in its global definition (economic, political, military, ...)" and six times "defence." The natural explanation for this emphasis on security issues is the Iraq-Kuwait war which ended only one and a half years before the interviews were conducted.

(iii) Improvements in the labor market were felt to be very important by the economic experts. Some pointed to the need for job opportunities for GCC nationals: "national participation in the labor force," "training of national manpower" and "streamlining of legislation regarding entry & residence of non GCC nationals." Others remained more general: "human development," "job opportunities" and four times "education."

(iv) It has been confirmed indirectly here (as was found in section B.3.6.) that a common GCC petroleum strategy is no major question. Only two answers dealt with the issue of oil: "energy strategy" and "expansion of oil production capacity."

(v) Similarly, the following areas received only few answers: "food security" (two answers), "healthy welfare," "unite the passports," "democracy" and "concentrate on more democracy to the people." In addition, the call for democracy and for women's right to vote was articulated by some ten interview partners who did not want to write it on the questionnaire or did not fill in one.

In summary, the interviewed experts push for much deeper GCC integration.[82]

---

[81] The last entry, "development funds," may refer to the funds which have been installed to support domestic development (cf. section B.3.4.). In this case, this answer would have been grouped under the heading 'economic union.'

[82] This corresponds to the findings of another survey. In fall 1984, Shamlan Yusif al-Isa and Kamal al-Manufi conducted an opinion poll on the GCC's acceptance in Kuwait. Sixty-two percent of the 1,000 respondents felt that the GCC was an organization of both governments and peoples, and that the GCC with its high ambitions expressed the will of the region's population (Nakhleh 1986, p. 90).

One important aspect of the GCC economic strategy is strengthening co-operation in the industrial sector. Arab intelligentsia is also convinced of the importance of sectoral integration and joint projects for economic integration within the GCC (Arikat 1986, p. 24). To find out how this goal can best be achieved, the interview partners were asked about the effectiveness of several GCC measures.

Question 4: From the point of view of economic cooperation between GCC companies, the following activity was:

of great practical value: 1 ... insignificant: 6

	1	2	3	4	5	6	x̄	SD
a) GCC Charter	6	4	4	5	3	3	3.1	1.7
b) Unified Economic Agreement	11	4	5	3	4	o	2.4	1.5
c) Joint Agricultural Policy	1	o	4	7	7	3	4.2	1.3
d) Exemption of GCC prod. from cust. tariffs and charges	12	7	5	o	2	1	2.1	1.3
e) Regulations governing transit goods	9	8	4	2	2	1	2.3	1.4
f) Right of ownership of landed property	8	3	7	7	1	o	2.6	1.3
g) Long-Term Development Plans	5	3	5	3	7	3	3.4	1.7
h) Uniform strategy for industrial development	7	2	5	6	3	4	3.2	1.7
i) Priority given to GCC prod. by gov. purchas. policy	13	5	4	2	2	1	2.2	1.4
j) Allowance to engage in wholesale and retail commerce	11	3	7	4	1	o	2.2	1.2
TOTAL	**83**	**39**	**50**	**39**	**32**	**16**	**2.7**	**1.6**

(one comment on f) was "... residential property: 1; trade: 4; industry: 2")
Notes: entries below the figures 1 to 6 are numbers of responses; x̄ = mean; SD = standard deviation; calculations of x̄ and SD include one answer "all 1.5"

Already after taking a casual look, it is natural to group the measures into two categories: those which received good scores (2.1 to 2.6 points) and those which received relatively bad scores (3.1 to 3.4 points). Only the Agricultural Policy (1985) was rated even worse with 4.2 points on average.

Typically enough, the practical regulations fall into category one (i.e., d, e, f, i and j) and the general strategies fall into category two or below (i.e., a, c, g and h), the only exception being the Economic Agreement (1982). The answers correspond to the detailed analyses of the GCC economic agreements in chapter B.3., which will not be repeated here.

With respect to the question of GCC achievements, it would be misleading to speak of a unanimity of opinions among economic experts. This can be seen from studying the standard deviations of the answers to questions 2 and 4. To get a better judgement of the reliability of the average answers, the complete sample has been compared to a *subsample of three economists* which were selected because they are known to be among the highest qualified GCC experts.[83]

The patterns of answers for Question 2 are very similar in each of the two groups, as can be seen from Figure 12. The correlation coefficient is 0.82. In addition, the level of scores is very similar. For Question 4 the correlation coefficient is also positiv, but only at 0.49. The selected three experts were more pessimistic about the practical significance of certain GCC decisions than the average of the complete sample, especially with regard to the following documents: Transit Goods (1983), Development Plans (1985), Industrial Strategy (1985), Government Purchasing (1987), Retail Commerce (1987) and Wholesale Commerce (1990).

When studying the Final Communiquès (several years) of the Supreme Council meetings, one gets the impression that the GCC leaders are not aware of the slow progress in the economic sphere which the GCC has made since its foundation in 1981. Is this also true for the GCC Secretariat General, especially the GCC Assistant Secretary General for Economic Affairs, Abdullah El-Kuwaiz? No. This definite answer is backed by many findings in this study. In addition, it is confirmed by the questionnaire which was returned by El-Kuwaiz. He is less optimistic than the average of the 28 interviewed GCC economic experts, as can be seen from Figure 13.

The correlation coefficient between the complete sample's answers and the answers of El-Kuwaiz is very high: 0.79 for Question 2 and 0.83 for Question 4. With respect to Question 2, El-Kuwaiz sees in particular the right of ownership and the cooperation between the GCC leaders and its business community as being underdeveloped. With regard to Question 4, El-Kuwaiz pronounces the difference in the evaluation of concrete decisions and more general agreements even more than the other experts.

El-Kuwaiz answered Question 1 as follows: "The [comparative advantages] of the [manufacturing sector] relate to resource endowment and the wide range of secondary and tertiary industries that find fairly cheap inputs from that resource and [its] derivatives. Moreover, high per capita income creates demand on manufacturing products. Incentives are an encouraging factor. On the other hand social services, banking and insurance, and transportation and communication are increasingly becoming inseparable of [the] development process.

---

[83] Of course, this is not to say that the other respondents are less qualified. However, it is not known to the author in any case whether they are well-prepared to answer specific questions concerning the GCC.

Figure 12: Comparison of Answers to Questions 2 and 4 of the Complete Sample and the Subsample of Three Highly Qualified GCC Economists

Question 2: Degree to which the following targets have been reached in the GCC:

100% 80% 60% 40% 20% 0%

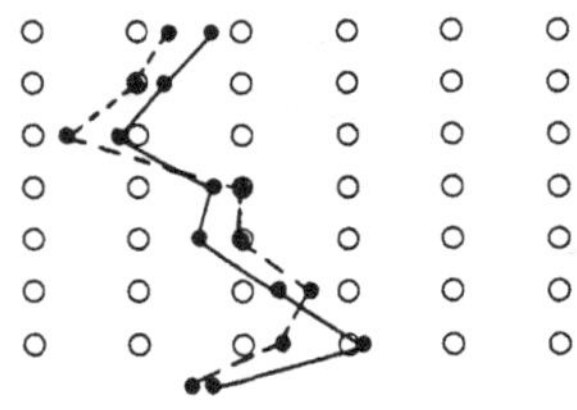

	all 28	three
a) Free trade within GCC	63	73
b) Transportation infrastructure within GCC	75	80
c) Right of movement of capital within GCC	81	93
d) Freedom for econ. activities in whole GCC	64	60
e) Right of ownership in whole GCC	68	60
f) Support of GCC by its bus. community	54	47
g) Firms' participation in GCC decision making	39	53
	64	67

Question 4: From the point of view of economic cooperation between GCC companies, the following GCC activity was:

of great practical value: 1 ... insignificant: 6

1 2 3 4 5 6

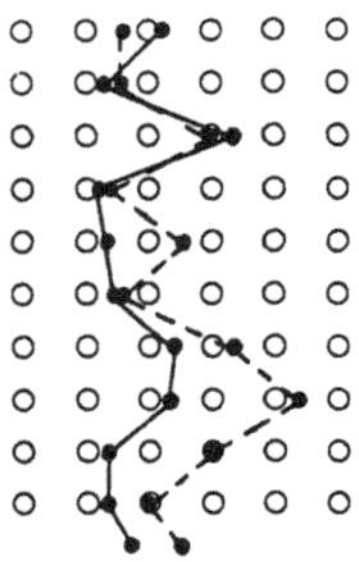

	all 28	three
a) GCC Charter	3.1	2.7
b) Unified Economic Agreement	2.4	2.7
c) Joint Agricultural Policy	4.2	4.0
d) Exemption of GCC prod. from cust. tariffs and charges	2.1	2.3
e) Regulations governing transit goods	2.3	3.7
f) Right of ownership of landed property	2.6	2.7
g) Long-Term Development Plans	3.4	4.3
h) Uniform strategy for industrial development	3.2	5.3
i) Priority given to GCC prod. by gov. purch. policy	2.2	4.0
j) Allowance to engage in wholesale and retail commerce	2.2	3.0
	2.8	3.5

Notes: "all 28" and "_____:" average of complete sample; "three" and "_ _ _:" average of the three selected highly qualified GCC economists

Figure 13: Comparison of Answers to Questions 2 and 4 of the Complete Sample and the GCC Secretariat General

Question 2: Degree to which the following targets have been reached in the GCC:

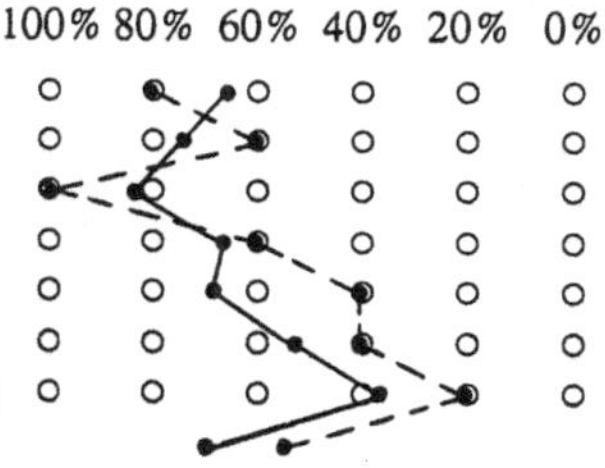

	all 28	GCC
a) Free trade within GCC	63	80
b) Transportation infrastructure within GCC	75	60
c) Right of movement of capital within GCC	81	100
d) Freedom for econ. activities in whole GCC	64	60
e) Right of ownership in whole GCC	68	40
f) Support of GCC by its bus. community	54	40
g) Firms' participation in GCC decision making	39	20
	64	57

Question 4: From the point of view of economic cooperation between GCC companies, the following GCC activity was:

of great practical value: 1 ... insignificant: 6

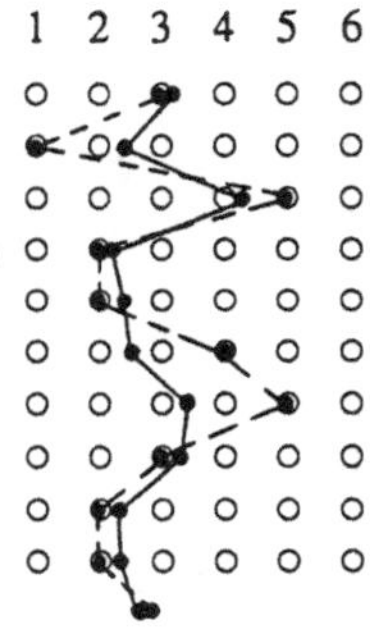

	all 28	GCC
a) GCC Charter	3.1	3
b) Unified Economic Agreement	2.4	1
c) Joint Agricultural Policy	4.2	5
d) Exemption of GCC prod. from cust. tariffs and charges	2.1	2
e) Regulations governing transit goods	2.3	2
f) Right of ownership of landed property	2.6	4
g) Long-Term Development Plans	3.4	5
h) Uniform strategy for industrial development	3.2	3
i) Priority given to GCC prod. by gov. purch. policy	2.2	2
j) Allowance to engage in wholesale and retail commerce	2.2	2
	2.8	2.9

Notes: "all 28" and "_____:" average of complete sample; "GCC" and "_ _ _:" GCC Secretariat General (viz., Abdullah El-Kuwaiz, Assistant Secretary General)

Advantages in both sectors have been augmented by easy access to foreign labor and strategic geographic location."

He saw the following GCC activities as deserving highest priority in the 1990s: "Common external tariff," "Freedom of economic activities and free movement of people and goods" and "Coordination of financial policies including exchange rate."

C.1.2. Intra-GCC Trade Flows

The GCC Free Trade Area was established in March 1983. In the preceding section, as well as in section B.3.2., several still existing barriers to intra-GCC trade have been analyzed. To demonstrate that the GCC Free Trade Area has been an empirical success, the GCC Secretariat General refers to simple trade statistics. As will be shown, although these statistics show a positive trend, they are are less convincing than it appears at first glance. To evaluate the impact of the Free Trade Area on intra-GCC trade (not to speak of impacts on investment, growth or income distribution), a more complex method is employed.

The Appendix Tables A9 to A12 provide *basic data on intra-GCC trade.* Some remarks may be helpful.

Table A9 shows the matrix of intra-GCC trade flows for 1977-1990, as derived from IMF's Direction of Trade Statistics. Oman's exports to the GCC (particularly to Saudi Arabia and the UAE) drastically increased from 1985 onwards. This is especially noteworthy because neither Saudi Arabia nor the UAE report such imports. The imports from Oman published by Saudi Arabia are less than 10% of Oman's stated exports, and the UAE doesn't report 1% of the value in question.[84] Similarly, the drastic increase in exports from the UAE to Oman is derived only from Oman's data. Finally, exports from Bahrain to the UAE are up to five times higher than the UAE's published imports.

Later, in the econometric test of the macroeconomic model, the trade data are derived from the importing countries' figures. In general, IMF experts expect the import data to be more accurate because GCC countries don't have export taxes, but they do have import tariffs. Therefore, they are eager to check incoming goods. The problem with the data and the likely superiority of the import statistics can also be seen by investigating Table A9. Part I of Table A9 presents trade flows from A to B as reported by the exporting country A; part II of Table A9 shows trade flows from A to B as reported by the importing country B. In part I, from the 420 possible entries, only 61% have been derived from the exporting country, 18% (marked by an asterix *) had to be derived solely from partner data, and 16% (marked with a y) had to be extrapolated for the entire year, sometimes by using partner data. The situation is somewhat better in part II, where from the 420 possible entries, 87% have been derived from the importing country, 0.5% (marked by an asterix *) had to be derived

[84] The original publications have been checked to make sure that no typing error occured in the IMF's publications.

solely from partner data, and 8% (marked with a y) had to be extrapolated for the entire year, sometimes with the use of partner data.

Table A10 first presents GCC country data on GDP and total exports. Then, summary statistics are provided. In absolute figures, intra-GCC trade experienced a decline from 1981 to 1985 and steadily increased from 1986 onwards. Total intra-GCC exports, which have been calculated from part I of Table A9, are compared to GCC's GDP as well as to GCC's total exports. Some politicians and even economists who analyse the GCC's internal trade argue that these figures clearly show an improvement in intra-GCC trade from 1985 onwards. Thus, they conclude the GCC Free Trade Area from March 1983 has been successful. Two comments have to be made. First, it is not necessarily the case that the increase in trade figures after the establishment of the GCC Free Trade Area is the cause of this establishment. In the following, a macroeconomic model is developed to investigate the impact of the GCC Free Trade Area. Second, the drastic increase in intra-GCC exports can be mainly attributed to the increase in exports from Oman to the UAE and from the UAE to Oman. Both flows are highly debatable. According to the UAE publications, they are much lower. Experts interviewed could not think of convincing explanations for the drastic increase in Oman's figures, other than that an error had been made. For a graphical analysis of the effect which arises from these debatable trade figures, see Graphs 5 and 6.

The upper line in *Graph 5* shows intra-GCC trade as a percentage of GCC's total GDP. The increase from 1985 onwards is impressive. The lower line shows the same ratio except that trade between Oman and the UAE as reported by Oman has been eliminated. The excitement diminishes somewhat. Similarly, the drastic increase of the share of intra-GCC trade in total GCC trade since 1985 (upper line in *Graph 6*) is partly due to the astonishing increase in trade between Oman and the UAE as published by Oman.

Table A11 gives some information on the development of specific parts of intra-GCC trade. These parts are the ones to which the Unified Economic Agreement explicitly grants freedom of trade. *Table A12* summarizes this information. Part (a) points to data problems. An asterix (*) marks the cases in which there is a great discrepancy between the reported values of both countries which report the same trade flow. Here, the deviation is called "great" if it is greater than 50% of the smaller flow value or greater than US$ 10 million. This is the case in 26 (i.e., 33%) of the 79 cases where matches are possible. Matches are not possible in 41 cases due to incomplete data.

Graph 5: ***upper line:*** **Intra-GCC Exports as % of GCC's Total GDP;** ***lower line:*** **Intra-GCC Exports without Oman-UAE and UAE-Oman as % of GCC's Total GDP, 1977-1990**

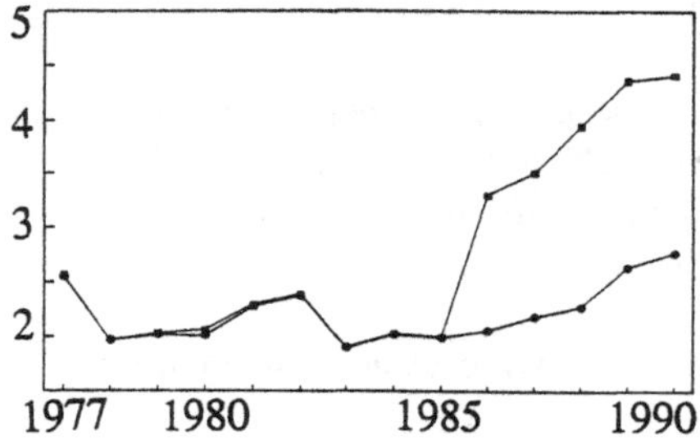

Graph 6: ***upper line:*** **Intra-GCC Exports as % of GCC's Total Exports;** ***lower line:*** **Intra-GCC Exports without Oman-UAE and UAE-Oman as % of GCC's Total Exports, 1977-1990**

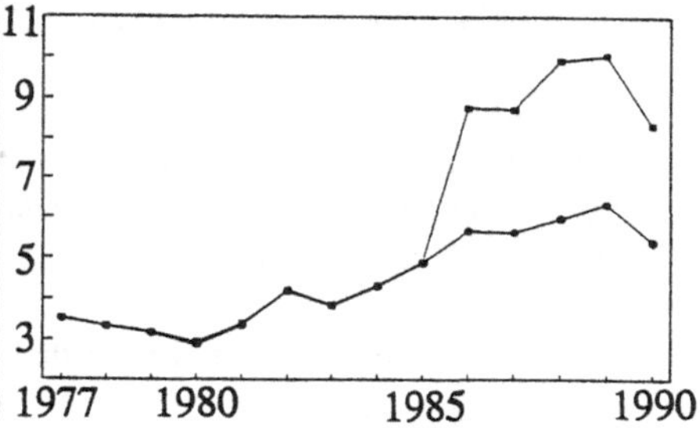

Sources: International Monetary Fund (1992a; 1992c); World Bank (1992)

Part (b) of Table A12, while still reporting only the exchange of products of national origin, refers to the total industrial exports to GCC countries and the total industrial imports from GCC countries, as reported by the individual GCC countries. It is interesting to look at the distribution of intra-GCC exports and imports for 1989, the only year for which almost complete data is available:

Table 13: Share in Total Intra-GCC Industrial Exports and Imports, by GCC Country, 1989 (%)

	share in total intra-GCC exports	share in total intra-GCC imports
Bahrain	9.1%	10.0%
Kuwait	10.1%	31.3%
Oman	6.6%	10.7%
Qatar	12.1%	8.7%
Saudi Arabia	43.3%	31.5%
UAE	18.9%	7.8% (only Abu Dhabi)

Source: GCC, Secretariat General (1991)

Thus, Kuwait was importing much more than it was exporting in 1989; whereas, Saudi Arabia was a net exporter of industrial products to its neighbors. This is different from previous years, when Saudi Arabia was a net importer (cf. Table 14).

Table 14: Saudi Arabian Industrial Imports from and Exports to the GCC, 1986-1989 ($ million)

	1986	1987	1988	1989
Imports	343	320	493	435
Exports	104	233	359	738

Source: GCC, Secretariat General (1991)

Econometric models are helpful in cases as here, where several factors influence intra-GCC trade flows, some of which are known and others are unknown. To begin with, *previous attempts to model the impact of a free trade agreement on intra-group trade* will be described.

Tinbergen (1962, p. 266) forwarded the following trade flow equation:

$$X_{ij} = a_0 Y_i^{a_1} Y_j^{a_2} D_{ij}^{a_3} N^{a_4} P_C^{a_5} P_B^{a_6} \quad (1)$$

where,

X_{ij} = exports of country i to country j
Y_i = GNP of country i
Y_j = GNP of country j
D_{ij} = distance between country i and country j
N = dummy variable for neighboring countries *
P_C = dummy variable for Commonwealth preference *
P_B = dummy variable for Benelux preference *

Note: * To obtain linear functional relationships, the logarithms of the variables have been taken; the logarithms of the dummies are 0 or 1, not the dummies themselves.

This equation provided the basis for estimating the coefficients a_0 to a_6 from cross-sectional data. Tinbergen himself admitted it is an important characteristic "of the present analysis that ... no separate demand and supply functions for exports are introduced – meaning that the equation is a turnover relation in which prices are not specified" (Tinbergen 1962, p. 263). At first glance, this seems to be a serious draw-back of the analysis.

However, Linnemann (1966) presented a general equilibrium model for international trade flows. His model is based on the following three basic equations:

$$X_{ij}^{D} = \gamma W_j^{\delta} p_i^{\varepsilon} t_{ij}^{\varrho} \quad (j \neq i) \tag{2}$$

$$X_i^{SF} = \omega W_i^{\sigma} p_i^{\pi} \tag{3}$$

$$X_i^{SF} = \sum_{\substack{j \neq i \\ j=1}}^{n} X_{ij}^{D} \tag{4}$$

where,

X_{ij}^{D} = demand for country i's goods by country j

X_i^{SF} = supply of export goods by country i

W_j = factors which determine country j's import demand, namely income and population of country j

W_i = factors which determine country i's export supply, namely income and population of country i

p_i = price level of country i's output as compared to the (exogenous) world price level

t_{ij} = trade impediments or trade supports between countries i and j (i.e., distance, adjacency, free trade agreements et al.)

Thus, (2) is a demand equation, (3) a supply equation, and equation (4) the usual equilibrium condition. It is straightforward to solve this model for p_i, and then to substitute this result into (2). The result is essentially equation (1), Tinbergen's equation. Finally, one might estimate this export equation. In the present case, one might take several Arab countries and run OLS (the ordinary least squares estimation procedure) for some years before the creation of the GCC's free trade area, as well as for some years thereafter. Now, one would judge the effectiveness of the free trade area by looking at the coefficient of the dummy variable for 'both countries being members of the GCC:' label the impact as positive if the coefficient was significantly higher after the creation of the free trade area.

In fact, this gravitity model approach has been applied several times (e.g., Aitken 1973, Sapir 1981 and essentially Amelung 1990 to evaluate the EEC, the EEC and EFTA, and four Asian groupings, respectively).

In the context of the GCC, the estimation result in this setting is that the creation of the GCC free trade area had no significant positive or negative effect on intra-GCC trade. However, the details will not be given here, because this approach faces several problems.

1) To begin with a theoretical one: the export supply equation (3) is not a structural equation of the economy, as is implicitly assumed in previous approaches. The inclusion of country i's income can not be justified in a macroeconomic setting. Export supply is not directly determined by the size of the exporting country's economy. Instead, export supply is one element of total supply. One might try to justify the above approach by stating that Y_i is determined by the country's real capital stock, which also determines export supply. However, the capital stock would only explain the supply side of Y_i; whereas, what is included in (3) is the actual (i.e., the equilibrium) value of Y_i. On the other hand, in an econometric sense Y_i could be interpreted as an instrument for the capital stock if data for the latter were not available. In this case one would have to overcome the simultaneity problem by statistical methods.

2) In the previous approach, T sets of coefficient estimates are obtained, one for every year t. Next, the t coefficient estimates for the relevant regional grouping dummy are compared. The dummy itself is 1 whenever both the exporting and the importing country are members of the regional grouping, 0 otherwise. If a considerable and significant increase in the coefficient's estimate is detected after the introduction of the free trade area, then the free trade area is labeled to be "successful." This approach is problematic when the estimated coefficients do not behave very "nicely." To be specific, when applying this approach to the GCC Free Trade Area, the estimates are for no single year significantly different from zero and some of the estimated coefficients after 1983 are lower than some of those before 1983. To get only one coefficient estimate for the success of trade liberalization, the regression procedure is applied once, but for all data. Two dummies have to be introduced: *Dummy* $D_{GCC\,ij}$ as just defined and *Dummy* $D_{GCC\,ijt}$ which is only 1 if both countries are GCC members *and* the figures are from 1984 or later. This allows to distinguish the trade effects which result from the creation of the GCC Free Trade Area in March 1983 (Dummy $D_{GCC\,ijt}$) from the trade effects which result from economic, cultural, historical or other links between GCC members (Dummy $D_{GCC\,ij}$). The latter effects may very well be negative (e.g., due to similar production structures or discrimination against GCC neighbors).

There are problems with this approach, too. If trade increases only gradually after the introduction of regional free trade, then the estimated coefficient for the Dummy $D_{GCC\,ijt}$ would be too small. Therefore, in the present study only the years 1980 to 1982 and 1986 to 1988 have been included in the sample.

3) In the import demand equation (2), it is implicitly assumed that the coefficients are constant over time and are not country-specific (i.e., they do

neither depend on the year t, nor on the exporting country i, nor on the importing country j). The nonindexation by t is common, in cases as here, where no plausible explanation for a change of coefficients into one direction or the other is available. The nonindexation by i can be justified if one assumes that import demand does not distinguish between the countries of supply. In other words, consumers are much more interested in the price they have to pay than in the country of origin.[85] It has to be recalled, however, that some dummies are indexed by i, such that, for example, a specific negative or positive evaluation by a GCC member for products of another GCC member will be detected (cf. the above-mentioned dummy $D_{GCC\ ij}$).

The non-indexation by j is most problematic. Even if two countries have the same characteristics with respect to the (few) variables included in the model, they may very well have different import coefficients. In the present context, the non-availability of some variables (cf. below) points especially to the necessity of indexation by j.

4) The inclusion of nominal figures for GNP and trade poses a problem. To illustrate, take the case where all real values remain unchanged and only inflationary effects occur over time. Because the GCC dummy and other variables would stay the same but GNP would move in line with the increase in nominal trade, the estimate of the coefficient for the GCC dummy would be too low. The correct answer to the problem is of course the use of real values, but price indices are missing for five of the eleven countries in the present application, including Qatar from the GCC.

Next, a more consistent model is provided, viz., a *macroeconomic, small-country model*. The target is the same as already one of Tinbergen's targets has been (although for other regional groupings than the GCC): to estimate from cross-sectional data the influence of the foundation of a free trade area on trade flows between the member countries.

In determining the supply side of country i's economy for year t, one of two models may be chosen:

$$Y_{it}^{S} = \begin{cases} \textit{Model I: nonrestricted} \qquad [\textit{unemployed capacities; Keynesian}] \\ \textit{Model II}: f_1(\underset{-}{q_{it}}, \underset{+}{p_{it} - p_t^*}) \qquad [\textit{Neoclassical}] \end{cases} \tag{5}$$

---

[85] However, because quality of products is often not easy to measure for consumers, the "Made in ..." label may very well influence the decision to buy.

where,

Y_{it}^{S} = country i's supply of goods and services in year t

q_{it} = input price level in country i (i.e., q_{it} is a weighted average of the real wage level, the real interest rate, etc.) in year t

p_{it} = price level of country i's output in year t †

p_t^* = world price level in year t

Notes: The + and − signs are the signs of the first derivatives; † changes in country i's nominal exchange rate are implicitely included in p_i; in the econometric test US Dollar values are employed for trade flows and national income.

The demand equation for country i's output in year t is:

$$Y_{it}^{D} = f_2(\underset{-}{r_{it}},\ \underset{-}{K_{i,t-1}},\ \underset{+}{M_{it}},\ \underset{-}{p_{it}},\ \underset{+}{Y_{jt}},\ \underset{+}{p_t^*},\ \underset{+/-}{tis_{ijt}},\ \underset{+}{G_i}) \tag{6}$$

where,

Y_{it}^{D} = demand for country i's goods and services in year t

r_{it} = real interest rate in country i in year t

$K_{i,t-1}$ = country i's real capital stock in period t-1

M_{it} = money supply in country i in year t

Y_{jt} = country j's GNP in year t

tis_{ijt} = trade impediments (e.g., distance) and supports (e.g., adjacency of two countries, regional groupings) for country i and its trading partners in year t

G_{it} = demand by government for country i's output in year t

The + and − signs for the first derivatives result from the following simplified functional relationships:[86]

$$\text{Investment} = K_{it}(\underset{-}{r_i}) - K_{i,t-1}$$

[86] In economic theory, different or more complex relationships are found. For example, one could consider only partial adjustment towards the new optimal capital stock. Keynesian theory would let the level of investment be dependent on the interest rate instead of linking the optimal capital stock to the interest rate as is done here in accordance with classical theory. However, a more thorough analysis would not change the present results, if only because the model has to be modified later anyway, due to data limitations, as is done below.

Consumption = f_3 (real wealth)
+

real wealth = K_{it} + M_{it}/p_{it} , with M_{it} = exogenous money supply†

Foreign Demand = f_4 (Y_{jt}, p_{it}, p_t^*, tis_{ijt}), cf. eq. (9) and its explanations,
+ − + ± (j = 1, ..., N; j ≠ i)

Government Demand = exogenous

where,
N = number of countries in the world

Note: † K_{it} and M_{it} are measured in US Dollar to be consistent with the definition of p_{it}

Ad Model I: In the case of unemployed capacities, trade flow from i to j (X_{ij}) would only depend on factors which determine foreign demand for goods of country i. Because data on prices are very insufficient, this Model I will not be tested. Moreover, it only makes sense in the short run, which is not considered here.

Some variables will be omitted in the following model specification, due to insufficient data for the countries concerned. This poses problems if the omitted variables are correlated with the included variables. In such cases, the included variables are no longer uncorrelated with the error term, and the coefficients are systematically over- or underestimated. The correct answer is of course an instrumental variables estimation procedure. The plausibility for correlation of omitted with included variables as well as the possibility of instrumental variables estimation are discussed in the following where necessary.

The general supply and demand equations (5) and (6) will next be specified for the present case, and the possibilities and limitations of estimating the trade flow equation are discussed.

For t = 1980, 1981, 1982, 1986, 1987, 1988 and for i= 1, 2, ..., n (where n is the number of countries included in the actual sample; n = 11: the six GCC countries, Egypt, Iran, Iraq, Jordan, Syria):

$$Y_{it}^S = a_0 + a_1 p_{it} - a_2 p_t^* + u_{1,it} \tag{7}$$

The input price index q_{it} is not included because data on wages, interest rates or other input prices are not available for the complete sample, not even for all GCC countries. This poses a problem because this renders it likely that the error term $u_{1,it}$ is positively correlated with the output price index p_{it}. In applying least square estimation methods it is implicitely assumed that $u_{1,it}$ and p_{it} are not correlated; because this is wrong, the estimate for coefficient a_1 would biased. Unfortunately, no instruments for p which are uncorrelated to u_1 are available.

$$Y_{it}^D = b_0 + b_1 \sum_{\substack{j \neq i \\ j=1}}^{N} X_{ijt}^D - b_2 p_{it} + u_{2,it} \qquad (8)$$

Again, the omission of r_{it}, $K_{i,t-1}$, M_{it} and G_{it} may pose problems if they are correlated to the included variables.

$$X_{ijt}^D = c_{0j} + c_{1j} Y_{jt} - c_2 pop_{jt} - c_3 p_{it} - c_4 dist_{ij} + c_5 D_{adj\ ij} \qquad (9)$$

$$+ c_6 D_{GCCij} + c_7 D_{GCCijt} + c_8 D_{ACMij} + c_9 p_t^* + u_{3,ijt} \quad ; \quad j = 1,\ldots,N; j \neq i$$

where,

pop_{jt} = population of country j in year t, to allow for different import demands for countries having the same GNP but different population figures; the coefficient is expected to be negative, mainly because a small population country can be expected to be more specialized and thus more dependent on trade than a country with a large population

$dist_{ij}$ = distance between two countries [87]

adj = adjacent; $D_{adj\ ij} = 1$ when i and j are neighboring countries, zero otherwise

ACM = Arab Common Market; free trade area since 1973; Egypt, Iraq, Jordan, Libya, Syria, Yemen (cf. section C.3.1.)

[87] Distance is not only relevant for transportation costs, but also for travelling costs of salesmen, transportation time, cultural differences, etc. This poses a data problem, as As-Sudais has already noted (1985, p. 257): "However, what is important is the economic distance rather than the mere mileage. Unfortunately no reliable data are available concerning the economic distances in the Gulf region." As a substitute, the shortest distances between the capital cities have been employed.

The inclusion of non-GCC countries is advisable because otherwise the GCC dummy could not be distinguished from the absolute term.[88]

The model is closed by the usual equilibrium condition:

$$Y_i^S = Y_i^D \qquad (10)$$

Algebraically, the system can be solved in a rather simple way. Statistically, these calculations and the subsequent estimation procedure can be justified when assuming that the error terms are normally distributed with mean zero, constant variance and that they are independently distributed with the exception of $E(u_{3,ijt}\, u_{3,kjt}) > 0$ (i.e., shocks on the importing country will effect all import demands of that country).[89] In general, even under these assumptions a simultaneous equations model as here has to be solved for its reduced form and estimated with a two- or three-stage procedure. Here, however, the specific results of the following summations and the nonavailability of some variables or of instruments leads to a restriction on the usual one-stage estimation procedure OLS.

First, substitute equation (9) into the sum in equation (8):

---

[88] Cain / Al-Badri (1989) calculate trade and restructuring effects (until the year 2000) which result from the GCC's decisions, with the help of an interregional programming model, using only GCC countries' data. This is not an econometric model but matrix algebra (i.e., a model with n equations and n unknowns). The results are highly debatable due to very specific assumptions and they will not be discussed here.

[89] In general, in a sample including successive years as here, one would have to worry about serial correlation and use a vector auto-regression model. Here, however, the problem is relatively unimportant as there are only 6 years, but each year contains 110 data sets (each of which comprises 14 observations; cf. Table 15 below). These 110 data sets are less likely to exhibit serious serial correlation, although there is always the possibility that some external shock shifts all trade flows of the sample countries to a higher or lower level.

$$b_1 \sum_{\substack{j \neq i \\ j=1}}^{N} X_{ijt}^{D} = b_1 \sum_{\substack{j \neq i \\ j=1}}^{N} c_{0j} + b_1 \sum_{\substack{j \neq i \\ j=1}}^{N} c_{1j} Y_{jt} - b_1 c_2 pop_{\backslash i,t}^{*} - b_1 c_3 (N-1) p_{it}$$

$$- b_1 c_4 \sum_{\substack{j \neq i \\ j=1}}^{N} dist_{ij} + b_1 c_5 \sum_{\substack{j \neq i \\ j=1}}^{N} D_{adj\, ij} + 5\, b_1 c_6 D_{i \in GCC}$$

$$+ 5\, b_1 c_7 D_{i \in GCC, t > 1983} + 5\, b_1 c_8 D_{i \in ACM} + b_1 c_9 (N-1) p_t^{*}$$

$$+ b_1 \sum_{\substack{j \neq i \\ j=1}}^{N} u_{3,ijt} \qquad (11)$$

$$\equiv - d_0 + b_1 \sum_{\substack{j \neq i \\ j=1}}^{N} c_{0j} + b_1 \sum_{\substack{j \neq i \\ j=1}}^{N} c_{1j} Y_{jt} - b_1 c_2 pop_{\backslash i,t}^{*} - d_1 p_{it}$$

$$+ d_2^{transp.} D_{1,it} + d_3 p_t^{*} + u_{4,ijt}$$

where,

$pop_{\backslash i,t}^{*}$ = world population in year t without country i's population

$d_0 = b_1\, c_4$ Dist

with Dist $\equiv \Sigma_j\, dist_{ij}$ = constant by assumption for the Middle East countries in question because they are all located close to each other and no country is more peripheral in the world than the others

$d_1 = b_1\, c_3\, (N-1)$

$d_3 = b_1\, c_9\, (N-1)$

The definitions of the two *vectors* d_2 and $D_{1,it}$ as well as of $u_{4,ijt}$ are obvious.

Solving for p_{it} , by setting (7) = (8) (from (10)), taking (11) into account:

$$p_{it} = \frac{1}{a_1 + b_2 + d_1} \left(-a_0 + b_0 - d_0 + b_1 \sum_{\substack{j \neq i \\ j=1}}^{N} c_{0j} \right.$$
$$+ b_1 \sum_{\substack{j \neq i \\ j=1}}^{N} c_{1j} Y_{jt} - b_1 c_2 pop^{*}_{\setminus i,t} + d_2^{transp.} D_{1,it} \tag{12}$$
$$\left. + (a_2 + d_3) p_t^{*} - u_{1,it} + u_{2,it} + u_{4,ijt} \right)$$

Substituting the equilibrium value of p_{it} from equation (12) back into (9) yields the equilibrium value of country i's exports to country j in year t:

$$X_{ijt} = f_0 + c_{0j} + c_{1j} Y_{jt} - c_2 pop_{jt} - f_1 \sum_{\substack{j \neq i \\ j=1}}^{N} c_{0j} - f_2 \sum_{\substack{j \neq i \\ j=1}}^{N} c_{1j} Y_{jt}$$
$$+ f_3 pop^{*}_{\setminus i,t} - f_4 \sum_{\substack{j \neq i \\ j=1}}^{N} D_{adj\,ij} - f_5 D_{i \in GCC} - f_6 D_{i \in GCC, t > 1983} \tag{13}$$
$$- f_7 D_{i \in ACM} - f_8 p_t^{*} - c_4 dist_{ij} + c_5 D_{adj\,ij}$$
$$+ c_6 D_{GCC\,ij} + c_7 D_{GCC\,ijt} + c_8 D_{ACM\,ij} + u_{5,ijt}$$

where,

$f_0 = - c_3 (- a_0 + b_0 - d_0) / (a_1 + b_2 + d_1)$
$f_1 = c_3 b_1 / (a_1 + b_2 + d_1)$
$f_2 = c_3 b_1 / (a_1 + b_2 + d_1)$
$f_3 = c_3 b_1 c_2 / (a_1 + b_2 + d_1)$
$f_4 = c_3 b_1 c_5 / (a_1 + b_2 + d_1)$
$f_5 = c_3 5b_1 c_6 / (a_1 + b_2 + d_1)$
$f_6 = c_3 5b_1 c_7 / (a_1 + b_2 + d_1)$
$f_7 = c_3 5b_1 c_8 / (a_1 + b_2 + d_1)$
$f_8 = [a_2 + b_1 c_9 (N-1) - c_9] / (a_1 + b_2 + d_1) - c_9$
$u_{5,ijt} = c_3 (u_{1,it} - u_{2,it} - u_{4,ijt}) / (a_1 + b_2 + d_1) + u_{3,ijt}$

Due to omitted variables which are correlated with the included ones, the error term $u_{5,ijt}$ is related in an almost nonpredictable (but probably systematic) way to the variables in equation (13). This makes the coefficient estimates unreliable which will be estimated from applying OLS to equation (13). However, no better method seems to be viable and the dependence of the most interesting variable in the present context ($D_{GCC\ ijt}$) on the omitted variables is unlikely, thus at least its coefficient's estimate is reliable.

Next, *results and interpretations* are provided. Equation (13) has been estimated with OLS, despite the short-comings already discussed. Data from 1980 to 1982 and 1986 to 1988 have been included; thus, up to 660 data sets comprising 14 observations each were present and degrees of freedom pose no problem.[90] Table 15 gives a summary of the variables included in the analysis, the signs which the coefficients are expected to have, the estimated coefficients and the t-statistics.

Table 15: Regression Results

Variable (cf. eq.(13))	*Meaning*	*Expected Sign* (cf. eqs. (7)-(13))	*Coefficient Estimate*	*t-Statistic*
X_{ijt}	flow of merchandise from i to j in year t, using import data from country j (in US$ mio)	(dependent variable)		
C	constant term †	+/−	-69.4	-0.26
Y_{jt}	importing country's GDP (in US$ bio; GNP would have been preferable, but data were insufficient)	+		
j = Bahrain			17.2	0.31
Egypt			-3.7	-0.37
Iran			-0.7	-0.28
Iraq			5.0	0.80
Jordan			48.2	0.82
Kuwait			3.7	0.49
Oman			24.3	0.63
Qatar			9.0	0.31
Saudi A.			0.5	0.27
Syria			13.9	0.80
UAE			3.5	0.91
pop_{jt}	j's popul. in year t (in mio)	−	3.4	0.91

[90] However, only the 516 data sets for which all 14 observations were available were included in the estimation procedure.

$pop_{\setminus i,t}^*$	world population in year t without i's popul. (in bio)	+	0.1	0.52
$\Sigma D_{adj\ ij}$	number of i's neighbors	–	-1.5	-0.39
$D_{i \in GCC}$	dummy for i in GCC	+/–	35.8	1.08
$D_{i \in GCC,\ t>1983}$	i in GCC, t = 1986-1988	– ‡	-62.1	-2.36
$D_{i \in ACM}$	dummy for i in Arab Common Market (i.e., Egypt, Iraq, Jordan, Syria)	+/–	-2.6	-0.11
p_t^*	world GDP deflator (1985 = 100)	+/–	-2.0	-0.53
$dist_{ij}$	geographical distance between i and j (air distance betw. econ. centers in km)	–	-0.043	-2.75
$D_{adj\ ij}$	dummy for i and j neighbors	+	62.5	3.55
$D_{GCC\ ij}$	dummy for i and j in GCC	+/–	-61.6	-1.67
$D_{GCC\ ijt}$	**dummy for i and j in GCC *and* t = 1986, 1987 or 1988**	**+ ‡**	**52.5**	**1.71**
$D_{ACM\ ij}$	dummy for i and j in ACM	+/–	-53.2	-1.37

$R^2 = 0.18$; adjusted $R^2 = 0.14$; F-statistic = 4.71

Notes: † because coefficient estimates for countries other than the eleven included are not available, the variables Σc_{0j} and $\Sigma c_{1j}\ Y_{jt}$ had to be excluded; +/– undetermined by economic theory; ‡ assum-ing that the creation of the GCC Free Trade Area had positive trade effects
Sources: International Monetary Fund (1992a; 1992c); World Bank (1982; 1983; 1984; 1988; 1989; 1990; 1992)

Before interpreting these results, first a note on the exclusion of the eleven constant terms c_{0j}, j = 1, ..., 11, (cf. equation (13)) is provided. Including these importing-country specific constants (instead of the constant term C) produced a too high collinearity between the explanatory variables; calculation of the estimates was not possible. On the other hand, including these "variables" and replacing the importing-country specific coefficients c_{1j} (linked to Y_j) by a single coefficient c_1 yielded very similar coefficient estimates for the most interesting variables $D_{GCC\ ijt}$ and $D_{GCC\ ij}$ as well as for most of the other variables.

As expected, important explanatory variables are missing; this is demonstrated by the low adjusted R^2 of only 14%.

As Table 15 shows, the signs of the coefficient estimates are almost all as expected. Specifically, adjacency of two countries ($D_{adj\ ij}$), higher GDP of the importing country (Y_{jt}) and smaller distance between two countries ($dist_{ij}$) are linked to higher bilateral exchange of merchandise. In addition, the coefficient estimates for the distance and adjacency variables are significantly different from zero.

Last, but certainly not least, the GCC dummies' coefficient estimates have to be discussed (i.e., $D_{GCC\ ijt}$ and $D_{GCC\ ij}$). They are significantly greater ('smaller' in the case of $D_{GCC\ ij}$) than zero with 95% probability.[91]

Assuming the estimates are correct, these estimates have the following interpretations. The general tendency of trade between GCC members is negative in the following sense: If one knows that both the importing and the exporting country are among the six GCC states, then one expects them to have an annual trade which is \$62 mio less than otherwise.[92] As has been explained before, this may be due to similar production structures or discrimination against GCC neighbors.

The introduction of the GCC Free Trade Area revised this negative tendency to some extent. The increase in average annual trade between two GCC countries which is attributable to the GCC Free Trade Area is \$53 mio. Because there are 30 such flows, the total trade creation was \$1,575 mio, or almost 50% of total intra-GCC trade in 1988 (cf. Appendix Table A9), or 2% of total GCC exports (cf. Appendix Table A10). Thus, the GCC Free Trade Area has been a reasonable success. However, as was just pointed out, this success is merely

---

[91] A coefficient estimate with a t-statistic above 1.64 is significant at the 5% level in a one-tailed significance test (i.e., a t-statistic above 1.64 means that given the true coefficient of a normally distributed variable is zero and the variance is the one estimated from the actual data, the possibility that the estimated or a higher ('lower' in the case of a negative estimate) coefficient value occurs is 5% or even less).

[92] Note that essentially the same is true for both countries being members of the Arab Common Market, which has been a free trade area since 1973.

a revision of the reduced intra-GCC trade before 1983. In addition, as has been pointed out by Viner (1950, chapter IV; cf. section B.2.2.), trade diversion and trade deflection may reduce the welfare improving effect from creating a free trade area which seems to be reflected by increased intra-area trade flows. This could have been avoided by the GCC by forming a customs union and reducing external tariffs.

C.1.3. Intra-GCC Factor Movements

Although a GCC Common Market has not yet been established, several steps have been taken to free intra-GCC factor flows (for details see sections B.3.4. and B.3.5.). Here, these flows are characterized. Where possible, comparisons to other regions and earlier years are drawn.

Several measures of the GCC were meant to stimulate intra-GCC investments, especially in the form of *joint ventures* with investors from several GCC countries. Overall, "as of 1990, there are 263 inter-GCC joint ventures, covering practically every business activity" (Al-Fayez 1992, p. 5). A study which has been prepared by the GCC Secretariat General and the Gulf Investment Corporation lists 249 joint enterprises of at least two GCC countries (GCC, Secretariat General, [1988]). These joint ventures have been established between 1952 and 1987 and often non-GCC investors have a substantial share in these companies' capital. Of these 249 joint projects, only 21% are reported to be from 1981 to 1987, 41% were established before 1981 and for 38% no year of foundation is provided. Therefor, it is not correct to ascribe all of the joint ventures to the blessings of the GCC decisions since its foundation in May 1981. The spatial distribution of the 249 projects is the following: Bahrain 23%, Kuwait 4%, Oman 20%, Qatar 0%, Saudi Arabia 26%, the UAE 27%.

In the industrial sphere, the GCC measures include the installation of a GCC technical committee which comprises officials in charge of issuing industrial licenses (cf. section B.3.5.) and the foundation of the Gulf Investment Corporation and the Gulf Organization for Industrial Consulting which are in charge of promoting joint ventures, partly in the industrial sector and as GCC joint ventures. Until 1992, 52 joint industrial ventures with invested capital of about $2 billion have been set up (Saudi Economic Survey 12 February 1992).[93]

Although not negligible, joint ventures in the GCC with at least two GCC participants are at present of limited importance. It is illuminating to compare the figures with other data:

- by the end of 1991, industrial investment in Saudi Arabia reached $25 billion (NCB Economist April 1992), more than 12 times the investment in GCC joint industrial ventures;

[93] Most probably, the majority of these industrial joint ventures were established before the creation of the GCC, as has been shown for all GCC joint ventures in the preceding paragraph. For earlier surveys of Gulf joint projects see Mohie El-Din (1984) and Mohyuddin (1984).

- the capital invested in Saudi Arabia by industrial joint ventures reached \$18.1 billion in 1991, of which at most \$1.1 billion was invested in projects with GCC partners (Arab News 7 October 1992);[94]
- the GCC countries have "an estimated \$350 billion or more invested outside the Arab World. Nearly \$160 billion is owned by the private sector" (Jordan Times 16 May 1993);
- public investment expenditures in the GCC countries in 1990 stood at \$17.4 billion (Al-Fayez 1992, Table 1).[95]

Muhammad Abdul Jalil Al-Fahim, the deputy chairman of the Abu Dhabi Chamber of Commerce and Industry in the UAE, summarized the situation in February 1993: investment revenues are higher overseas; the Arab market is too small, opportunities are limited and guarantees inadequate; investment laws are basically good but they are not implemented; the GCC decisions to allow for movement of goods and factors are not implemented (Arab News 11 February 1993). Here, the latter is of special interest. Al-Fahim refered to the following failures of the GCC (most of which have also been treated in this study):

- other GCC members fail to enforce the decisions allowing Emirates nationals to have full ownership of business projects;
- other GCC countries impose restrictions on buying land for investment purposes: the one plot of land one can buy is not enough for Emirate investors which have diverse and large commercial interests and industrial investments; in some member states even this one plot is not sold to investors from the UAE;
- obstacles and difficulties are faced by investors applying for business licenses;
- red tape, delays at border points and other barriers limit the movement of goods and individuals among GCC countries.

In this context, Al-Fahim noted that "[i]ronically, deals between Gulf businessmen and those from Japan, Europe and the United States are usually successful but they fall through when we deal among ourselves." Thus, he accuses the GCC officials (and the businessmen themselves?) of a lack of willingness to promote GCC economic cooperation. Al-Fahim adds that financing for investment is difficult to obtain because "most banks in the region prefer to

---

[94] \$669 million are invested in Saudi-Kuwaiti projects, \$166 million in Saudi-UAE ventures.

[95] The distribution among the six member countries is the following: Bahrain 2%, Kuwait 6% (estimates for fiscal year 1989/90), Oman 5%, Qatar 2%, Saudi Arabia 53%, the UAE 32%.

extend credit to foreign rather than GCC investors." This points to the possibility that GCC investors are less reliable than others.

A special role in the integration process is designated to the *Gulf Investment Corporation (GIC)* (see section B.3.5.; Gulf Investment Corporation 1982a; 1982b; 1990; 1991; 1992). Its task is to contribute to the integration of the GCC economies, assist in diversifying sources of income and encourage private sector activities, albeit with the purpose of realizing profits. GIC serves this purpose in the following ways:

- lending for industrial, agricultural and fishery activities in the GCC where its comparative advantages lie in the ability to provide long term finance;
- undertaking technical and economic feasibility studies and providing project selection or rejection, which is a positive externality to other investors;
- involvement in selected new investment projects either by long term investment of 20 percent or more and exerting significant influence (associated companies), or by otherwise simply participating (participations);
- investing in existing companies, assisting them in expanding, and providing them with management and financial expertise;
- cooperation with the GCC Secretariat General in organizing conferences or undertaking research and consulting for the GCC.

In evaluating these activities, two questions may be posed: Did GIC make progress with respect to these criteria? Does the whole undertaking make sense, or does such involvement of the GCC governments bear economic risks? The second question will be dealt with in section C.2.2. As for the first question, keeping in mind that total assets at 31 December 1991 were $1752 million:

- Total outstanding loans amounted to $150 million at the end of 1991; and according to 1990 figures, undrawn loan commitments were probably about half this size. GIC played a major role in the $650 million syndicated loan for an expansion of the Aluminum Bahrain plant. After GIC took over the Gulf International Bank (GIB) in 1991 (for details see B.3.5.), lending and related risk taking activities were de-emphasized by GIC because such activities are more appropriate for GIB.
- Until the end of 1991, GIC had chosen 199 projects for appraisal and evaluation. For less than half of them a full technical and economic feasibility study is conducted, and less than 10 percent are finally accepted. GIC holds only 10 to 26 percent of the capital in its 12 direct investment projects. This analysis points to a lack of profitable projects in the GCC region,

especially because GIC has no scarcity of resources [96] and its projects are fully supported by the GCC governments, which are GIC's shareholders.

- GIC invested in 7 associated companies and in 5 others. Of these 12 companies three were in the agricultural sector (dairy and poultry) and 9 in the industrial sphere (pharmaceutical, aluminum, pigment, military uniforms, aircraft maintenance, electronics, pesticides, propulsion). GIC's direct investment in these 12 projects, a total cost of $2.3 billion, is $504 million. However, only $54 million had been disbursed by the GIC by the end of 1991. Although all projects were in the pipeline by December 1989, only five of the 12 projects were producing by December 1991. The regional distribution of projects is fairly uneven if one considers that all GCC governments subscribed equal amounts to GIC's total capital of $2,100 million.[97] Six projects are in Saudi Arabia, two are in the UAE and one each in Bahrain, Kuwait, Oman and Qatar.
- GIC is increasingly interested in investing in existing projects. In 1991 it made one such offer, a second was under review at the end of the year.
- GIC prepared a study on the issue of certificates of origin for products of national origin and the meaning and measurement of "value added" (as was discussed previously, this is an important task, although the main problem is a political one). GIC was the co-organizer of a GCC-EC conference on joint-ventures in October 1992 in Doha. GIC is the financial advisor to the GCC committee which studies the integrated GCC electric-power grid intended to reduce generating reserves; and it made major contributions to other studies of potential GCC joint projects such as a regional reinsurance company and a regional commuter airline project.

To summarize, GIC has not been an overwhelming success if it comes to the mere amount of investment in the GCC region, but at least it is in a healthy financial situation and undertakes serious and in-depth studies before it engages in projects which can only be subsidy-cured in the end.[98] GIC's collective

---

[96] The ratio of shareholders' equity to total assets lay well above 40% before the acquisition of GIB. Although the Articles of Association stipulate that 100% of the nominal value of shares should have been paid in by 1989, only 26% were paid in by 1991.

[97] The author does, however, not know each country's share in the actually paid-up capital of $540 million. Perhaps Saudi Arabia contributed the major part?

[98] This contrasts to loss of the capital the GCC governments and Iraq invested in the Gulf International Bank and which can only partly be ascribed to Iraq's invasion in Kuwait. Another source is the loss incured from too optimistic loans to LDCs. This is not to say that GIB's management made mistakes (other banks were in similar positions), but every such setback is a setback for GCC governments' willingness to cooperate.

expertise is of greatest help to several GCC bodies when evaluating specific project proposals, assessing steps to create a GCC Common Market and searching for ways to improve the business environment in the GCC states.

The *Gulf Organization for Industrial Consulting (GOIC)* is of similar importance to the GCC (see section B.3.5.; Gulf Organization for Industrial Consulting 1981; 1982; 1984; 1985; 1988; 1989; 1990; 1991; 1993). Its Secretary General, Abdul Rahman Ahmed Al Jafary, likes to think of the GOIC as an acronym of "Good On Industrial Concepts" (Al Jafary 1992). Indeed, the GOIC has acquired considerable expertise in conducting the following tasks:

- conducting industrial studies to get comprehensive and detailed pictures of the development role of certain industries, especially iron and steel, aluminum, petrochemicals, electrical appliances, glass, rubber and cement;
- provision of industrial consulting services for private and public institutions and bodies on investment and policy questions; e.g., GOIC conducted in 1984 five tasks for the GCC Secretariat General: a study on industrial development strategies (jointly with the Kuwait Institute for Scientific Research, KISR), a conference organized on the same topic, a draft law stipulating a model industrial organization, and prefeasibility studies for the manufacturing of telecommunications equipment and telephone cables and wires;
- collection and dissemination of industrial data through the GOIC Industrial Data Bank;
- organization of and participation in industrial conferences and training courses;
- publication of conference proceedings, studies, and specialized periodicals and bulletins, such as the quarterly "Industrial Cooperation in the Arab Gulf" (bilingual), the "Monthly Bulletin" (arabic) and the quarterly "Gulf Industrial Focus" (bilingual);
- serving as a catalyst for coordination and cooperation among operating Gulf industries (e.g., by organizing technical meetings of experts).

However, when it comes to one of its most important tasks, the picture changes. This task is the identification, evaluation and promotion of joint industrial projects. As Secretary General Al Jafary (1992) points out, examples of GOIC researched joint venture manufacturing projects are to be found particularly in chemicals, metals, glass, rubber and engineering. In 1980, GOIC was quite optimistic: It had identified a number of projects and summarized that "it is possible to conceive, for the first time, the existence of a sound technical and economic basis for regional industry." When providing an overview, it is revealing to study the most promissing projects (almost all of which date back to 1980) in some detail.

1. Projects which actually reached the production stadium:

– The Gulf Aluminium Rolling Mill Company (Garmco) is GOIC's first industrial project, owned by six Arab Gulf governments (North Africa and the Middle East 1990, 1991, p. 338). It was established in Bahrain in February 1981, work commenced on the plant in 1983, production of some 60,000 tons of aluminum sheets and can stock p.a. started in 1986 (Saudi Basic Industries Corporation 1991, p. 29). Garmco was then the largest downstream aluminum industry in the Gulf (Arab Communicators [1989], p. 30).
– A prefeasibility study for production of aluminum foil in 1982 resulted in the adoption of the project by Garmco; production start was scheduled for 1988 (Arab Communicators [1989], p. 30).

2. Projects which have come up for discussion several times:

– A float sheet glass project which was already "under implementation" in 1980 had passed its first hurdles by 1988, and by then it was likely that the production company would be set up soon. Nothing was said in the annual reports 1989 and 1990.
– A petroleum coke project was under study in 1980; in 1988 it was reported that an international consulting group would conduct a full-fledged techno-economic study, to be finalized in 1989. The project was not mentioned in 1989 and 1990.
– A ferro-silicon project was under study in 1980; in 1990 a feasibility study for this project was undertaken, or better: updated for the third time.
– A joint project for producing aluminum was under study in 1980 with a proposed capacity of 2 million tons per year; in 1990 the project was still under consideration and the prefeasibility study was updated once again.

3. Projects which were declined after considerable efforts:

– An acetic acid and derivatives complex, which was recommended in 1980 and for which Qatar had been suggested as a location in 1981, suffered from a lack of technology suppliers; until 1988 all international suppliers declined participation, and GOIC started searching for alternative technologies. The question of technology transfer will be addressed in section C.1.5.
– A feasibility study for production of aromatics was successful in 1980, but the project was declined in 1981 because Saudi Arabia and Kuwait were already considering the establishment of aromatics projects.
– The same is true for a refractory bricks project.

4. Seven projects were studied and reported to have been adopted by investors, which does in general mean that feasibility studies (or even prefeasibility studies) had yet to be undertaken.

5. At least 26 projects were studied but were not reported to have passed a further hurdle.[99]

This is a rather poor balance, especially because GOIC hired highly qualified and experienced experts. The conclusion which may be drawn (and which is reinforced by the fact that GIC's record is only slightly better) is there are only few viable projects in the Gulf region, despite intense research by GCC specialized agencies (GIC and GOIC) which coordinated their activities, at least to some degree. The "technical and economic basis for regional industry" is not as sound as the GOIC hoped for in 1980.

The GCC worked towards a GCC Common Market by the agreements on the *establishment of firms* (Firms 1983; Firms 1984) and on the *engagement in various professions* (Professions 1983; Professions 1984). It has been shown in section B.3.4. that the freedom which has been granted by these agreements is a limited one. However, they are an improvement when compared to the earlier situation in which these freedoms were not available. Tables 16 provides data on the extent to which these rights have been used.

Table 16: Licenses Granted by GCC Countries to Citizens from Other GCC States Permitting Them to Practice Economic Activities, 1983-1989 (Number; %)

	Number	%
Bahrain	75	8
Kuwait	132	14
Oman	46	5
Qatar	9	1
Saudi Arabia	263	27
UAE	439	46
GCC	964	101

Note: the total number of licenses granted between 1983 and 1988 has been 854
Sources: GCC, Secretariat General (1991, p. 98; 1990, p. 111)

This shows that border-crossing activities by GCC businesspeople concentrated on the UAE and, to a lesser extent, Saudi Arabia.

---

[99] Please note that this number does not include general industrial studies or consulting studies, as it is not surprising if their use is not reported by GOIC in subsequent years.

GCC nationals have a comparative advantage over expatriates especially in cross-border services. Expatriates need in general not only the agreement of their sponsors (in general the employers), but also a visa to travel from one GCC country to another. This requirement has been dropped for GCC nationals in August 1987. For example, Bahrainis who are increasingly specializing in selling software to their neighbors can profit from this (Arab News 15 February 1993). For low-skill jobs, especially drivers of vehicules, the visa requirement poses a cost-effective problem because multi entry and exit visa are not granted, visa application is a time consuming activity and GCC citizens are reluctant to accept low-skill jobs (Tim 1992; Varghese 1992).

Another step towards the GCC Common Market has been the introduction of the right of *ownership of landed property and buildings* for personal use in March 1985 (Land Ownership 1985). Table 17 gives an overview of the intra-GCC real estate investments since then.

Table 17: GCC Owners of Real Estate in Other GCC States, 1989 (%)

in / *from*	Bahrain	Kuwait	Oman	Qatar	Saudi A.	UAE	*Total*
Bahrain	-	0.5	0	1.3	0.3	3.2	5.3
Kuwait	44.0	-	0	0	2.4	10.7	57.2
Oman	0.1	0	-	0.2	0.2	3.1	3.7
Qatar	0.4	0.6	0	-	0.1	5.5	6.7
Saudi Arabia	16.5	4.8	0	0.7	-	3.3	25.3
UAE	0.6	0.5	0	0.7	0.1	-	2.0
GCC	61.6	6.3	0.1	2.9	3.2	25.9	**100**

Note: the total number of holdings in 1989 was 4869
Source: GCC, Secretariat General (1991, p. 99)

According to Table 17, at least until 1989, intra-GCC real estate purchases have been mainly made by Kuwaitis investing in Bahrain and the UAE. In addition, many Saudis invested in Bahraini real estate. Since the Gulf crisis, such Kuwaiti investment in GCC real estate has increased. Saudi Arabia has become increasingly interesting for these investors. Kuwaiti real estate investment in Saudi Arabia has exceeded $400 million in 1992 and is spread over major cities. In most cases the flats are hired to youths or expatriates. According to the coordinator of Saudi-Kuwaiti real estate dealings in Riyadh, the Kuwaiti dealer Muhammad Al-Azemi, "some other Gulf countries have often stood in the way of Kuwaitis purchasing real estates in their territories" (Arab News 16 October 1992). Although this would in many cases not be in conflict with the GCC's agreement because ownership of land and buildings has only been allowed for personal use (Land Ownership 1985), the data in Table 18 does not support this view.

Given that the impact of the GCC agreements have been limited, has the GCC at least been successful in the international arena, especially in strengthening its bargaining position vis-à-vis other regional groupings? This will be investigated next.

C.1.4. Attainment of GCC's International Economic Objectives

The main economic interests of the GCC in the international arena are
- high and stable oil revenues,
- open markets for their exports such as refined products and petrochemicals and
- attraction of foreign workers, capital goods, technology, production know-how, and operating skills.

While the GCC states were able to hire foreign workers of all kind, they have made little progress in achieving the other objectives. Oil revenues are vulnerable and have dropped considerably since 1983. In 1984, the EC introduced tariffs for GCC petrochemicals which exceeded a certain low limit. The situation for Gulf petrochemicals in the US and Japan is not any better. Talks with US, Japanese and EU officials about joint ventures to acquire technology have failed to produce concrete results; for example, El-Kuwaiz attacked Japan after the failure of talks in June 1993 (Arab News 18 July 1993).

Some reasons for these failures could be overcome by joint GCC actions. Primarily, the GCC could form a customs union, which is a precondition for the European Union to sign a trade agreement. A major obstacle against investment from industrialized countries is the system of sponsorship. Another concern of foreign partners is the insufficient protection of property rights.

Given these introductory and summarizing remarks, consider the concern about comprehensive energy taxes that would hurt GCC's oil revenues, protectionist measures by its trading partners against GCC's downstream petroleum products and its international competitiveness, as well as aspects of attracting foreign technology.[100]

To stabilize carbon dioxyde emissions "motivated by serious environmental preoccupations" (Doha Declaration 1992), the EC decided in October 1990 to levy a comprehensive *EC energy/carbon dioxyde tax* (European Community 1992). This would have hurt the GCC's oil revenues substantially, presumably by $6 billion p.a. (Arab News 26 January 1993). Rightly, OPEC and the GCC argued that a reduction of coal subsidies should be a complementary policy element (Okogu / Birol 1992; cf. also Subroto 1992). GCC ministers threatened to impose retaliatory import tariffs on EC countries which introduce an energy

---

[100] The importance of a reduced GCC market segmentation for the EU has been discussed in section B.2.3., and the frequent postponement of establishing a GCC Customs Union has been documented in section B.3.3. The problems of the sponsorship system for foreign investors have been dealt with in section B.1.3.

tax that hurts GCC's petroleum revenues. The GCC chief negotiator, Mamoun Kurdi, even spoke of a possible trade war (Arab News 23 January 1992). The whole subject has lost its importance in 1993. In October 1993, EC environmental ministers decided to postpone the introduction of an energy/carbon dioxyde tax. The UK was especially responsible for this decision as it strictly opposed the proposal. Similarly, in the USA President Clinton has not been able to enforce his plans of a comprehensive energy tax. Only a fuel tax of US$0.043 per gallon ($1.806 per barrel) passed the Senate and the House of Representatives in August 1993.

Given the discussion here, it is interesting to note that the GCC countries still insist on the predominance of its crude oil exports. The oil and energy related industries (e.g., refining, petrochemical and aluminum) would have gained from the introduction of comprehensive energy taxes in the EU and the USA. This was of course the reason why Great Britain and others opposed the EU energy tax. The GCC could argue that the EU might increase its import tariffs on refining and petrochemical products if its industries are hurt after the introduction of an energy tax. However, in a joint declaration which has been attached to the EEC-GCC Cooperation Agreement from 1988, the two groups agreed not to aggravate existing trade barriers and, after official negotiations about a trade agreement have commenced, to impose no additional trade obstacles. These negotiations began in May 1990.

In the 1980s, major GCC petrochemical plants began production (cf. Appendix Table A5; Horndasch 1990, p. 159). A plant in Saudi Arabia, which annually produced 600,000 tons of methanol, started in February 1984. Four months later, the European Community imposed, at a Dutch request, a 13.5 percent duty on Saudi methanol imports because they had climbed to twelve times the EEC ceiling of $191,870; the ceiling was transformed into a quota[101] (Dietl 1988, p. 368; Middle East and North Africa 1991, 1990, p. 235; Ramazani 1988, p. 102). The background is the European Union's preferential treatment of developing countries. Since 1971, industrial countries are allowed to grant preferential treatment to developing countries in the framework of GATT. One week later, the EC introduced its General System of Preferences (GSP) which grants duty free ceilings on imports from developing countries

---

[101] In the past, EU's GSP ceilings (General System of Preferences, see below) have not been enforced in the case of refinery imports from the Gulf, although the duty free ceilings have often been exceeded (Horndasch 1990, p. 146). The import duty is imposed automatically if a *quota* is exceeded, but only at request of an EU member if a *ceiling* is surmounted. It is often pointed out that the 13.5 percent duty compares to an average 4 percent EU tariff rate on other imports.

(Hummer 1993, pp. 37f). In the 1970s and 1980s, the GCC countries were among the privileged, but in 1990 six Saudi Arabian petrochemical products were completely eliminated from EC's GSP because its shipments exceeded certain limits (NCB Economist April 1992, p. 4).[102] Of course, the ceilings or quotas were also applied to the other GCC countries when they began exporting ammonia, methanol and nitrogen fertilizer to the EC (for the 1990 duty free ceilings and quotas cf. Arab-British Chamber of Commerce 1990, p. 34). In addition, urea exports from Saudi Arabia are subject to EU anti-dumping duties (NCB Economist April 1992, p. 4).

Immediately in 1984, the GCC began talks with the EC and in December 1987 the Supreme Council commissioned the Ministerial Council to start official negotiations with the EC (Final Communiqué 1987). The USA and Japan also impose the GATT import duties on GCC petrochemical products. Even worse, the USA never granted GCC's OPEC members Kuwait, Qatar, Saudi Arabia and the UAE access to its GSP (Heynitz 1989, p. 5). When Japan announced to increase its import protection against GCC products, the Supreme Council attacked, in an unprecedented step, another country directly when it expressed its "worry regarding the protectionist policies, especially those which Japan is determined to apply with regard to the imposition of duties and taxes on imports of crude oil and petroleum products."

Although an agreement has been reached in 1988 with the EEC about some elements of economic cooperation, no trade agreement has been signed yet with any GCC international partner. In December 1989, the EC proposed a step by step reduction of its barriers against petrochemical imports from the GCC, conditioned on the GCC's foundation of a customs union. Import tariffs would be reduced from 14% to 0% within 8 to 16 years (Saudi Gazette 12 June 1990). The products which would have been most important for the GCC (46 kinds of petrochemicals, refining and aluminum products) would have been regarded sensitive and not granted free access for at least 12 years (Heynitz 1989, p. 15; Kuwait Times 4 January 1990; Saudi Gazette 17 June 1990).

The GCC objected that this period was too long and refused to agree. This was hardly a wise decision, especially because the EC would have permitted the GCC to impose infant industry protection tariffs of 20 percent on young industries as long as at least 90 percent of total imports are duty free (Kuwait Times

[102] Saudi Arabia's plafond on certain petrochemicals was already in 1989 reduced by 50% since its import share exceeded 20% (Heynitz 1989, p. 12). Coming into effect 1 January 1996, Kuwait, Qatar and the UAE were cancelled from the OECD list of developing countries. This may lead to the cancellation of their EU's GSP ceilings or quotas, too.

4 January 1990). The EU will hardly uphold its proposal. The recession in Europe assists the European petrochemical industry in their call for protection. They argue, otherwise 10 to 15 percent of the jobs would be lost (MEED 1992, p. 4), in part due to the fact that the GCC competitors would concentrate on the EU market as the USA and Japan are not likely to lower their import barriers (Heynitz 1989, pp. 13f). Currently, the Saudi Basic Industries Corporation exports one forth of its output to the European Union (NCB Economist April 1992, p. 4). One reason for the GCC's rejection of the EC's proposal may have been the unwillingness of GCC officials to introduce a customs union.

The whole subject might come to an end if all GCC countries become members of the General Agreement on Tariffs and Trade. For the GCC's relationship to GATT, see section C.3.1.

How harmful is the 12 to 14 percent import tariff to GCC's petrochemical industry? This leads to the question of GCC's *international competitiveness in the field of petrochemicals*. Keep in mind that a 12 to 14 percent nominal tariff may mean a much higher effective protection, if EU tariffs on those raw material imports, which serve as intermediaries, are not changed. Heynitz (1989, pp. 12f) calculates the effective tariff protection to be 20 to 30 percent, which is equivalent to a reduction of $4 per barrel for crude oil input.

Besides individual companies (e.g., the Saudi Basic Industries Corporation), the GCC-owned Gulf Organization for Industrial Consulting in Doha has made major contributions to providing feasibility studies for Gulf petrochemical industries. Some are published in its journal Industrial Cooperation in the Arab Gulf States. The major determinants of GCC petrochemical producers' international competitiveness are production, transportation and marketing costs. As a reference point, in Graph 7 the influence of the world oil price level on the competitive power of GCC polyethylene producers on the West European market is shown. The following analysis is based on Horndasch (1990).

The sensitivity analysis of Graph 7 demonstrates that Gulf producers' costs for plastic products in the ethylene line are inelastic with respect to oil price changes. Raw material and energy costs are low and constant because the methane and ethane fraction of the wet gases occuring in oil extraction, which are used as feed stocks and energy source have no alternative economic use. Without considering depreciation allowances, Gulf producers become competi-

Graph 7: Oil Price Level and Competitive Power of GCC Polyethylene Producers, 1988

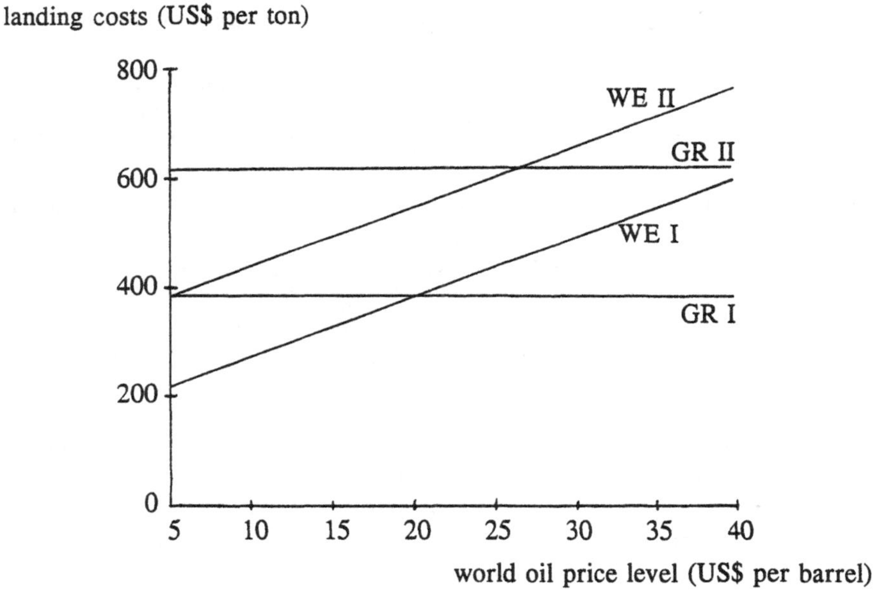

I: "cash costs" (raw material, labor, energy, transportation, marketing)
II: total costs (cash costs + depreciation)
GR: plant location Gulf region (Saudi Arabia)
WE: plant location Western Europe (North Sea coast)
landing costs = production costs + transportation costs + marketing expenses
capacity utilization: 90%
Source: Horndasch 1990, p. 151

tive in Europe when the world market price of oil surmounts $20 per barrel.[103] If the EU import tariffs on petrochemicals are taken into consideration, the oil price would have to rise to even $23-24 per barrel.

Taking depreciation costs into account, Gulf producers have to wait for oil prices of $26.5 before they earn money by exporting to Europe. Construction

---

[103] Horndasch's analysis depends, of course, on specific assumptions about supply and demand (e.g., the assumption of constant returns to scale or of price-inelastic world demand), as well as on the hight of future trade barriers on the relevant markets.

costs are higher in the Gulf because of long transportation distances, lack of infrastructure and special climatic conditions.

How does this specific result change when market location and sort of product are altered?

- market location: On the South Asian market, GCC producers of basic plastics are competitive against US suppliers when the oil price is above $9, and against European firms when oil is priced above $14. This shows that transportation costs are a decisive factor.
- product: When it comes to selling methanol, GCC plants are profitable in Western Europe if the oil price exceeds $18 (in South Asia a $6 oil price is sufficient). Thus, Gulf producers are good at selling basic and intermediate products, but petrochemical end products require more expensive marketing efforts. Accordingly, planned GCC large projects for the 1990s are based on methane and ethane, an exception being the Naphta Cracker in Jubail (Gulf Industrial Focus December 1991, p. 2).

Foreign know-how has been indispensable for most of these petrochemical projects. However, the GCC aims at "creating an indigenous base for research, applied sciences and technology" (Development Plans 1985; Industrial Strategy 1985). This is only possible if the industrialized countries provide initial training (at home and abroad), equipment, know-how and experts. However, the transfer of know-how is problematic because many suppliers fear their intellectual property rights are not sufficiently protected.

Before investigating the problems that have to be overcome collectively or individually by the GCC countries to attract adequate amounts of foreign know-how, consider the dimension of foreign investment into the GCC economies. GCC governments feel direct investment of companies from industrial countries in the Gulf region is minor. Total non-GCC direct investment in the GCC region amounted to $8 billion at the end of 1988 (Murtfeld / Azzam 1990, pp. 76f), whereas GCC foreign investments in bank deposits, real estate and stocks in the industrialized world are estimated at some $350 billion (e.g., Jordan Times 16 May 1993). Most of the foreign investment in the GCC region stems from the USA. For the end of 1990, Saudi Arabia reviewed all Saudi joint ventures with foreign partners and found 360 projects existed with a total foreign capital of $6.4 billion invested (Al Jafary 1992).[104] Again, US companies were detected to be the main capital contributors and were mainly

---

[104] The 360 projects represented 15% of the 2,400 manufacturing establishments in Saudi Arabia; the $6.4 billion equaled 43% of total capital of the 360 projects.

engaged in large scale projects. In contrast, EC joint venture partners concentrated on medium size projects, as can be seen from Table 18.

Table 18: Regional Distribution of Partners in Saudi-Foreign Joint Ventures, End of 1990

partner from	share of the 360 projects	share of total $6.4 billion foreign capital
EC	23%	5%
other Europe	10%	5%
America	16%	67%
Asia	9%	15%
Arab	42%	8%
	100%	100%

Source: Al Jafary (1992)

GCC officials view the $8 billion stock of foreign investment also as small when they compare it to their imports from the trading partners: $43 billion in 1989.

Lack of foreign technology provision is the "major implementation problem" for projects actively promoted by the Gulf Organization for Industrial Consulting (Atalla 1992). This problem of projects which have already been licensed, results from difficulties with technology holders such as Hoechst, Olin Corporation, Mitsubishi, Dow Chemical, British Petroleum etc. Similarly, the Saudi Ministry of Industry and Electricity proposed the participation in or supplying of technology to more than 100 potential joint venture projects (Ministry of Industry and Electricity 1992). All of these projects had already been licensed and awaited finding a foreign partner for four years in some cases.

As shown in section B.3.5., the GCC is more or less intensively discussing the following issues related to concerns of foreign investors:

- general abolition of the requirement that GCC nationals own 51 percent of any joint venture,
- establishment of a patent office to protect industrial patents,
- guidelines for trademarks,
- establishment of an arbitration center to handle disputes arising from investment activities.

The importance of the abolition of *ownership restrictions* has been emphasized by empirical studies. "Involuntary joint ventures ... are viewed by foreign investors as a major disincentive to investment" (Weigel 1990, p. 74).

It was not accidental that the abolition of the ownership and sponsor restriction was a major action taken by Bahrain when it decided to effectively promote foreign investment inflows. Foreign investors demonstrated they do not like to be in a minority position when they provide technical, production and marketing know-how. For example, although Saudi incentives to joint ventures with 51 percent Saudi or GCC capital are much higher than to joint ventures with non-GCC capital majority, 14 Italian-Saudi industrial joint ventures in Saudi Arabia were established with an Italian capital majority during the 1980s (Gald 1988, p. 26).[105]

Protection of *intellectual property rights* is another sensitive issue for potential foreign investors in the GCC. Since at least 1985, the GCC discussed unified patent legislation to deal with the increasing problem of counterfeit goods in the region (Middle East and North Africa 1991, 1990, p. 234). In July 1992, the US Department of Commerce presented a report to the GCC Secretariat General urging GCC states to adopt laws in this respect (Jordan Times 6 February 1993). The UAE was attacked specifically for inducing a loss of $156 million per year to US firms, in part by sales of counterfeit products and pirated works of art. A safer legal environment, with regard to property rights, would help to overcome the above-mentioned "major implementation problem: technology provision."

Meyer-Laucke / Meyer-Reumann summarized the situation of intellectual property rights legislation in the Arab countries of the Gulf (i.e., GCC and Iraq) in 1990 (p. 504, author's translation): "The current situation [of intellectual property rights] can be sketched as follows:
- the business name is protected by law in all countries;
- most Gulf countries (exception: the United Arab Emirates) have a legal regulation for the registration of trade marks;
- patent laws are existing in some cases, but they have not yet gained importance in the jurisdictional practice. Regulations for patterns or designs are until today only existing in rudiments (for example, in Kuwait);
- copyright protection is until now legally regulated only in Saudi Arabia."

---

[105] In the US-GCC talks, the potential American investors have been advocating to have the same rights and obligations as the nationals. It is even a major problem to obtain multiple-entry visas (Dietl 1988, p. 372).

Meanwhile the first UAE intellectual property rights legislation came into force, consisting of three laws: a trade mark law, a patent law and a copyright law (Jordan Times 6 February 1993).

One way to promote joint ventures is via *industrial conferences* where businessmen from the GCC and other regions meet. At these events, they also have a chance to talk to officials about removing trade and investment barriers. Two such EC-GCC conferences have already occurred (Doha Declaration 1992).

To attract foreign investment and technology transfer, GCC governments have the intention to link imports to investment (Al-Attiyah 1992). The GCC countries have already taken steps in this direction. To increase Western countries investment and transfer of technology and managerial know-how, *offset investment programs* have been established. In 1985, Saudi Arabia was the first to require that foreign suppliers invest part of their return from arms sales in Saudi industrial joint venture projects. Since then, a total of three offset programs have been concluded with suppliers from the USA (Peace Shield), the U.K. (Al-Yamamah) and France (SWARY II) (Arab News 7 October 1992). The arms deals are worth more than $30 billion and have generated offset pledges worth some $10 billion, of which $3 billion have to be invested in local arms industry (Jordan Times 26 July 1993). The UAE have signed an offset contract with a French supplier of tanks; equity reinvestment is worth about $500 million which will be matched by a similar amount from local partners (Arab News 6 July 1993). The offset deals in the UAE and Kuwait do not require investment in arms manufacturing.

These offset programs could have provided a good opportunity for the GCC countries to specify common terms; and thus, to coordinate their incentive schemes and industrial policies in an important field. This, however, is not the case. They do not even seem to have a common purchasing policy to get a well-structured and compatible military force.

Two fields that could help GCC countries in improving their export and industrial stand are information collection about extra-GCC markets, and specifications and standards. Collecting *information about foreign markets* is viewed as a natural monopoly good and, therefore, often provided by governments at low fees. This reasoning applies, a forteriori, to the GCC region and points to high gains from cooperation. The Federation of GCC Chambers strongly supports the foundation of a joint GCC "highly effective information system" to overcome "the lack of adequate and professional information about the EC markets" among others (Council of Saudi Chambers of Commerce & Industry 1992, pp. 9, 13).

Common efforts towards *standardization* have two advantages. They are a technical precondition for the functioning of regional economic exchange and help GCC producers in overcoming difficulties with imported machinery from industrial countries. Although the Standardization and Metrology Organization for G.C.C. Countries has been established in 1985 (see section B.3.2.), a 1992 field study showed 29 percent of the GCC sample importers from the EC complained that "Gulf specifications and standards represent a real obstacle [because they are] inconsistent with European specifications" (Council of Saudi Chambers of Commerce & Industry 1992, p. 12). The latter argument does not necessarily call for common standardization efforts, but if the difficulties are similar and preliminary costs for hiring experts and conducting research are high (which they generally are), then common measures are advisable.

C.1.5. Conclusions

The impact of the GCC's establishment on its member economies has been positive in the field of intra-GCC flow of merchandise, but with respect to intra-GCC flow of merchandise, labor and capital, the influence of the GCC has been rather limited. The same holds for its international bargaining position.

This is not astonishing when one recognizes that economic experts in the GCC (among them many government employees and the GCC Assistant Secretary General) believe the GCC has still a long way to go before economic integration is achieved. However, the experts are divided in their opinions. Take, for example, the question of the GCC Free Trade Area. It has been established in March 1983. In practice, many obstacles still exist, as has been discussed. The average of the interview partners holds that the goal of "free trade within GCC" has been achieved to the degree of 63%, but 4 of them marked 100% and 2 marked only 20%.

To understand the limited impact of the GCC, one has to inquire in its internal mechanisms and the decisions which have been taken (and those which have not) should be judged from the point of view of economic theory. Later, the motivations of the agents have to be analyzed.

C.2. Intrinsic Explanations for GCC's Economic Performance

Appropriate decisions are not carried out; implemented decisions have a negative impact; no decisions are taken: these are possible intrinsic sources for failures in GCC's economic integration. In the following, implementation procedures, the appropriateness of decisions and the decision making process are analyzed and evaluated to find out intrinsic sources for progress and delays in GCC's economic cooperation and integration.

C.2.1. Implementation of Decisions

The Council's Secretary General from 1981 to 1993, Abdulla Yacoub Bishara, was well aware of the importance of credibility for economic agencies. If economic agents are sceptical about the future validity of today's announcements and decisions, they will not adjust their expectations and actions. To take just one example: If US investors expected in 1983 that a GCC Common Market would be realized in 1989, they would have adjusted their investment decisions to take advantage of the future large GCC market. It was not by accident that Bishara spelled out in 1983 before a gathering of US diplomats and businessmen the GCC's goal "that by the end of the 1980s, the Gulf will be one common market, with all the obligations and privileges which that step entails" (Bishara 1984, p. 41). The large market was the carrot, and the protective external tariffs which were written down in the Unified Economic Agreement from 1982 were the stick which should have convinced US investors of the advantages of investments in the Gulf. However, as the GCC was only 2 ½ years old, the missing link was GCC's unavailable record of carrying through of decisions. Therefore, Bishara told his audience that

> "[i]n the GCC we follow scrupulously the principle that our actions should be credible. If we advanced pronouncements and issued declarations that we could not implement, our credibility would be jeopardized and our ability to fulfill our ambitions would be questioned" (Bishara 1984, p. 44).

Measured by this yard-stick, the GCC has a serious credibility problem. The GCC delayed the implementation of its pronouncements time and again:

- The Unified Economic Agreement stipulated that by November 1987 a uniform minimum protective external tariff should be in force. It is generally accepted that the common tariff range of 4 to 20 percent, which was established in September 1983, is not the aspired tariff because it is not protective. In 1987 the Supreme Council decided on "rapidly" creating a GCC Customs Union. The GCC owned Gulf Investment Corporation wrote in 1990 that "[a]t the last summit meeting in Oman [in December 1989] the heads of states, while endorsing several measures for joint regional action, also pledged to develop a unified external tariff regime within three years, i.e. by March 1993" (Gulf Investment Corporation 1990, p. 11). In fall 1993 the customs union still was not in sight. For further details cf. section B.3.3.

- The GCC Common Market which had been announced by Bishara to be established by 1990 (see above) will at best be completed by the year 2000. In May 1992 the GCC finance and economic ministers decided on a seven-year timetable to establish a common market (Arab News 23 November 1992). El-Kuwaiz outlined in October 1992 the specific elements of the timetable towards the GCC Common Market: four years for the customs union, seven years for "the alignment of currency rates, share ownership and establishment of banks in member states" (New Arabia 12 November 1992, p. 15). But, the Supreme Council did not endorse this proposal at its next meeting in December 1992. However, some measures to free labor and capital movements were taken in the 1980s. Specifically, professionals were allowed to practice in the whole GCC region, GCC nationals were permitted to establish and run a wide range of firms (including wholesale and retail commerce) all over the GCC, and the equal treatment in obtaining subsidized industrial loans was decided upon. For details and the various specifications applying cf. section B.3.3. and B.3.4.
- Neither the Trans-Gulf Railroad, nor the GCC gas pipeline network, nor the GCC electricity grid, nor the GCC export oil refinery in Oman, nor the GCC crude oil pipeline to Oman's Indian Ocean coast have gone beyond the stage of feasibility studies (cf. section B.3.5.).
- The Gulf Investment Corporation and the Gulf Organization for Industrial Consulting which had been established to promote numerous of joint ventures were not able to achieve these goals (cf. section C.1.3.).

The implementation of actual and concrete decisions which have been taken are investigated next. As discussed in chapter B.3., the labels of the specific agreements were the one thing and the real contents were another. For example, the "Right of Ownership of Landed Property" (Land Ownership 1985) has been a rather limited one. It was only granted to personal residence, but not to production units which are owned by businesspeople from other GCC countries (cf. section B.3.4.). Not before December 1993, the Supreme Council allowed to own property for commercial purposes, too (Arab News 23 December 1993). The discussion here will be confined to the GCC trade accords.

Since September 1983, the agreed-upon minimum external tariff has been 4% and the maximum tariff 20%. However, the tariffs in the different GCC member countries are not only different within this range, but they lie also outside this range.

In every GCC country, certain imports are duty-free. Not surprisingly, this is the case for personal effects of residents, for shipments to embassies and for business samples. In addition, goods sold to the ruling families are duty-free (at least in Bahrain and the UAE, but probably also in the other GCC states; Dubai Ports & Customs 1992, p. 1; World Customs Clearing 1992). There are still other more or less large groups of goods on which no import tariffs are levied:
Bahrain: machinery, raw materials and semi-manufactured goods for manufacture; imports required for development projects; transhipments or re-exports; printed matter; dates; living plants, animals, birds (Arab Communicators [1989], p. 38; Bahrain Marketing & Promotions Office [1992], p. 2; World Customs Clearing 1992);
Kuwait: foodstuffs; medicine; some industrial establishments' imports of machinery and equipment, spare parts and raw materials (International Monetary Fund 1991b, p. 282; GCC, Secretariat General [1990], p. 4);
Oman: essential consumer goods such as foodstuff and medicine; in some cases equipment and materials for use on government projects (Ernst & Young 1990a, p. 13);
Qatar: fruit, vegetables, livestock, medicine, raw materials (Ernst & Young 1990b, section D.7; GCC, Secretariat General [1990], p. 4);
Saudi Arabia: military equipment; machinery, equipment and raw materials for Saudi industrial companies and joint ventures licensed under the Saudi Foreign Capital Investment Code; hospital supplies and electrical supplies (such as gas turbines, generators and transformers) for regional electricity companies; food products such as grains, livestock, meat, tea, coffee, sugar, rice and milk for infants; medicine; books; gold, silver and platinum (Ernst & Whinney International 1989b, p. 17);
UAE: a wide range of products of all kind are exempted from import duties (inputs, basic consumer products); government departments, certain non-profit organizations, oil exploring or producing GCC firms, UAE industrial licence holders and "firms granted exemption by H.H. The Ruler" can import goods duty-free (Dubai Ports & Customs 1992); duty-free are also imports into Dubai's Jebel Ali Free Zone, but they can not be resold duty-free in the UAE except as inputs in goods with 40% local value added if a National Industrial License is obtained from the UAE Ministry of Finance and Industry (Jebel Ali Free Zone Authority 1992a; Ernst & Young 1990c, p. 9).

It is not clear whether any of these duty-free goods are also produced in the GCC, albeit it is most probable that this is the case. In June 1984 the Ministerial Council reiterated that it is important for member countries to stick to the agreed-upon minimum tariff of 4% because it was the goal that this creates a price priority for GCC national products (GCC, Secretariat General, 1988, pp. 176f).

On other goods (e.g., pork, drugs, alcohol) tariffs higher than 20% are levied or they are forbidden to be imported. The existing economic boycotts of Israel and South Africa were thought over in 1993 and probably will be completely abolished soon.

To see just how far GCC countries are from having unified external customs tariffs, it is illuminating to take a closer look at today's rates for imports into the GCC countries which lie within the range of 4% to 20% (for the pre-GCC tariff rates cf. Table 10). All GCC countries except the UAE impose protective tariffs on imports. In the case of Kuwait, these exceed even the agreed-upon 20%, and in the case of Oman they are even levied on GCC products of domestic origin.[106] This suggests the GCC countries, except the UAE, seek to impose nontariff barriers on GCC products, too. The complaints of GCC industrialists about specific nontariff barriers when exporting to other GCC countries (see section C.1.2.) are all the more credible, as many of the protective tariffs have been implemented step by step in the course of industrialization without consulting the GCC.
Bahrain: The standard rate is 5% on the CIF value of imports. Mostly for fiscal reasons, 10% is applied to imports of "general luxuries" (electrical goods, cloth, spare parts, decoration items, furniture, shoes, gold, jewellery, machinery, office equipment, hydraulic oil) and 20% on vehicles. To "encourage manufacturing, the Government actively promotes Bahraini products and protects the manufacturer through import tariffs" (Bahrain Marketing & Promotions Office [1992], p. 10) on products such as screws, nails, plastic bags and tissues (World Customs Clearing 1992).
Kuwait: The standard rate is 4% on the CIF value of imports. To protect local manufacturers, depending on the degree of local value added, tariffs between 15% and 100% were introduced (e.g., on imports of gypsum, portland cement, fiberglass, paper products, biscuits, glass bottles, linens, paint, building materials, reinforced glass products, commercial refrigeration units, central air-conditioning units, electric and telephone cables, synthetic sponges, air filters, wooden nails). "In total, some 58 items receive tariff protection from the

[106] Kuwait also levied customs tariffs on products of national origin from GCC partner countries. It was not before 1993 that the tariff on lubricants was lifted (Arab News 2 January 1993).

Government" (International Monetary Fund 1991b, p. 282; Ernst & Whinney 1989a, p. 11).[107]

Oman: The standard rate is 5% on the CIF value of imports. As incentives for domestic industrial installations, higher import tariffs are levied on pipes, cement, polyurethane products, paints, glass fibre reinforced plastic, PVC, vitrified clay, cast iron (Ernst & Young 1990a, p. 13). Let the reader be reminded that Oman even imposes import tariffs on specific goods which fall under the GCC Free Trade Agreement (see section B.3.2.). For protective reasons, Oman imposes seasonal bans on the importation of fruits and vegetables that are grown locally and on importation of domestically produced refinery products (International Monetary Fund 1991b, p. 367).

Qatar: The standard rate is 4% on the CIF value of imports. Protective rates are possible, e.g., 20% apply to cement and steel (Ernst & Young 1990b, section D.7).

Saudi Arabia: The standard rate is 12% on the CIF value of imports. Exceptional rates are as follows: 7% on medical equipment; 20% for protection of certain national industries on iron, steel pipes and tubes, high-pressure steel pipes used in hydro-electric power stations, certain kinds of steel wire, iron or steel mesh or mesh slabs, steel electric poles, steel reinforcement rods, cement, and furniture, soaps, organic detergents and ordinary liquid detergents (Ernst & Whinney International 1989b, p. 18; Saudi Economic Survey 18 March 1992).

UAE: The standard rate is 4% (sometimes 2%) on the CIF value of imports. No tariff protection is available to domestic producers (Jebel Ali Free Zone Authority 1992a, p. 40; GCC, Secretariat General [1990], p. 4).

Another example of slow implementation of decisions is connected to Article 1, Paragraph 1, of the Unified Economic Agreement, which establishes that the "Member States shall permit the importation and exportation of agricultural, animal, industrial and natural resource products that are of national origin." This has been put into force by the Ministerial Council and came into effect 1 March 1983 (GCC, Secretariat General, 1988, pp. 170f). Article 27 of the Unified Economic Agreement establishes that its provisions prevail over local laws and regulations of member states. However, Saudi Arabia restricts exportation of certain commodities, in part for the legitimate reason of protection of cultural heritage, in part for the reason of preventing subsidies which are intended to help domestic consumers from being spread to outside consumers. Examples of the latter are wheat (unless exportation is approved by the Grain Silos and Flour Mills Corporation), petroleum products (unless approved by the

[107] During Iraq's invasion of Kuwait in 1990/91 most production units were heavily damaged. Subsequently, Kuwait did not charge any import duties until mid-1992. It is expected that protective tariffs will be re-employed as local producers resume production.

Petroleum and Minerals General Corporation) and agricultural plant and machinery (unless approved by the Saudi Arabian Agricultural Bank) (Saudi Economic Survey 18 March 1992). This leads to a separation of markets, not to a common GCC market. It is well-known that if consumers are to receive preferential treatment, it is better to grant direct income aid than to influence specific prices.

Still another topic in the trade context is related to joining forces when importing or exporting goods. It is one of the specific goals of the GCC members to improve their positions as buyers and sellers on the world market by collectively negotiating with foreign partners (Economic Agreement 1982; Industrial Strategy 1985). From what can be determined, efforts to reach this objective have not been successful. In the oil sector, OPEC is where negotiation takes place; in the area of arms, every member negotiates on its own; in the field of petrochemicals, the GCC has not reached an agreement with the EU nor with the USA nor with Japan; with regard to airplanes, each of the four Gulf airlines buys its planes on its own; when it comes to selling gas, every GCC country finds its own ways to market its supply, sometimes in conflict to other partners.[108] This undermines the credibility of the GCC.

A credibility gap was sensed less than five years since the first GCC decisions were made. Nakhleh (1986, p. v) notes that approval might have been even higher if media and politicians had been more cautious: "Intentionally or not, it [the GCC] has become a major media event, a fact that has contributed to the credibility gap between raising expectations based on public pronouncements and real achievements" (Nakhleh 1986, p. v).[109] As has been demonstrated, it was the political leaders which made the public pronouncements, not the media. In section C.2.3. it will be shown that the decision making structure of the GCC is one of the problems and that a powerful supranational GCC

[108] Because Oman will be faster with building its underwater gas pipeline to India, the Qatari plans to erect an underwater gas pipeline to Pakistan may be partly obsolete. Qatar may be forced by economic reasons to bargain with Oman about the possibility of joining lines (Egyptian Gazette 2 July 1993).

[109] Another reason for public frustration about the GCC are inappropriate or ineffective decisions, as As-Sudais (1985, p. 290) points out: "It is important here to realize that priority should be given to economic integration in which economic development can be achieved. ... Taking ineffective integrational economic steps ... may serve the short-run public relation purposes, but shortly the public will realize what is actually taking place." The following section deals with the appropriateness of steps.

organization should be established to supervise implementation of the economic agreements (As-Sudais 1985, p. 290).

In demanding more power for the GCC Secretariat General to see that the integration steps which are already approved by the Supreme Council are "firmly put into action," El-Kuwaiz (1987, p. 82) discloses that the Supreme Council is unwilling or unable to do so.

True, it is wiser to question one's own decisions from time to time and move slowly and carefully in the right direction, rather than to advance quickly in the wrong. However, the GCC always emphasized it was sure it made the right decisions. For example, at its December 1981 meeting the Supreme Council approved the Unified Economic Agreement and wrote in the Final Communiquè that this Agreement is the "ideal path for ensuring progress and prosperity for all the states of the Council" (Final Communiqué 1981b). Although this is true, the actual GCC decisions may be questioned to have been ideal, as it will be shown in the following section.

C.2.2. Appropriateness of Decisions

The natural way to study the economic cooperation measures of the GCC is to ask whether they helped to stimulate economic development of the GCC countries (i.e., by reducing Dutch Disease and rentier state problems and by increasing international competitiveness) or whether they aggrevated the problems. To begin with, two notes are called for.

In the context of the appropriateness of decisions taken, there are at least two criticisms which are correct, but are too far-reaching to be dealt with here. The first deals with non-economic measures which would have a great economic effect. The reasoning is as follows: One should not expect too much from regional GCC economic integration. In particular, there are political measures which could be adopted immediately and which could help GCC economies significantly. One example is the economic boycott of South Africa. Suleiman Al-Shahin, Kuwait's Foreign Ministry Under-Secretary, said that "Kuwait's support of anti-apartheid sanctions against Pretoria had lost it millions of dollars because it had had to forego potential investments in the South African economy, especially in its oil refineries" (Egyptian Gazette 10 June 1993). This boycott has been reduced significantly in 1992 and 1993. A more important example is the economic boycott of Israel. In a so-called indirect boycott, all foreign firms doing business with Israel have been blacklisted for four decades by the Arab League. After the Israel-Palestinian Washington Agreement from September 1993, it is expected that these measures will be abandoned soon. Already some months before, Kuwait disengaged from the indirect boycott for "considerations related to its national interest" (Arab News 9 June 1993).[110] Another example of measures which could help individual member countries (especially Saudi Arabia) is the full integration of women into the production

[110] It is noteworthy that the GCC did not take joint action on this issue. Numerous examples exist where important foreign policy decisions have not been taken by the GCC as a group. This applies to the relationship to Iran after the Iraq-Iran war and to the employment of Hindu workers from India after the distruction of the historical Babri Mosque and massacre of Muslims in India, which prompted only Saudi Arabia to ban the employment of Hindus from India (Tehran Times 17 July 1993). It even applies to the policy vis-à-vis Iraq after the Iraq-Kuwait war. While Oman as the only GCC country kept its ambassador in Baghdad throughout the war (New Arabia 12 November 1992, p. 8), Qatar send back its ambassador to Bagdad in November 1992, which "was seen as a gesture of defiance against other states of the Gulf region" (Arab News 15 November 1992). At that time Qatar and Saudi Arabia had a serious border conflict about Saudi Arabia's violent enforcement of its claim that part of the road between Qatar and the UAE passes Saudi territory (Tim 1992; Arab News 15 October 1992). The conflict was resolved by mediation of Egypt's president Mubarak, not GCC mediation (Arab News 21 December 1992).

process, including the permission for women to drive cars. Still another example is the integration of foreigners in the GCC economies. At the moment, it is almost impossible for them to become nationals or to own residential property or GCC stocks. This leads to commitment problems and disincentives. Finally, those GCC countries granting development aid (i.e., Kuwait, Qatar, Saudi Arabia and the UAE) might gain from tying aid to purchase of their products. Azzam proposes this in the context of Saudi Arabia: "One way to boost exports of manufactured Saudi products, is to tie the implementation of projects abroad financed by Saudi development loans and grants to purchasing of Saudi products" (NCB Economist October 1992, p. 8).

The second correct, while too far-reaching, criticism says that the decisions taken were not outright wrong in that they did harm to the patient, but they were wrong as they did not cure all diseases. For example, As-Sudais (1985, pp. 287f, emphasis added) holds that the GCC "[s]teps that have been taken so far are the *most ineffective ones*. The GCC eliminated tariffs between the members even though tariffs were already extremely low, imposed a 4 percent common external tariff, and freed the movement of physicians, lawyers, pharmacists, and other professionals while all members have a severe shortage in such professions and in domestic manpower in general." He adds (pp. 295f) that "[p]olicies of licensing, financial assistance, regulations, and other issues that affect private investors' confidence are more urgent and more important than eliminating the already very low tariffs." True, the GCC leaders did *not yet* take decisive policies in these regards. However, they have often stressed that it is their intention to do so later. For example, in December 1987 the Supreme Council "affirmed its determination to increasingly bring policies closer together and to unify rules, regulations, laws and procedures in order to achieve economic integration and facilitate collective work in encouraging competitive development in economic activity as well as to continue the diversification and expansion of a balanced economic base in the Council States" (Economic Declaration 1987).

Note, however, that here GCC decisions which explicitely or implicitely eliminate certain actions from the set of policy options will be discussed, too.

Does the cooperation within the framework of the GCC help the member countries to overcome the problem of *Dutch Disease* (i.e., does it help to favor industrialization as opposed to the production of nontradables?). A rather trivial answer is: "Yes, because the GCC Free Trade Area creates a larger market; and thus, increases the profitability of regional industrial production." However, this needs some elaboration. Assume some nontradables have been restricted by artificial barriers from being traded and these obstacles are removed in the GCC. Then, there will be a real appreciation in the countries with low oil income and they will suffer from Dutch Disease more than before (cf. section B.1.2.). The primary example is Bahrain, where this situation has intensified since 1987 because the causeway to Saudi Arabia was opened and tourism was stimulated. Members with high oil income experienced a relief from Dutch Disease.

On the other hand, Dutch Disease can decrease in the course of the development process if regional integration enables the GCC citizens to acquire production experience which can later be used to build internationally competitive industries. The GCC acknowledges this when it places emphasis on the "development of small and medium industries that supply local market needs which technically and psychologically prepare the society of the GCC States for developing into an industrial society" (Industrial Strategy 1985).[111] In other words, if "local" manufactured goods become "regional" goods due to boarder elimination in a free trade area, then citizens can acquire technical know-how through more efficient production and increased learning by doing which later enable them to produce "international" products.

However, all of this depends on the assumption that the GCC region becomes increasingly integrated with regard to trade flows and factor movements. As mentioned in the previous chapter C.1., the GCC has only been of limited success in this regard.

As a consequence of the effects of Dutch Disease (i.e., of the problems to establish a tradable goods sector which is internationally competitive), the GCC countries actively promote their industrial sectors. Because they face difficulties in selling goods on the world market, they increasingly rely on import substitution and protectionism. A pseudo-scientific argument in favor of this says "that local market demand is still larger than available production capacities" (Gulf Organization for Industrial Consulting 1991, p. 11; here, market demand is a synonym for actual consumption). The upshot of this argument is that the GCC thrives for self-sufficiency (which would be extremely costly in terms of foregone welfare) or that it tries to achieve at least a balanced trade balance with respect to manufactures. This would imply, however, a high surplus in the trade balance as long as oil is exported; consumers would have to accumulate much greater savings abroad than they are willing to. Again, the best strategy seems to be the promotion of regional industries by nondiscriminating incentives in open economies. The industries which are viable will get established;

---

[111] For the fact that government incentives, at least in Saudi Arabia, are biased towards large industries see NCB Economist (August/September 1993).

especially those which produce goods with only imperfect substitutes on the world market (Benjamin / Devarjan / Weiner 1989) and those which have international comparative advantages and can export (cf. section B.1.4.).

Does the GCC cooperation help to overcome the problems of *rentier states*? In describing the situation, one is tempted to quote Voltaire: "Work preserves us from three evils: tediousness, vice and misery." Although certain passages in the GCC document on development plans stress that rent distribution should be limited and work ethics should be improved (for details cf. section B.3.6.), every country works on its own (if at all) towards achieving these objectives.

One fundamental characteristic of the GCC countries' strategic approach towards the GCC seems to be that other GCC nationals are allowed as little as possible to participate in national economic rents. For example, Saudi Arabia made it clear that the permission for GCC nationals to engage in contracting activities does not include the permission to be an agent (sponsor, guarantor) for foreign companies in whatever domain (GCC, Secretariat General, 1988, p. 47). Not before December 1993, the Supreme Council decided to allow at least Gulf air carriers to operate in the member states without the need for a sponsor (Arab News 23 December 1993). In addition, although other GCC nationals are allowed to engage in agricultural activities, "[d]irect subsidies, fallow land grants and incentive purchasing programs will be confined to Saudi citizens" (GCC, Secretariat General, 1988, p. 48).

What about GCC's importance in improving *international competitiveness*? The creation of the GCC Free Trade Area, insufficient as it may be, was an appropriate measure. The completion of the common market would be another. However, even if the GCC countries would form a textbook common market with complete mobility of national factors, major parts of the production factors would still be restricted from moving: foreign factors. As to the mobility of foreign know-how, due to restrictions by the foreign partners, know-how from abroad cannot easily be transferred from one company to the next. The refusal of the GCC to free expatriate labor is problematic from an economic point of view, although it is quite understandable from a cultural and political point of view.

The difficulties of expatriate workers with respect to changing their employer or occupation and with respect to getting visa for other GCC countries has to be seen against the background of a 80 percent share of foreign workers in total GCC labor force (Saudi Gazette 4 February 1992). Foreign workers not only have to stick with their present sponsor, but even to their present function if the concerned GCC government does not explicitely permit the change. This permit is in most cases difficult to get (Küppers 1990, pp. 440 (Bahrain), 446 (Kuwait), 452 (Oman), 456f (Qatar), 459 (the UAE); Westerich 1990, p. 467 (Saudi Arabia); Arab Communicators [1989], p. 42 (Bahrain)). This measure is designed to provide nationals with ample time to apply for vacancies in the private sector (Ernst & Whinney 1989b, p. 59). The extreme example is the UAE, where, according to a 1992 study of the UAE Labor and Social Affairs Ministry, more than 93 percent of the labor force in the public sector and 99 percent of the labor force in the private sector are foreigners (Arab News 7 November 1992). Equal situations prevail in Qatar and Kuwait, but the situation is somewhat less dramatic in Oman, Bahrain and Saudi Arabia. Nationals as a percentage of total populations were as follows in the second half of the 1980s: Qatar 27%, the UAE 31%, Kuwait 39%, Bahrain 68%, Saudi Arabia 77% and Oman 82% (Ramazani 1988, p. 199).[112] In connection with increased mobility of foreign workers, their work permits should be unlimited and they should be interested in the countries' economic development by allowing them to attain citizenship, to buy homes and shares and to open businesses. To repeat, these are just economic considerations. However, it might be interesting to combine these measures with a drastic reduction of foreign workers, a cut in unproductive rent payments and an increase in women's labor market participation.

When assessing the Gulf Investment Corporation (GIC), which is wholly owned by the GCC governments, in section C.1.3., it was shown that its financial and industrial know how is of great importance for the GCC and helps in improving competitiveness of GCC countries. Against GIC, one might object that it is engaged in 12 projects which are inappropriate because none are an infrastructural project which links GCC countries, and none is an extremely capital intensive project which can only be managed by all GCC countries together. Indeed, this argument cannot be discarded altogether. In sections B.2.4. and B.2.5. in the context of Balassa's package approach it was pointed out that the establishment of joint companies in all member countries raises questions of practicability, sustainability, efficiency and fairness. The critics might add that the individual GCC country which hosts one of these projects is tempted to provide special tariff or nontariff protection because each loss is a direct financial loss to the country itself as a co-owner of the project. However,

[112] At first glance one is tempted to argue that immobility of expatriate workers has important economic advantages. Training costs are internalized; industry specific know how, as opposed to firm specific know how, is effectively tied to the firm. Several objections can be raised. The loss of mobility in the course of a dynamic development process is costly to the economy; expatriates are very often unskilled workers anyway; the training costs could be paid by the governments or by the workers themselves in the form of low initial pay or by commutation payments from the new employer; most expatriates have a time limit for their work permits.

as every GCC country hosts at least one project, the GCC countries will jointly come to the conclusion that they are better off if all members refrain from such action. Thus, GIC is an ideal forum to discuss the advantages of regional cooperation and joint elimination of barriers to flows of merchandise, services and capital.

Unfortunately, the discussions of GCC officials deal with more than eliminating barriers and enhance competitiveness. The GCC countries rely "on free-enterprise economy as the base for development" (Development Plans 1985), but this does not automatically imply a commitment to full market competition.

The Supreme Council often stressed the need for economic viability in connection with joint projects and industrial policies. In Article 12 of the Economic Agreement (1982), the GCC announces that it will "allocate industries between member states according to comparative advantages and economic feasibility." This strengthens the position of proponents of market mechanisms. On the other hand, the GCC often insists that "harmful competition" has to be avoided. For example, in the present context the GCC governments are urged to promote "coordination between GCC States, joint ventures and Arab joint ventures, to avoid duplication, conflict, waste of financial and human resources, and market competition" (Industrial Strategy 1985). One gets the feeling that at least two different economists assisted in writing the texts.

Several additional examples of the GCC's fear of harmful competition can be found:

- The Economic Agreement (1982) calls for implementing an external customs tariff for "protection of national products from foreign competition." Limited subsidies would be a much better tool.
- Licenses for new industrial projects are in general only granted if "supply is less than demand" for the product at the prevailing price. In combination with tariff protection this, and not the possible competition, is quite harmful, as Al-Fayez (1992, p. 15) points out: "As to tariff redundancy, a recent study shows that it is minimal where protection is provided; that is, producers do take advantage of it by raising their local prices in proportion to the protection level. Furthermore, given past and current government policies of rationalizing the issuance of industrial licenses to avoid multiplicities of competing industries in the same product within a certain local geographical region, there exists a measure of monopolistic competition or even pure monopolies in the market place which encourages producers to exploit the full extent of the protection provided through tariffs." Let the reader be reminded that economic and technical feasibility studies are required when companies apply for licensing of new projects. Useful as this may be, when

an investor applies for subsidies or loans on preferential terms, it is harmful if generally enforced. By the way, licensing procedures provide, of course, ample scope for rent seeking activities.

- As-Sudais (1985, p. 267) notes that "[m]ore recent legislation requires that license applications for any industrial projects of certain size in any GCC member must have approval from the GCC General Secretariat." Similarly, according to Middle East and North Africa 1991 (1990, p. 234) "[i]n December 1987 the Supreme Council discussed a system for regulating regional industry in order to avoid duplication. Under the proposed system, member states would have to obtain approval from the GCC Secretariat for any major new industrial project." Interesting as these proposals are, they have not yet been implemented. In direct contrast, the Economic Declaration of the 1987 Supreme Council summit underlined the importance of competition when it noted that the Unified Economic Agreement "enables the productive energies of the Gulf to serve a wider market" (Economic Declaration 1987). The necessity to encourage "competitive development in economic activity" has been declared, too.
- Foreign direct investment by foreign contractors and sub-contractors to government projects is unwelcome if it is for the purpose of "making the materials which are necessary for the projects. Instead, he must purchase all such requirements from among national products and products of national origin if any such products exist" (Government Purchasing 1987, Article 6).

The latter example is especially harmful because international competitiveness can be increased by foreign investment. In this context, a dynamic and operational problem in the GCC Free Trade Area is the requirement that GCC citizens' ownership "of the producing plant" shall not be less than 51%. At the time of the creation of the GCC Free Trade Area in 1983, the absolute capital majority in GCC plants had to be held by a national. Only Saudi Arabia allowed for foreign capital majority, but its incentive schemes were biased towards favoring companies with a Saudi capital majority. True, the GCC condition is less stringent because other GCC nationals are also allowed to contribute to the 51% share. A problem arises in Saudi Arabia, the Jebel Ali Free Zone in the UAE (which was established in 1985 and where no lower limit for GCC nationals' capital contribution to production units is required) and in Bahrain (which dropped the 51% condition for its whole territory in 1991). Bahrain's intention when allowing for foreign capital majority was to attract foreign capital and know how to compensate for diminishing oil resources and to answer heavy complaints by foreign investors about the undue reliance on their sponsor. Often foreign investors view the production within a free trade area as a mean to get access to the market under avoidance of the import tariffs. However, market access is denied to investors which possess absolute capital majority. Moreover, it is open to dispute between the GCC partners whether the 51% GCC-ownership condition applies only to the plant which produces the final product or whether it applies also to each of the GCC plants which supply intermediaries and contribute to the 40% GCC value added of the final product.

The 40% value added clause is not unusual for free trade areas because partners want to eliminate trade deflection. A better way to eliminate it is of course a uniform external tariff with a mechanism to share the revenues from the import tariffs. Among the ports which gain from a customs union would most probably be the UAE ports; and thus, the UAE would be among the net payers to other GCC countries in a GCC Customs Union.

For reasons of trade deflection and trade diversion, already the establishment of a free trade area has an effect on collected import duties (cf. section B.2.2.). Some interview partners (cf. section C.1.1.) were convinced that Bahrain was one of the losers in the GCC Free Trade Area (e.g., in terms of revenues from import duties). First, there is no theory which states that customs duties which maximize revenues are optimal from a macro-economic point of view. Second, as can be seen from Table 19, data do only confirm a moderate decrease in Bahrain's import duties since 1983, both in absolute figures and as share of total imports.

Table 19: Bahrain's Revenues from Import Duties, 1981-1989 (Bahraini Dinar million; % of "Other" Imports *)

	import duties (Mio Bahr. Dinar)	import duties (% of "other" imports *)
1981	27	9.5
	33	6.6
	49	8.9
1984	49	8.3
	42	8.6
	37	8.9
1987	31	7.2
	34	6.9
1989	37	6.3

Note: * excluding imports of crude petroleum and imports into the bonded area
Sources: International Monetary Fund (1991a; 1991c)

The question of finding a just mechanism to distribute import tariff revenues is a technical one and could be solved by the mediation of IMF, World Bank, EU or other experienced organizations. Another question is the creation of a GCC Regional Fund for assisting poorer countries. This will be discussed when studying economic disparities between GCC members in section C.3.2.

C.2.3. Decision Making Process

The GCC made slow progress in its economic cooperation in the sense that it was not able to stick to its own timetable. The major reason is of course the divergence of interests. Institutional arrangements reflect and aggravate some of the problems. The principle of consensus in "substantive matters" by the Supreme Council slows down the negotiations. "As everyone has the right to veto not only each individual item but also the whole outcome, even the smallest participant can require his point of view to be fully respected, and obtain considerable concessions from the others. ... The whole procedure is much lengthier and more devious than majority voting" (Mühlen 1989, p. 11). In fact, an even stronger voting rule than consensus is applied in the GCC: unanimity. It is not enough that no more objections are made; every party participating in voting has to agree. The principle of consensus by itself shows that the GCC is still immature: "The more practical majority voting is based upon a higher level of social maturity, and a more sophisticated political system, the members of which share a basic consensus and the respect for enforcement mechanisms" (Mühlen 1989, p. 8).

Slow progression to the next stage is not necessarily negative. Wellconsidered and generally accepted agreements are preferable to quick majority decisions which leave some members discontent. However, when evaluating unanimity voting rules, it should be kept in mind that minorities are able to block any progress until their demands are fully met (foot dragging) and that the least willing participant determines the pace of the negotiations (convoy effect).

At first glance, in the GCC the principle of self-steering by the heads of state is applied. All essential matters have to be submitted to the Supreme Council for appropriate action. This could provide quick results. On the other hand the Supreme Council meets only once a year [113] and often hands the proposals back to the Ministerial Council for further elaboration in its remote-controlled negotiations. Each head of state has to render the decisions into national law.[114] Two examples: a) The Unified Economic Agreement was initiated by the ministers of finance and economy on 8 June 1981; it was approved

[113] The first version of the Charter of the GCC stated that the Supreme Council "shall meet in normal sessions twice a year" (Decision to Establish 1981). Maybe this would have speeded the integration process.

[114] Oman is an exemption because "no ratification is required for the [Unified Economic] Agreement to which His Majesty the Sultan has personally and graciously affixed his signature" (GCC, Secretariat General, 1988, p. 1).

by the heads of states on 11 November 1981 which decided that it should come into effect on 12 March 1982; it came into effect on 1 November 1982 when Kuwait ratified it (GCC, Secretariat General, 1988, p. 1). b) The Cooperation Agreement between the GCC and the European Economic Community was signed on 15 June 1988; the Agreement was set into effect by the EC Council of Ministers on behalf of the EEC on 26 February 1989 (EEC-GCC Cooperation Agreement 1989); the last signatory, the UAE, ratified the agreement more than half a year later.

Thus, a "loser" always has the power to challenge results. This makes a strategy of taking others by surprise ineffective, but it also slows down the carrying out of the GCC's ambitious objectives even more. The vulnerability of the GCC decision making has been described by Dietl (1988, p. 367) with the following ironic words: "Its deliberations are closed-door, the agenda is not necessarily adhered to, and the records are not published. Its philosophy is condensed in 'We belong to the world and that is dynamic.'"

The role of the GCC Secretariat General in the decision making process is not easy to assess. Formally, it has to carry out specific secretarial tasks. This is underlined by its relatively small etat of US$ 27 million for 1985/86 (Middle East and North Africa 1991, 1990, p. 234).[115] This amounts to 0.014% of GCC's 1989 GDP. For comparison: the budget of the EU accounts for 1.15% of the EU's 1992 GNP; the EU's administrative machinery alone gets 0.054% of the EU's 1992 GNP. On the other hand, it can influence the integration process by employing its superior knowledge. Especially the Assistant Secretary General for Economic Affairs, El-Kuwaiz, is renowned for being a "pusher." This helps in implementing many small steps which sum up to considerable progress, but it has only limited influence when it comes to the relevant questions such as the "three c": customs union, common market, currency union.

As-Sudais (1985, pp. 288-290) underlines that the "Supreme Council monopolizes authority and all of the GCC institutions are given only an advisory role." He rightly argues that a powerful GCC Integration Council should be established which is responsible for implementing the various and far-reaching integration measures proclaimed in the Unified Economic Agreement. El-Kuwaiz also demands that with its "far-reaching comprehensive objectives, it is imperative the GCC and its institutions develop themselves to increasingly assume the role of a *supranational government*" (El-Kuwaiz 1987, p. 82, emphasis added).

---

[115] According to another source, the Secretariat General has 290 employees, 50 of which are security agents.

C.2.4. Conclusions

If one would view the GCC as being a 'joint venture' that was formed in 1981 by merging their 'firms,' the situation could be described as follows. The GCC began business operations with high aspirations. However, as the directors were unwilling to execute agreed-upon decisions, to delegate implementation rights and refrain from the consensus principle, common gains were low. Clients and employees lost patience and trust in the whole enterprise. One of the leading employees of the GCC spoke of the GCC as suffering from "weak collective organization and inadequate joint action" (El-Kuwaiz 1990, p. 196). He adds that the "process of restructuring" at the six firm levels to gain from synergy effects "still lags behind the institutional and legal requirements of integration."

What has driven the partners to pay little attention to the economic success of their joint business? This question will be dealt with in the following.

C.3. Underlying Reasons for GCC's Economic Performance

The GCC was good in identifying fields of economic cooperation, but it was slow in realizing the possible gains from cooperation. This is almost the same conclusion as drawn by Peterson in 1988 when he wrote "much of the progress to date in the economic realm has been simply the identification of specific means by which the larger GCC objectives may be realized" (1988, p. 175). Although this would surely deserve a study on its own, this study will attempt to shed some light on the fundamental reasons behind this record.

When speaking about potential and actual economically important conflicts of interest between GCC countries, one should perhaps first recall inhabitants of the Arabian Peninsula were in the past often involved in "tribal, nationalistic, and dynastic rivalries and feuds" (Ramazani 1988, p. 102). Thus, it is important for economic cooperation and integration that the GCC societies find peaceful ways to deal with each other, especially through the foundation of the Gulf Cooperation Council itself. The degree of unity and cohesion could especially be felt during Iraq's invasion in Kuwait. The fact that soldiers from Bahrain, Qatar, Saudi Arabia and the UAE fought for Kuwait's liberation, that Bahrain and Saudi Arabia made available military bases and that financial assistance was made available to allied troops by Saudi Arabia and the UAE can be explained by the fear that Iraq might occupy the whole Arabian Peninsula. However, the generous allotment of adequate housing for the expelled Kuwaitis in all GCC countries can hardly be explained only by this argument.

C.3.1. Limited Need for GCC Economic Cooperation Due to Membership in Other Associations?

One of the reasons for little achievements of the GCC may have been the following. In many possible cooperation areas there was no more need for joint GCC measures because other regional of international arrangements provided more appropriate frameworks. The other side of the coin is that the GCC might have been necessary to make the membership in other bodies more effective. These questions will be addressed next.

Economic cooperation of the Gulf countries was present in the decade before the foundation of the GCC in 1981. Many bilateral and multilateral agreements were concluded without the GCC framework, often involving Iraq. Examples of organizations which have already been discussed in sections B.3.5. and B.3.6. and which were transfered into GCC bodies in the early 1990s are the Gulf Organization for Industrial Consulting, the Gulf International Bank, the

Arab Bureau of Education for the Gulf States with its Arab Gulf University, and the Federation of Arab Gulf Chambers (which became later the Federation of GCC Chambers). Along the same lines are the Gulf Ports Union and the Arab Gulf Labour Organization which were established by the six GCC countries plus Iraq in the 1970s. The United Arab Shipping Company was established in 1976 by the GCC countries without Oman, but with Iraq. The Gulf Organization for the Protection of Marine Environment was founded in 1983, during the Iran-Iraq war, by the GCC members plus Iran and Iraq (Bauer / Oehme 1989, pp. 106, 132).

In addition, other broad based Arab and international bodies provide the framework for sometimes far-reaching economic arrangements and are listed below. The *competitive* as well as the *complementary* nature of these organizations will be studied; i.e., it is asked to what extent they fulfill tasks which could otherwise have been fulfilled by the GCC (thereby weakening the GCC), and to what extent they support the GCC as an organization in achieving its objectives (thereby strengthening the GCC).[116] Much of the information is from "Middle East and North Africa 1991" (1990); this source will not be mentioned in this section unless it is quoted.

The United Nations Organization (UN)
founded: 1945; *seat:* New York; GCC's share in UN budget 1989/91: 1.5%; *members:* world-wide membership, including the GCC countries.
Activities: The UN "aims to maintain international peace and security and to develop international co-operation in economic, social, cultural and humanitarian problems" (Middle East and North Africa 1991, 1990, p. 205). During Iraq's occupation of Kuwait from August 1990 to February 1991, the UN Security Council authorized the international allies to take appropriate actions to liberate Kuwait. Economic cooperation is conducted by the Economic and Social Commission for Western Asia (ESCWA, a UN principal organ) in conjunction with other UN bodies, such as UN Industrial Development Organization (UNIDO), Food and Agriculture Organization of the UN (FAO), UN Development Program (UNDP, human resources development), UN Fund for Population Activities (UNFPA), International Labour Organization (ILO), UN Conference on Trade and Development (UNCTAD) and UN Environment Programme (UNEP). UNDP will provide $1.2 billion for environmental rehabilitation in the Gulf region from 1992-96, inter alia for coordination of regional efforts to strenghten environmental protection capabilities (Arab News 26

[116] It almost goes without saying that the question of whether these bodies are worth their membership fees for individual GCC members is not dealt with here. Rather the membership is taken as given and not questioned.

November 1992). Monetary and financial cooperation is promoted by the IMF, a UN specialized agency (see below).
Comments: In the past, Bahrain and Oman received some development aid by UN bodies (e.g., Oman received between 1947 and 1989 eleven loans from the International Bank for Reconstruction and Development). More important for the GCC is the coordinating and advisory function of the UN bodies. For instance, the GCC Secretariat General commissioned a study on the resource base for industrialization to UNIDO (GCC, Secretariat General, 1985); UNIDO co-organized in May 1993 a seminar in Saudi Arabia on appraisal and implementation of industrial projects for experts from Islamic countries (Arab News 8 March 1993). These measures clearly assist the GCC in achieving its objectives.

International Monetary Fund (IMF)
founded: 1945; *seat:* Washington, DC; GCC's share in quotas since November 1992: 4.7%;
members: world-wide membership, including the GCC countries; Saudi Arabia with its relatively high contribution of 3.5% appoints one of seven permanent members of the 25-member Board of Executive Directors which is responsible for the day-to-day operations.
Activities: Member countries with balance of payments problems can draw (i.e., purchase) from the IMF foreign exchange for the equivalent amount of their own currencies. According to the situation, there are several drawing arrangements. Besides, the IMF offers technical assistance on every aspect of economic management, not only during the annual consultations.
Comments: The GCC countries are not facing balance of payments problems, except Kuwait. Starting with $100 billion overseas assets in summer 1990, payment for the operation Desert Storm to defeat Iraq as well as subsequent budget deficits led to an estimated $15 to $35 billion assets by May 1993. The IMF then "called on Kuwait to reduce the deficit by cutting civil service wages and salaries ... and imposing fees for many state services currently free or charged at nominal cheap rates" (Arab News 19 May 1993); wage cuts, however, were ruled out by Finance Minister Nasser Abdullah Al-Rodhan. It would be hard for GCC partners to make such requirements and force Kuwait to accept them. IMF activities (including annual missions, seminars, discussions, technical assistance and training) are very welcome by the GCC countries, even though they are partly reimbursable. For example, the IMF gave advice on unifying financial markets, on forming a monetary union and on the unification of import tariffs. The IMF helps the GCC instead of diminishing its right to exist.

International Bank for Reconstruction and Development (World Bank)
founded: 1945; *seat:* Washington, DC; GCC's share in subscribed capital as of 31.12.1991: 3.2% (Deutsche Bundesbank 1992, pp. 88-91);
members: world-wide membership, including the GCC countries.
Activities: The World Bank is a UN specialized agency which assists economic development by making loans and giving advice.
Comments: The technical and financial assistance was welcome by Oman which received loans of $157.1 million between 1947 and 1989. More important for the GCC are the publications of the World Bank and its participation in seminars on regional development. To the extent that the World Bank intervenes in the GCC economies at all, it is rather helpful.

General Agreement on Tariffs and Trade (GATT)
founded: 1946; *seat:* Geneva; *members:* 111 countries world-wide (July 1993); from GCC only Kuwait, but its participation is minimal; e.g., it did not ratify or even sign any Tokyo round (1973-79) agreement; Bahrain, Qatar and the UAE "maintain a de facto application of the GATT pending final decisions as to their future commercial policy" (General Agreement on Tariffs and Trade 1992, pp. 151-156). Saudi Arabia is an observer to the GATT at the moment, but GATT's world trade body agreed in July 1993 to work for early approval of Saudi Arabia's application to become a full member (Egyptian Gazette 22 July 1993).
Activities: GATT is an autonomous organization within the UN system which aims at fair international trade. It will soon be transformed into a Multilateral Trade Organization (MTO) with increased power.
Comments: GATT would provide a framework for fair intra-GCC trade if all GCC countries were members. GATT would allow for the preferential trade arrangements in a GCC free trade area or customs union, especially as the relevant Article XXIV of the GATT (which requires that preferential regional arrangements do not raise outside trade barriers on the whole) has gained a negative reputation for its lax implementation (Torre / Kelly 1992, pp. 42-44). GATT is not a free trade organization, but to the extent that the Uruguay Round (1986-1993) and further rounds reduce trade barriers, GATT would reduce the necessity for GCC agreements on free trade. On the other hand, such GATT achievements would assist the GCC in its attempt to reach free access for its tradables, especially its petrochemicals.

The Organization of Petroleum Exporting Countries (OPEC)
founded: 1960; *seat:* Vienna;
members: 4 from GCC: Kuwait, Qatar, Saudi Arabia, the UAE; 8 others: Algeria, Gabon, Indonesia, Iran, Iraq, Libya, Nigeria, Venezuela.

Activities: controlling oil prices; coordinating oil supplies and sales; in the beginning: oil sales to international concessionaries. In 1973/74 and 1979/80 OPEC was quite successful in controlling output and thereby rising prices for crude oil (see Graph 3 in section B.1.1.), but the "oil-war" in 1985/86 proofed that OPEC's power is limited. Currently, the price of oil is far below OPEC's agreed-upon price of $21 per barrel.
Comments: Due to the existence of OPEC, GCC's necessity to coordinate oil-price policies is small.

The League of Arab States (LAS)
founded: 1945; *seat:* Cairo;
members: GCC countries, Algeria, Djibouti, Egypt, Iraq, Jordan, Lebanon, Libya, Mauritania, Morocco, Palestine, Somalia, Sudan, Syria, Tunesia, Yemen.
Activities: The Pact of the LAS from 1945 stipulates in Article 2 as a purpose of the LAS "the close co-operation of the member states ... on the following matters: (a) Economic and financial affairs, including commercial relations, customs, currency, and questions of agriculture and industry. (b) Communications: this includes railways, roads, aviation, navigation, telegraphs and posts" (League of Arab States 1945). A host of specialized organizations deal with these issues (Bauer / Oehme 1989, pp. 116-118). In the following, some of them will be mentioned: OAPEC, AFESD, AMF, ATFP, IAIGC, CAEU. In Article 9, the Pact allows member states to conclude agreements to "establish closer co-operation and stronger bonds than are provided by this Pact" (League of Arab States 1945).
Comments: Overall, the LAS has had only very limited success in economic co-operation (Arikat 1986, p. 7). This is mainly due to the diverse situations and interests of its members, as well as to the requirement of unanimity for most decisions (Amin 1984, pp. 177f; Arikat 1986, p. 9). Some specifications will be given in the following. Of course, full implementation of all LAS objectives would render the GCC's economic right of existence close to zero.

The Organization of Arab Petroleum Exporting Countries (OAPEC)
founded: 1968; *seat:* Kuwait;
members: 5 from GCC: Bahrain, Kuwait, Qatar, Saudi Arabia, the UAE; 5 others: Algeria, Egypt, Iraq, Libya, Syria.
Activities: OAPEC determines ways and means for cooperation in various forms of economic activity in the petroleum industry. It organizes conferences on exploration and tries to promote intra-Arab trade in petroleum products and petrochemicals. The members jointly operate several undertakings which are located in GCC countries: Arab Maritime Petroleum Transport Company (AMPTC; founded 1973; headquarter in Kuwait; tanker transport industry;

subscribed capital $500 million), Arab Petroleum Investments Corporation (APICORP; 1975; Dhahran, Saudi Arabia; petroleum and petrochemicals; $400 million), Arab Shipbuilding and Repair Yard Company (ASRY; 1974; Bahrain; dry dock for ship repairs and servicing; $340 million).
Comments: OAPEC is rather competitive with GCC, and together with OPEC it questions the necessity that the GCC establishes an own oil policy.

The Arab Fund for Economic and Social Development (AFESD)
founded: 1972; *seat:* Kuwait; GCC's share in 1988: 59.4%;
members: the 21 members of the League of Arab States.
Activities: The AFESD finances development projects in Arab countries. In addition, it acts as the secretariat of the Co-ordination Group of Arab National and Regional Development Institutions, which comprises the most important Arab development funds, such as the AFESD, the Saudi Fund for Development, the Kuwait Fund for Arab Economic Development, the Abu Dhabi Fund for Arab Economic Development and the Arab Bank for Economic Development in Africa (Bauer / Oehme 1989, p. 12). In all these funds, including the AFESD, the GCC countries Saudi Arabia, Kuwait, Qatar and the UAE are the major donors: Saudi Fund 100%, Kuwait Fund 100%, Abu Dhabi Fund 100%, Arab Bank for Africa 61% (shares as of Dec. 31, 1986; Koppers 1992, p. 44). These four GCC countries are also major contributors to the OPEC Fund for International Development in Vienna (49%) and to the Islamic Development Bank in Jeddah (54%). On the other hand, Bahrain and Oman are recipient countries.
Comments: Because coordination of development aid is not an economic objective of the GCC, the activities of the AFESD do not compete with desirable GCC activities.

The Arab Monetary Fund (AMF)
founded: 1976; *seat:* Abu Dhabi; GCC's financial share: 36.6%;
members: the 21 members of the League of Arab States.
Activities: The AMF is comparable to the IMF in its lending policy and in the settlement of current payments among member countries. Moreover, the AMF promotes economic development and cooperation, especially in the field of inter-Arab trade and Arab capital markets (Arab Monetary Fund 1981, pp. 5-9; 1992b; Bauer / Oehme 1989, pp. 71-73). Subscribed capital of the AMF as of 31 December 1991 is 326 million Arab Accounting Dinars, equivalent to $1400 million. 99.3% are paid-in. The individual shares of the GCC countries in subscribed capital are the following: Saudi Arabia 14.8%, Kuwait 9.8%, the UAE 5.9%, Qatar 3.1%, Bahrain 1.5%, Oman 1.5% (Arab Monetary Fund 1992a, pp. 47, 56).

Comments: The more successful AMF is with regard to promotion of co-operation in trade and capital markets, the less important are GCC activities in these fields. However, because AMF has a very diverse membership, it can only achieve the most basic common standards and there is ample scope for GCC actions which go beyond these minimum standards.

The Arab Trade Financing Program (ATFP)
founded: 1989; *seat:* Abu Dhabi (AMF);
members: the 21 members of the League of Arab States.
Activities: Share-holders are the AMF (50% share of the US$ 500 Mio capital), the AFSED (20%) and Central Banks and commercial banks of the LAS member countries. The ATFP promotes intra-Arab trade by refinancing trade in goods and associated services (without crude oil, used goods and re-exports) with interest rates between Libor and Libor + ½ and by the establishment of the Intra-Arab Trade Information Network. The ATFP's goal is to finance an additional 33% of trade between Arab countries until the end of this century (Bingaradi 1992).
Comments: The ATFP is increasingly important for the GCC countries in the course of diversifying their export structure. Thus, it is complementary to the GCC because the GCC can, if it wants, be one of the bargaining groups in the ATFP and use it as a platform for trade links with other Arab countries.

The Inter-Arab Investment Guarantee Corporation (IAIGC)
start of operations: 1975; *seat:* Kuwait;
members: the 21 members of the League of Arab States.
Activities: IAIGC offers export credits against commercial and non-commercial risks and guarantees direct investments, equity participations and loans against non-commercial risks (Moore 1990; NCB Economist November 1993, p. 7).
Comments: Its relevance for the GCC lies in promoting trade with *extra*-GCC Arab countries, because "intra-GCC trade partners have established a credit-worthiness that makes trade financing – overwhelmingly as letter of credit (L/C) confirmation – something of a formality" (Moore 1990, p. 21).

The Council for Arab Economic Unity (CAEU)
founded: 1957; first meeting: 1964; *seat:* Amman;
members: 1 from GCC: the UAE (Kuwait quit the CAEU in March 1990), 10 others: Egypt, Iraq, Jordan, Libya, Mauritania, Palestine Liberation Organization (PLO), Somalia, Sudan, Syria, Yemen.
Activities: Amongst other goals the CAEU aims at creating a customs union. In January 1965 the Arab Common Market (ACM) was established. It does not constitute a separate organization and groups Egypt, Iraq, Jordan, Libya, Syria and Yemen. By 1971 the ACM had become a free trade union.

Comments: The CAEU was ineffective and did not attract new members. On the contrary, Kuwait quit the Council in 1990 because it "had only achieved a small number of its objectives" (Arab News 26 March 1990). Much the same is true for the ACM. In practice, "the trading of national products has not been freed from all monetary, quantitative and administrative restrictions" (Middle East and North Africa 1991, 1990, p. 236). Four of its members, namely Egypt, Iraq, Jordan and Yemen, formed in 1989 the Arab Cooperation Council (ACC), which is not only in its name, but also in its goals similar to the Gulf Cooperation Council (Koppers 1992). Thus, the CAEU is only in theory an alternative to the GCC.

To conclude, current international or Arab regional agreements are not substitutes for intense GCC economic cooperation. If all GCC countries would become GATT members and GATT would reach a world-wide free trade agreement, then the GCC Customs Union would be unnecessary; but GATT is a forum to negotiate fair trade, not necessarily free trade. A comprehensive Arab economic cooperation would render GCC integration partly useless, but this not in sight. In fact, the GCC was created partly because the League of Arab States was unsuccessful. However, the above-mentioned organizations provide platforms for more intense GCC cooperation and some of them, such as the IMF, assist the GCC in reaching its goals.

C.3.2. Motivations of the Heads of State

Even though the GCC economies are rightly viewed as very similar, there is some potential for divergent economic interests. GCC members are different in economic strength, resources, production structure, infrastructure and human capital. Consider some of the concrete issues.

Saudi Arabia has a large petrochemical sector and suffers from import restrictions by the EU, Japan and the USA, while Oman has not yet shown ambitions to create an extensive petrochemical industry. The reduction of import restrictions against petrochemicals is the most important GCC demand in its free trade negotiations with the EU. Therefore, "[w]ithin the GCC, there are countries that feel the Saudis have hijacked the talks with the EEC" (Dietl 1988, p. 370).

The UAE profits heavily from entrepôt trade and wants to agree on a very low common external tariff in a GCC Customs Union. Other countries, such as Saudi Arabia, want to protect their national industries and demand a high prohibitive import tariff.[117]

It is in the interest of poorer partners, such as Bahrain, to agree upon a far-reaching system of incentives for industrial companies which is nevertheless little cost-intensive. This might be achieved through establishing a GCC Common Market and abolishing capital-ownership restrictions. An agreement to limit subsidies is, however, hard to achieve because richer GCC partners can buy themselves a locational advantage for industries by granting higher pecuniary incentives. It is general belief, as well as the result of scientific studies, that by far the highest subsidies are granted by Saudi Arabia (Girgis 1992; Al-Sharhan 1992). Oman successfully negotiated to exempt important groups of goods from profiting of free import to Oman in the GCC Free Trade Area (Free Trade 1983; cf. section B.3.2.). As-Sudais (1985, pp. 179f) believes the reason was Oman's unability to match the great financial and technical assistance which other GCC products receive.

However, how would one want to consistently explain slow integration just by economic disparities? In such situations a compromise is, in general, found to be in the interest of all members. What such a compromise could look like has been outlined by the Supreme Council itself. One fundamental cause of

---

[117] For example, the GCC has hired Warwick Research Institute from the UK to propose a common tariff structure for a GCC Customs Union, but the UAE has asked another institution to do the same exercise and propose very low tariffs (Fayez 1992).

conflicts between the GCC members is the effort of each country to achieve its own development at the expense of its neighbors. To avoid situations such as the prisoners' dilemma, the GCC partners agreed on the following principles:

a) The "disparities in development levels among member states" shall be reduced (Development Plans 1985).
b) Industrialization shall be achieved "in all the GCC States, on an integrated and balanced basis" (Industrial Strategy 1985).
c) The "differences in the industrial growth rates of the GCC states" shall be narrowed (Industrial Strategy 1985).[118]

Particularly, a GCC Regional Fund could help to achieve these objectives. El-Kuwaiz praises the EC for its mechanism, whereby "financial resources are allocated on a collective basis to benefit the Community's other less developed members" (Arab Times 17 January 1992). A GCC instrument to compensate members which profit less from certain decisions could increase decision finding significantly. In the GCC, no official mechanism of this sort exists. Saudi Arabia financed the Bahrain-Saudi Arabian bridge and made a special contribution to the building of the GCC Secretariat General headquarter. As positive as this may be, such grants are based upon unilateral decisions and are almost unpredictable.

Single members are reknown for joining the GCC because they wanted to achieve coordination in fields other than the economy. Indeed, although not mentioned in the GCC Charter, common security concerns were the most important motivation for founding the GCC.[119] The most imminent concern

---

[118] If one views development and industrialization as two words for the same phenomenon, then these principles are only compatible if all members are on the same level of development. Otherwise the country lagging behind has to have higher growth rates than the frontrunning country if the gap is to be narrowed. Moreover, a country with depleting oil reserves such as Bahrain; Oman or even Qatar might argue that it has to have a higher level of industrialization for a long time to make up for the missing income from exporting crude oil.

[119] The first joint document of the GCC foreign ministers four months before the official foundation of the GCC names "development and stability" as objectives of the GCC (Riyadh Communiqué 1981). This reference to stability (i.e., internal and external security) has not been repeated in the GCC Charter, but the GCC Working Paper by the Supreme Council one day later speaks of "the preservation of stability and security" (Working Paper 1981). Moreover, the ministers of defense, the chiefs of staffs and the ministers of interior each met more than once a year to discuss security matters; not to mention the meetings of the Supreme Council and the Ministerial Council which often had the security situation as their main topic (cf. Final Communiqués and, for the first seven years, Ramazani 1988, pp. 205-228, and Peterson 1988, pp. 225-227).

was neither the Soviet Union's occupation of Afghanistan (1979 - 1989), which created the threat of launching the imperialist expansion in the Gulf, nor the fear that the Iran-Iraq war (1980 - 1988) might spread to the GCC; rather it "was the perceived threat of the contagion of the Iranian Revolution" that "impelled the leaders of the six states to create the GCC" (Ramazani 1988, p. 10). When the GCC was founded, Oman was especially interested in security and military cooperation and in establishing ties with the Western world, while Kuwait insisted on economic, social and cultural cooperation. Even in this setting, a compromise should be found which permits the GCC to pursue the economic as well as the other goals.[120]

Of course, any concrete compromise may be broken. For such cases, legal steps should be possible for the injured party. For example, some firms (e.g., from the UAE) are accused to buy foreign products and sell them as domestically produced with 40% value added to get the GCC free-trade privilege. This hurts other GCC countries which lose import tariff revenues and protection of their own industries. The GCC has already established mechanisms to deal with this. A special commission visits the company in question and submits a report. When GCC economic cooperation gains momentum, further mechanisms are necessary.

As was shown in section B.3.1., no GCC Supreme Court exists. The Commission for the Settlement of Disputes can only be formed by the Supreme Council, it has no decision making power and it can only deal with conflicts between member states or about the GCC Charter. It has not been formed yet (October 1992), although there have been economic disputes which might have called for investigation by such a commission. One example is the long-standing border problem between Qatar and Bahrain over a cluster of potentially oil and gas-rich islands and reefs. Instead of asking the Supreme Council to establish the Commission for the Settlement of Disputes, Qatar submitted the conflict to the United Nations' International Court of Justice in The Hague in July 1991 (Arab News 9 October 1991). Another example is the erection of a Saudi Arabian checkpoint on the road between Qatar and the UAE in 1990, "although these two countries would say that the road passed directly from one to the other" (New Arabia 6 June 1991). Saudi Arabia and Oman did not request mediation before they reached an agreement solving their border conflict in March 1990 and the UAE and Oman set up a bilaterale Supreme Committee in

[120] Here it is assumed that at least one government has a genuine interest in economic cooperation. The alternative assumption cannot be discarded altogether and will be dealt with in the next section.

May 1991 to discuss bilateral issues, including border issues (New Arabia 6 June 1991).

So what is it really that hinders GCC countries to take decisive economic decisions if not unsurmountable disputes about economic policies?

A prominent answer is that the decrease in oil revenues in the 1980s made governments reluctant to deal with luxuries such as regional cooperation. However, this is not a rational policy because it is regional cooperation which could have given GCC economies additional stimulus. One can already imagine the inventors of this explanation in the next boom, saying that now that the crisis is over, it is not any more necessary to pursue regional cooperation and to jointly find ways to overcome dependence on oil revenues (Ramazani 1988, p. 104). This is not to deny that a slowdown in economic growth will also slow down economic integration in the form of new joint ventures and regional infrastructure. However, by definition this is also true for the national economic activities. There are good reasons for believing that freeing of factors, reduction of trade barriers and improvement of competitiveness help to overcome the crisis.

The most appropriate answer seems to be for most observers that economic success is just one objective of GCC heads of state and their pressure groups, and that extensive regional cooperation efforts would conflict with other more important objectives. These objectives are generally described by the term "*sovereignty*." For example, El-Kuwaiz (1990, p. 196) wrote that "[m]ember countries are jealous of their sovereignty."

This argument is hard to understand from a purely economic point of view. Take, for example, the argument in favor of national barriers which holds that the people may be afraid of "foreign infiltration" by an excessive inflow of goods, factors of production and ideas from the GCC partner countries. However, culture, religion and heritage are very similar on the Arabian peninsula and foreigners from non-GCC countries account for more than half of the population. It is argued that the inflow of foreign capital might lead to a national sellout. A net sellout is only possible if consumers are willing to run down their assets and increase consumption.

It cannot be denied that GCC integration did hardly ever touched the question of national sovereignty. Numerous interview partners underlined this observation, and many academic studies point to this explanation for major failures of the GCC. Peterson (1988, pp. 228f) draws the following Figure 14. He suggests that the GCC has achieved a free trade area in 1983, but members

Figure 14: Peterson's View of the Relationship Between Legal Sovereignty and Balassa's Classification of Economic Cooperation

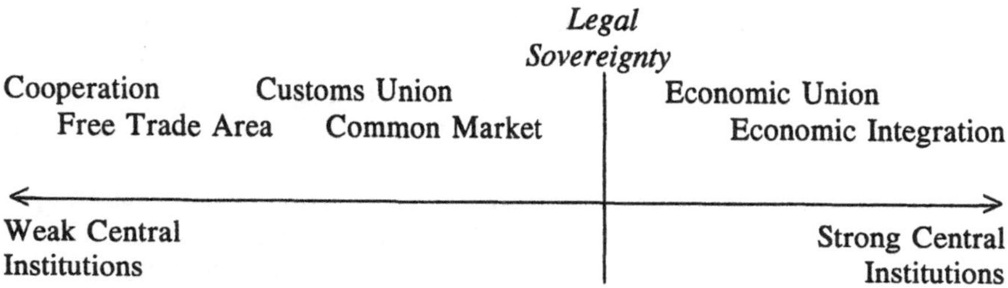

Source: Peterson (1988, p. 228)

were extremely reluctant to take measures which touch the issue of legal sovereignty.

Such a view is problematic because, in the economic sphere, there is no sharp point which separates a country which has still its national sovereignty from another which has just lost its sovereignty. Rather, in the economic field, sovereignty is lost gradually. GCC partners agreed to give in national sovereignty already now, for example, by joining the GCC Free Trade Area or by agreeing to permit GCC professionals to work in their countries.

Peterson (1988, p. 229) points out that not even the program as laid down in the Unified Economic Agreement "has transcended national sovereignty. ... In the final analysis, then, the GCC is moving from the stage of customs union to that of common market."[121]

What is at stake is the liberty of action for each of the heads of state, or their ability to control on a case to case basis. Although the GCC partners agreed to measures which seem to limit the individual influence of each ruler, they implemented in fact mechanisms which leave the final dećisions in the hands of each country. Investors and professionals have to undergo licensing and registration procedures, goods have to pass border controls, industrial loan applications are evaluated case by case. If partners don't act as agreed upon, nobody can force them to. The Gulf University cannot move into its new

---

[121] This is not absolutely true; for instance, the Unified Economic Agreement envisages a GCC Currency Union.

building and teach its students as planned because some GCC countries simply didn't pay their bills.

Thus, there is no limit to GCC cooperation as long as governments find possibilities to have their way in problematic cases, disguised as these ways may be. Such free-riding attitudes might ruin the whole concept of regional cooperation, especially if contracts are not binding. One of the solutions which suggest itself is to grant the GCC people and business sector more influence in the decision making processes. As-Sudais (1985, p. 295) views this as being a general aspect of regional cooperation between developing countries: "One of the obstacles facing LDC [Least Developed Countries'] integration is the problem of national sovereignty. Such a problem may be overcome if decisions are made by the people."

Still, there remain several puzzles. For example, one might object that the it is not consistent to start a complicated process, conduct many conferences and sign a host of documents which demonstrate one's determination – only to stop the whole process at this preliminary stage.

Therefore, an *alternative explanation* for the slow progress of GCC economic cooperation is forwarded. Imagine that rulers are eager to promote economic integration. This is not as unlikely as it might seem from just studying the facts of the GCC process. GCC heads of state actively promoted the industrialization and modernization efforts of their own countries, so why should they prevent improvements for the business environment and for consumers through regional agreements? This leads to the conclusion that the Supreme Council does not want to jeopardize the whole process by offending an influential group in their countries. Slow progress may be more appropriate.

An example from another sphere may illustrate this. The Saudi royal family submits itself completely to the religious law of Islam (sharia). Law memoranda (fatwa) of official interpreters of Islamic law (mufti) decide whether a proposed governmental decision is in accordance with Islamic law. In the past, the royal family was in most cases able to receive affirmative memoranda for their modernization efforts. First, it was decided that not everything could be forbidden that was unknown to the prophet (guns, tobacco, telephon, television). Rather, 'good innovations' were permitted; the Islamic experts were allowed to distinguish between 'good' and 'bad' innovations.

The important aspect here is that rulers didn't use force to pursuade the religious leaders, but they argued until agreement was reached. Although this was tedious, it lead to stable and satisfactory solutions. Maybe that the same concept is followed in the GCC in getting agreement from many groups (e.g., from the influential merchant families).

The upshot is that GCC countries revealed their preferences not to pursue the route to economic cooperation as fast as they should have; and that one has to understand the interests and influences of the different groups in the GCC societies to start understanding who is in the end responsible for these slow moves and how the whole process may develop in the future.

C.3.3. Interests of Different Groups in the GCC Societies

In general, one would expect that there are potential conflicts between and within the following economic groups: governments, consumers, producers, merchants. In the following, potential conflicts which have relevance for the GCC as a regional body will be considered. Two of the more interesting economic questions which arise in the GCC are: 1) Who is pushing for regional cooperation with open markets and a competitive environment? and 2) Which groups have large influence on the heads of state?

As for the first question, one would expect that potential entrepreneurs and consumers are pushing for open markets, while established industrialists want to protect their market shares and advocate for tariff protection, subsidies and no new industrial licenses. The role of influential merchant families has to be assessed, too.

The interaction of different entrepreneurial groups can be felt when studying the position of the Federation of GCC Chambers (FGCCC) on the GCC. On the one hand, it complained about the low international competitiveness of national products. In a 1992 study FGCCC revealed that the factors to which this has to be attributed include "high production costs, nonutilization of production capabilities, low standard of administrative and technical qualifications and the shortage in research and development activities" (Arab News 14 August 1992). It presses for the implementation of the remaining articles of the Unified Economic Agreement. To stress this desire, a symposium of the Gulf private sector, entiteled "GCC ... Without Barriers," was held in Abu Dhabi in June 1993. Muhammad Al-Mulla, Secretary General of the GCC Federation of Chambers of Commerce and Industry, spoke of fulfilling the "dream of a common market in a few years when [the GCC countries'] currencies are aligned, stock markets linked and customs barriers torn down" (Arab News 16 June 1993). This is in line with claims from flexible and innovative industrialists which are not afraid of competition.

On the other hand, FGCCC recommended concentration on large-size and integrated projects, on introducing a comprehensive system of export incentives and on encouraging cooperation and coordination among producers of similar goods "so as to avoid harmful competition" (Arab News 14 August 1992). Thus, instead of advocating the improvement of international competitiveness by coordinating industrial incentives in the GCC, a common GCC international bargaining position to open foreign markets and attract foreign know-how (which would also include the establishment of an outward-oriented GCC common market), the FGCCC advocates rent-opportunities, avoidance of competition and subsidy-cured projects.[122] This part of the FGCCC position is influenced by the economic establishment. For example, as has been revealed by a series of interviews in 1986, the majority of Saudi industrialists producing for the domestic market is convinced that foreign competitors employ dumping practices (Soufi / Mayer 1991, pp. 51, 54). They advocate protectionism, a ban on foreign-product commercials, etc.

It seems that these influential lobbyists have convinced policy-makers at least partially. As was shown in detail in section C.2.2., the harmful view that competition is harmful and that duplication of projects should be avoided by regional coordination and by granting industrial licenses only if the new project is "economically viable," has been adopted in the GCC agreements.

When investigating in the economic establishment, the dominance of some influential families can hardly be exaggerated. These are in the first place the ruling families. Dominant ministries (prime ministership, ministry of foreign affairs, ministry of the interior, ministry of defence) are distributed among the members of the ruling families in the GCC countries (Al-Naqeeb 1990, p. 104). For example, the importance of the ruling Al Saud family in business can be seen from the genealogical tree of the Al Saud in business (Carter 1979), but the leading merchant families are perhaps even more important (Crystal 1991). They had time to concentrate on their businesses, and their monopolistic positions as importers were protected by sponsorship rules.

These merchant families were able to transfer their dominance to the industrial sector. The chairmen of the industrial companies are often merchants (Al-Sharhan 1992; Soufi / Mayer 1991, p. 59). The long-standing dominance of merchant families and of mercantile thinking has at least two significant negative impacts on the industrial sectors in the GCC economies. First, the understanding of the market mechanism is very limited. Often it is their belief that new licenses should only be granted if 'demand is greater than domestic supply,' without reference to the prevailing price or quality; and that industry must not only be guided by price instruments but also by quantity restrictions (Al-Sharhan 1992; Soufi / Mayer 1991, p. 56).

Second, the mercantile experience of getting relatively fast return on investment is contrary to the needs of industrial development, where long-lasting

---

[122] Similarly, it recommends (jointly with the Council of Saudi Chambers of Commerce & Industry) for the future relationships between GCC and EC "co-operation and integration between them but, for sure, not competition and conflict" (Council of Saudi Chambers of Commerce & Industry 1992, p. 15).

engagements are necessary. Murtfeld / Azzam (1990, p. 74, author's translation) combine this diagnosis with the hope that the new generation is less reluctant to get involved in long-term investments: "[For the attraction of foreign investors to get know-how in technology, management and training] a fundamental change in mentality is helpful, which means that the thinking in categories of fast realization of profits and rents, which frequently characterizes the old generation in the Gulf countries, gives way to the readiness of the young generation to work and to assume entrepreneurial responsibility. Many of the young are seeking for chances to employ their specialized knowledge which they have sometimes acquired abroad."

The conflict of interest between potential investors and governments is reflected by the criticism against private investors by GCC governments which urge for higher investments in the domestic economy; the private sector, however, complains about the limited investment opportunities with reasonable return (Jordan Times 16 May 1993). These are in part due to the above-mentioned system of sponsorship and licensing. At least with respect to another important aspect the GCC Assistant Secretary General for Economic Affairs, Abdullah El-Kuwaiz, supports the private sector interests. He urged the GCC governments to open the oil sector (oil and gas production, refining) to private investors (Arab News 9 August 1992). The oil sector has been kept to public companies because it is considered a strategic industry. Prevailing budget deficits and the necessity of upgrading the existing facilities (estimated at $70 billion) might help GCC governments to change their mind.[123]

One governmental answer to consumers and competitive producers which ask for GCC economic integration is to set up plans and non-binding agreements with non-specific general statements. This assumes that GCC leaders had a greater interest in other objectives and pursued the economic route to disguise their real objectives, such as internal and external security enhancement. Indeed, Peterson (1988, p. 175) argues that "GCC officials did not want the organization to be regarded solely as a military response to the regional instability generated by the Iran-Iraq war" and, therefore, directed public attention towards economic cooperation.[124]

---

[123] The 1992 budget deficits as percent of total expenditure were as follows for the GCC countries: Bahrain -21%, Kuwait -86% (1991/92 fiscal year), Oman -13%, Qatar -28% (1991/92 fiscal year), Saudi Arabia -17%, the UAE -8% (NCB Economist January 1993; February/March 1993).

[124] In addition, as Peterson points out, achievements in the economic field might help to increase adherence between the countries and assist efforts "to achieve higher degrees of cooperation in the political as well as defense and security domains." To be sure, Peterson

This points to the possibility that the rulers are not just influenced by the direct threat from the members of the ruling families,[125] but also by the threat of internal security problems due to a discontent of merchant families, consumers, young academics, religious groups and others. As in all social relationships, a complicated net of deterrent potential, subsidies and privileges has been woven to secure the power structure and to buy legitimacy.

However, the high budget deficits may force GCC governments to pursue jointly their objective to reduce subsidies in the form of inexpensive public utilities. The GCC calls upon its member countries for "proceeding with the aim of making the beneficiaries from public services share in bearing the expenses of producing them" (Development Plans 1985). This is not at all easy, as can be seen from the fact that since the Supreme Council has decided upon this principle, almost no action has been taken. On the contrary, in 1991 Saudi Arabia increased subsidies for basic consumer goods even more because it felt that this was important for political stability.

One-dimensional thinking is not adequate in this context. To illustrate, consider the Uniform GCC Strategy for the Industrial Development (Industrial Strategy 1985). It is in many respects a remarkable document. It shows that the GCC places high priority on the development of a strong industrial sector and on modernization. This is not at all obvious because the rulers might fear that a new technical elite may ask for more political participation, too. In addition, it has sometimes been argued that Islam in the conservative Wahhabit specification of the GCC countries is fundamentally opposed to technology, science and industrialization. Thus, the rulers are not only trying to preserve their power by making only those changes which are inevitable, but they also want to act, create, form and influence. After all, even though they are absolutistic rulers which combine legislative, executive and jurisdicti al power, they can hardly be described as despotic, cruel and incalculable.

---

believes that GCC officials had also a genuine interest in economic cooperation, as is demonstrated by the many conferences and meetings.

[125] To give examples that this threat of overthrow by the own family is real: In Saudi Arabia two of the four recent changes of ruler were unvoluntary (1953 Abdulaziz died a natural death; 1964 Saud was overthrown by his brother Faisal; 1975 Faisal was killed by a family member; 1982 Khalid died a natural dead and Fahd became his successor); in Abu Dhabi all of the four recent changes in power were unvolantary, three involved killing (1922, 1926 and 1928; only 1966 the ruler was overthrown without killing).

C.3.4. Conclusions

The future pattern of GCC economic integration is not at all predetermined. On the one hand, if progress remains slow, members may lose interest in the whole issue and go on with pursuing policies they think are in their own best interests. Examples of regional groupings which lost importance are numerous. In section C.3.1. it was shown that other Arab groupings also, such as the Council of Arab Economic Unity (CAEU), suffered when implementation of decisions was slow and members had increasingly divergent interests.

Open or covert non-participation in specific economic GCC measures are a tempting option. No enforcement mechanism exists, every member has a veto right and economic interests are diverse. Some differences culminate in the GCC's foreign bargaining position. The reduction of tariffs on GCC petrochemicals by the EU, the USA and Japan is mainly in the interest of Saudi Arabia, but it is of no issue for Oman. It is in the interest of the UAE that a GCC Customs Union (which is a prerequisite for a GCC-EC free trade agreement) is outward oriented with minimal tariffs. Other partners which do not serve as a center for regional entrepôt trade insist on relatively high protective import duties. Bahrain with its low oil and gas reserves is less interested in a stable oil market and more in improving the foreign investment climate. As the GCC partners were not willing to abolish national capital majority requirements and sponsorship obligations, Bahrain decided to go it alone. However, foreign investors, which now hope for serving the whole GCC market from Bahrain by fulfilling the 40 percent regional value added precondition are disappointed. Their products may only participate in GCC free trade if the GCC capital share in the companies is 51 percent or more. This limits the negative externalities to other Gulf producers substantially, but it also reduces the healthy competitive pressure on them and possible positive effects for consumers.

On the other hand, much points to the possibility that the pressure of its own industrialists and consumers, as well as bloc building in other regions, will provide the GCC leaders with the necessary backing to give the integration process a decisive push in the next few years. The institutional and cultural similarities between GCC members are great, and no alternative grouping can be thought of, as was the case for Kuwait when it quit CAEU in 1990. Also, a reduction of GCC membership is unlikely.

D. Summary and Perspectives

The GCC Supreme Council which groups the six heads of state and is the primary decision-making body is well aware of the difficulties which arise from their oil revenues. It stated at the end of its founding meeting that the "oil on which we are relying at present is an exhaustible wealth. It generated high tension and changes in human behavior. The peoples of the Gulf look to their governments to solve the difficult equation of achieving real development on the one hand, and safeguard social peace, security and progress on the other" (Working Paper 1981). It is misleading to include oil revenues in Gross Domestic *Product* because it is merely asset reduction and not production which takes place. If the current level of consumption is to be maintained after depletion of oil one (Bahrain, Oman), two (Qatar) or three generations (Kuwait, Saudi Arabia, the UAE) from now, asset transformation through saving and investment should take place.

One obvious way to proceed is the investment of oil revenues in international capital markets, but this may lead to increased political dependence and to the prolongation of the rentier status. A more sustainable development path is the development of human resources and international competitiveness, mainly through industrialization. During the first years, however, industrialization calls for subsidies. One reason is that imperfect capital markets or short-sighted investors are reluctant to make the initial investments to achieve learning-by-doing effects and minimum-size requirements. This is the well-known infant-industry argument. Another reason is called 'Dutch Disease:' The rent income from oil revenues induces a real appreciation (due to increased demand for nontradables) which hampers the production of tradables (i.e., mostly industrial goods). If oil revenues are later reduced for one reason or another, the economy lacks the necessary international competitiveness and marketing know-how in other sectors, again assuming imperfect capital markets or short-sighted consumers. As has been shown additionally, Dutch Disease even prevails if the usual assumption of international immobility of factor movements is dropped.

In this setting the strengthening of competitive forces and the optimal allocation of regional resources is essential. Both of these are furthered by regional economic cooperation, specifically by creating a GCC Common Market. Indeed, a GCC Free Trade Area came into effect in March 1983 and in the following years labor and capital movement was liberalized. According to empirical findings of this study, the GCC Free Trade Area has been successful in creating additional intra-GCC trade. However, as data and opinion surveys show, there are still major intra-GCC trade barriers; and competition on the labor and capital market remains low due to government intervention.

Labor mobility is limited because nationals seek and find jobs in the governmental administrations and companies, and expatriates do not profit from the liberalization of labor movement. Efficient capital mobility in the especially important industrial sector is limited because licensing is often denied when demand is already met by another regional producer. In general, the initial impression that GCC economies are free market economies with considerable scope for private sector competition has to be questioned. Competition is viewed as waste of resources and GCC's decisions often aim at avoiding competition.

Another characteristic of GCC decision making is the fear of GCC governments to touch the issue of national sovereignty. Even when agreements are signed which seem to limit national sovereignty, each head of state is eager to have a backdoor which allows for the circumvention of decisions. In the GCC Free Trade Area this is possible through red tape at the borders and through questioning the fulfillment of the 40% share of local value requirement. Even in a GCC Customs Union red tape would be possible if internal border controls are not eliminated altogether. As licensing and registration is mandatory, factor mobility can be controlled. Especially Saudi Arabia, which dominates in terms of GNP and is also the major producer of petrochemicals in the GCC, should be pushing for a GCC Customs Union with few border controls. The reason is that for the European Union this is a precondition for a free trade agreement with the GCC, especially in the field of petrochemicals imports from the GCC. However, to protect its infant industry on the domestic market, Saudi Arabia advocates a high external tariff and is known for erecting non-tariff barriers against imports from GCC partners.

Nevertheless, as has been pointed out in sections C.3.2. and C.3.3., there are good reasons for arguing that the GCC rulers are willing to proceed much faster with economic integration, but that they have to pursuade influential interest groups first.

The slowness in the realization of GCC's high objectives has its positive aspects: GCC governments have not yet established a supranational agency which decides upon the locations and sizes of new industrial plants, thereby further reducing regional competition. Similarly, a GCC Customs Union would be of limited or even negative impact if the common external tariff were prohibitively high, which was the goal when the GCC Supreme Council decided in 1981 to establish a GCC minimum common external tariff until November 1987. The theoretically more appealing solution is the coordination and fixing of industrial subsidies. The GCC did not achieve this, either.

Among the GCC cooperation and integration efforts which still have to be made are the establishment of a GCC Customs Union with low external tariffs, the coordination of industrial incentive schemes, an effective GCC Intellectual Property Rights Legislation, an effective GCC Foreign Markets Information System and later, after the coordination of fiscal policies, perhaps even a GCC Currency Union. Important institutional arrangements include the establishment of a GCC Consultation Council with representatives of consumers, the business community and other non-governmental groups having the right to propose and to comment, a GCC Integration Council which implements the far-reaching decisions of the Supreme Council, and a GCC Supreme Court to which governments and private persons or groups may appeal to identify and enforce their legitimate rights. A pecuniary GCC Compensation Fund might help to distribute duties of a customs union and a GCC Regional Fund would help to achieve the GCC objective to reduce development level disparities (Development Plans 1985).

True, the GCC countries "have embarked upon the *ultimate joint venture* – the economic and political combination of nations" (Al Jafary 1992, emphasis in original). But their boat has not covered much distance yet and one has the impression that there are six captains, each of which wants to (or is pressed to) retain his independence.

While the present study could serve as a basis for comparing GCC's achievements to those of other regional groupings, one cautionary note is called for. The GCC countries are rather special cases as the "GCC economies are best described as a hybrid of developed and developing economies" (Al-Fayez 1992, p. 2). While their per capita incomes are as high as those in many industrialized countries, GCC countries' production structures are not more diversified than those of many developing countries. This does not facilitate the task of comparing the GCC experience in regional cooperation to other groups.

Much of this study has been dedicated to demonstrating that the GCC economies and the GCC as an organization face serious economic problems and shortcomings despite their relatively great wealth and their high objectives. This may be an unjust view given the number of agreements initiated by the GCC and the positive outlook on the future if the plans are implemented, as well as the immense problems other regional groups have encountered. In addition, while other regions have to contend with external or internal wars, the GCC countries have managed to deal with each other almost cordially.

E. Appendix

Table A1: National Accounts in GCC Countries, 1989 (% of GDP)

	Bahrain	Kuwait	Oman	Qatar	S.A.	UAE	GCC
I. Structure of Expenditure on GDP							
private consumption	42	47	40	32	47	41	**45**
government consumption	29	24	30	39	31	20	**28**
gross fixed cap. formation *	14	20	14	15	21	23	**20**
trade balance	16	10	16	14	1	14	**7**
exports of goods & serv.	100	55	48	42	38	59	**47**
imports of goods & serv.	-84	-45	-32	-29	-37	-44	**-40**
net factor income fr. abroad	-7	35	-13	-	4	-	**9**
GNP	93	135	87	-	104	-	**109**
II. Structure of GDP by Kind of Economic Activity							
Commodity Sectors							
agriculture, fishing, forestry	1.2	0.7	3.6	1.0	7.3	1.7	**4.7**
mining, quarring & fuel	17.5	40.9	45.8	29.4	27.6	39.0	**32.5**
manufacturing industry	17.8	14.4	4.2	13.0	8.1	8.6	**9.4**
refining †	12.7	6.3	1.3	1.4	3.0	1.2	**3.3**
electricity, water, gas	2.1	-0.6	1.5	1.5	0.2	2.2	**0.6**
construction	6.5	2.3	3.3	4.8	10.4	9.2	**8.2**
	45.1	*57.7*	*58.4*	*49.7*	*53.6*	*60.7*	***55.4***
Service Sectors							
commerce, restaurant, hotel	10.2	8.2	12.2	6.0	8.4	10.9	**9.0**
transp., traffic, storage	11.3	4.0	3.5	2.8	7.4	5.2	**6.2**
finance, insurance, banking	0.5	1.5	1.4	7.3	4.1	3.8	**3.6**
Housing	5.5	8.9	6.6	-	2.0	6.4	**4.1**
Government Services	22.2	18.9	17.0	31.6	18.6	12.0	**18.0**
Other Services	5.2	-	-	2.1	3.7	2.6	**2.7**
	54.9	*41.5*	*40.7*	*49.8*	*44.2*	*40.9*	***43.5***
Net Indirect Taxes	-	*0.9*	*0.9*	*0.6*	*2.2*	*-1.6*	***1.1***
Memo.: GDP 1989 ($ billion)	3.6	23.0	8.4	6.5	83.0	27.5	**152.0**

Notes: - not available; * including 1 to 2 percentage points "increase in stocks"; † the share of refining in GDP has been approximated for the non-Saudi GCC members by the following procedure: (a) Saudi Arabia's refining contributed $2.51 billion to GDP in 1989 (NCB Economist April 1992, p. 2); (b) this corresponds to a throughput of 1.3559 million barrels per day (Arab Petroleum Research Center 1992, p. 542); (c) thus 1 barrel throughput "created" $5.072 on average; (d) assuming that this ratio is also correct for the other GCC refining industries, their contribution to GDP has been calculated from their throughputs
Sources: Arab Monetary Fund (1991b); Arab Petroleum Research Center (1992); Gulf Organization for Industrial Consulting, Industrial Data Bank, as reported in As-Sultan / Al-Matrak (1992); International Monetary Fund (1992b)

Table A2: Central Governments' Budgets in GCC Count. 1989 (% of GDP)

	Bahrain	Kuwait	Oman	Qatar*	S.A.	UAE†	GCC‡
I. Revenues	***32.7***	***32.9***	***35.7***	***24.7***	***37.3***	***12.5***	***31.4***
Current Revenues & Grants	*32.7*	*32.7*	*35.6*	-	*32.5*	*12.5*	***28.9***
tax revenues	*8.5*	*1.2*	*2.0*	-	*8.8*	*0.6*	***5.7***
corporate (w/o oil comp.)	1.2	0.2	0.6	-	-	0	**0.2**
social security funds	2.9	0	0	-	-	0.0	**0.2**
taxes on goods & serv.	1.3	0.0	0.3	-	-	0.5	**0.3**
import duties	2.7	1.0	0.9	-	-	0	**0.6**
other	0.4	0.0	0.3	-	-	0.0	**0.1**
nontax revenues & grants	*21.4*	*31.4*	*33.6*	-	-	*0.5*	***22.6***
petroleum	14.9	30.1	29.0	-	23.7	0	**20.3**
gas	2.1	0	-	-	-	0	**0.1**
grants	2.8♪	0	0.9	-	-	11.2¶	**5.2**
other	1.6	1.3	3.7	-	-	0.8	**1.4**
Capital Revenues	*0.0*	*0.3*	*0.1*	-	*4.9*	*0.0*	***2.8***
II. Expenditures	***34.7***	***42.9***	***44.1***	***48.6***	***45.2***	***13.1***	***38.9***
by Function							
general public services	10.5	4.2	4.8	-	10.1	0.6	**7.1**
defense	5.5	8.5	18.5	-	15.4	5.7	**12.4**
public order & safety	§	3.0	-	-	#	1.7	**2.3**
education	5.2	6.0	4.6	-	7.7	2.0	**6.1**
health	2.7	3.2	2.3	-	3.4	0.9	**2.8**
social security & welfare	0.8	5.4	-	-	@	0.4	**2.6**
housing & commun. amenit.	1.5	3.4	2.5	-	1.7	0.1	**1.7**
recreation, culture, relig. aff.	0.6	0.9	0.9	-	-	0.4	**0.7**
fuel & energy development	2.4	4.4	2.7	-	1.6	0.3	**1.9**
transport. & communication	3.9	1.1	0.9	-	2.7	0.0	**1.9**
other	1.7	2.7	1.6	-	2.5	0.9	**2.1**
by Economic Type							
current expenditures	*26.3*	*33.4*	*38.4*	*42.2*	-	*13.0*	***26.3***
wages & salaries	17.1	12.9	10.0	-	-	4.4	**9.0**
other purch. goods & serv.	5.7	11.5	22.5	-	-	7.6	**10.9**
interest payments	1.0	-	2.9	-	-	-	**2.4**
subsid. & oth. curr. transf.	2.5	8.9	3.1	-	-	1.0	**4.3**
capital expenditures	*8.4*	*9.5*	*5.7*	*6.4*	-	*0.1*	***5.0***
acquis. of fixed cap. assets	4.8	5.0	5.0	-	-	0.1	**2.8**
capital transfers	3.6	3.3	0.7	-	-	-	**2.7**
domestic	3.6	3.3	-	-	-	-	**3.4**
others	-	1.2	-	-	-	-	**1.2**
III. Lending minus Repayments	***6.6***	-	***0.5***	-	-	***0***	***0.7***
domestic	2.0	-	0.1	-	-	-	**0.7**
abroad	4.6	-	0.5	-	-	-	**1.7**
IV. Deficit = I. - (II.+III.)	***-8.6***	***-9.9***	***-9.0***	***-23.9***	***-7.9***	***-0.6***	***-7.6***

Notes: - not available; * for fiscal year 1989/90; † central government; total government revenues per GDP = 22.6%; total government expenditures per GDP = 32.7%; (Arab Monetary Fund 1991a, pp. 10f) ‡ share of GDP from countries for which data are available; ♪ from Saudi Arabia; ¶ from UAE members Dubai and Abu Dhabi; § included in general public services; # included in defense; @ included in health

Sources: International Monet. Fund (1992c); NCB Economist (Jan. 1993; Feb./March 1993)

Table A3: Balance of Payments in GCC Countries, 1989 (% of GDP)

	Bahrain	Kuwait	Oman	Qatar	S.A.	UAE	GCC*
Current Account	*-0.5*	*36.6*	*3.8*	*-0.1*	*-11.1*	*16.5*	**2.7**
merchandise	*0.3*	*20.6*	*22.8*	*21.8*	*10.9*	*21.6*	***15.2***
exports f.o.b.	79.0	49.4	48.2	42.2	34.1	58.4	**43.0**
oil sector	59.4	44.7	43.0	-	28.9	37.1	**34.5**
crude petroleum	10.8	-	-	-	22.7	-	**22.2**
refined petroleum	48.6	-	-	-	6.3	-	**8.1**
imports f.o.b.	-78.7	-28.7	-25.4	-20.4	-23.2	-36.8	**-27.8**
crude petroleum	-34.6	-	-	-	-	-	**-34.6**
services	*8.7*	*-12.6*	*-6.5*	↑	*-21.1*	↑	***-17.5***
credit	24.4	5.8	0.1		3.1		**4.1**
debit	-15.6	-18.3	-6.7		-24.2		**-21.5**
income	*-7.0*	*35.1*	*-3.2*	-21.8	*11.7*	-5.0	***14.7***
credit	13.8	38.4	3.8		12.6		**17.0**
inv. income off. sect.†	5.3	25.0	0.4		12.6		**13.9**
debit	-20.7	-3.3	-7.0		-0.8		**-2.4**
labor income	-13.8	-	-		-		**-13.8**
unrequited transfers	*-2.6*	*-6.5*	*-9.2*		*-12.7*		***-10.9***
private	-5.5	-5.6	-9.4		-10.1		**-9.0**
workers' remittances	-5.5	-5.6	-9.4		-10.4		**-9.3**
official	2.8	-0.9	0.2	↓	-2.7	↓	**-1.9**
Long-Term Capital	*2.6*	*-4.1*	*1.9*	-	*-2.5*	↑	***-2.4***
direct investment	5.0	-2.2	1.3	-	-0.4		**-0.4**
portfolio investment (public)	-	-1.4	-	-	-2.2		**-2.0**
other	-2.4	-0.5	0.6	-	-		**-0.4**
resident official sector	-	-0.6	0.6	-	-		**-0.3**
Short-Term Capital	*-7.7*	*-29.3*	*-1.7*	-	*9.4*	-11.1	***0.6***
resident official sector	0.5	-26.5	-	-	-		**-22.8**
deposit money banks	-11.0	-2.1	-0.9	-	0.6		**-0.4**
other	2.9	-0.7	-0.8	-	8.9	↓	**6.1**
Net Errors and Ommissions	*0.4*	*2.2*	*-0.8*	-	-	-	***1.4***
Reserves (increase: -)	*5.2*	*-5.4*	*-3.4*	-	*4.2*	*-5.5*	***0.5***

Notes: - not available; * share of GDP from countries from which data are available; † investment income resident official sector
Sources: International Monetary Fund (1991a; 1992c); NCB Economist (February/March 1993)

Table A4: Refinery Industries in the GCC, 1 January 1992

	Location, Start-up	Ownership	Capacity (Throughput in '000 b/d)
Bahrain	Sitra, 1936	Bahrain Petroleum Co. BSC [60% gov. Bahr., 40% Caltex Bahr. (USA)]	**243**
Kuwait	Mina Abdulla, 1958	Kuwait National Petr. Co. [100% gov. Kuwait]	190
	Mina Al-Ahmadi, 1946	Kuwait National Petr. Co.	370
	Shuaiba, 1969	Kuwait National Petr. Co.	187
			747
Oman	Mina Al Fahal, 1982	Oman Refinery Co. [100% gov. Oman]	**80**
Qatar	Umm Said I: 1960s; II: 1983	National Oil Distribution Co. [100% Qatar Gas and Petr. Co., which is owned 100% by gov. Qatar]	**60**
Saudi Arabia	Ras Tanura, 1945	Saudi Aramco * [100% gov. Saudi Arabia]	300
	Ras Al-Khafji, 1966	Arabian Oil Co. [10% S.A., 10% Kuw., 80% Japanese]	30
	Riyadh, 1974	Riyadh Oil Refining Co. [100% Saudi Aramco *]	134
	Jeddah, 1980	Jeddah Oil Refining Co. [100% Saudi Aramco *]	91
	Yanbu, 1982	Saudi Aramco *	170
	Yanbu, 1983	Petromin 50% / Mobil 50% [100% Saudi Aramco * / 100% USA]	280
	Jubail, 1984	Petromin 50% / Shell 50% [Shell: USA]	250
	Rabigh, 1989	Petromin 50% / Petrola 50% [Petrola: Greece]	325
			1580
UAE	Ruwais, 1981	Abu Dhabi National Oil Co. [100% gov. Abu Dhabi]	120
	Umm Al-Nar, 2: 1983	Abu Dhabi National Oil Co.	72.5
			192.5

Note: * Saudi Aramco merged in June 1993 with Samarec, which before owned most of the Saudi shares

Sources: International Petroleum Encyclopedia [1992]; NCB Economist (May/June 1992)

Table A5: Petrochemical Production Capacities in GCC States, 1988 ('000 tons)

	Bahrain	Kuwait	Oman	Qatar	S.A.	UAE	GCC
Basic Products							
Ethylene				280	1,980		**2,260**
Intermediates							
Ethylene Glycol					580		**580**
Ethylene Dichloride					560		**560**
Styrene					360		**360**
Vinyl Chlorid Monomer					300		**300**
Ethanol					300		**300**
Methanol	330				1,410		**1,740**
Ammonia	300	1,000		640	1,030	330	**3,300**
End Products							
Low Density Polyethylene				140			**140**
Linear LDPE / High DPE					902		**902**
Polyvinyl Chloride					200		**200**
Nitrogen Fertilizer (Urea)		792		744	930	495	**2,961**
Methyl Tertiary Butyl Ether					500		**500**
Total	*630*	*1,792*	*0*	*1,804*	*9,052*	*825*	***14,103***

Source: Horndasch (1990, p. 158)

Table A6: GCC Countries' Ministries of Economic Importance

Bahrain	Kuwait	Oman	Qatar	Saudi Arabia	UAE
Foreign Affairs	Foreign Affairs	Foreign Affairs	Foreign Affairs	Foreign Affairs	Foreign Aff.
Finance & National Econ.	Finance	Finance	Finance & Petroleum	Finance & National Economy	Finance & Industry
Development & Industry	Commerce & Industry	Commerce & Industry	Industry & Public Works	Industry & Electricity	
	Planning			Planning	Planning
Commerce & Agriculture			Economy & Trade	Commerce	Economy & Commerce
Labor & Social Affairs	Labor & Social Affairs	Labor & Voca-tional Training	Labor, Social Aff. & Housing	Labor & Social Affairs	Labor & Social Aff.
		Social Affairs			
		Agriculture & Fisheries	Municipal Aff. & Agriculture	Agriculture & Water	Agriculture & Fisheries
	Oil	Petroleum & Minerals		Petroleum & Mineral Resources	Petroleum & Mineral Res.
Transport		Communications, Civil Aviation, Ports & Roads	Communications & Transport		
Public Works, Power & Water	Electricity & Water	Electricity & Water	Electricity & Water	Public Works & Housing	Electricity & Water
		Environment & Water Resources			
	Public Works	Public Works			Public Works & Housing

Source: Middle East and North Africa 1990 (1991)

Table A7: Questionnaire which has been Distributed to Scientific or Governmental Institutions in the GCC

1. **Institution's profile:**
   a) We provide you with the following information (e.g. annual reports):

   b) Scope of activities:
   c) Approximate number of employees:
   d) Year of foundation:
   e) Name and address:

2. **The international comparative advantages of the GCC lie in the following area:**

   o Service o Manufacturing

   (Please comment:)

3. **Degree to which the following targets have been reached in the GCC:**

	100%	80%	60%	40%	20%	0%
a) Free trade within GCC	o	o	o	o	o	o
b) Transportation infrastructure within GCC	o	o	o	o	o	o
c) Right of movement of capital within GCC	o	o	o	o	o	o
d) Freedom for economic activities in whole GCC	o	o	o	o	o	o
e) Right of ownership in whole GCC	o	o	o	o	o	o
f) Support of GCC by its business community	o	o	o	o	o	o
g) Firms' participation in GCC decision taking	o	o	o	o	o	o

4. **Among the GCC activities which should receive highest priority in the 1990s are:**

   a)

   b)

   c)

5. **From the point of view of economic cooperation between GCC companies, the following GCC activity was: of great practical value: 1 ... insignificant: 6**

	1	2	3	4	5	6
a) GCC Charter	o	o	o	o	o	o
b) Unified Economic Agreement	o	o	o	o	o	o
c) Joint Agricultural Policy	o	o	o	o	o	o
d) Exemption of GCC products from customs tariffs and charges	o	o	o	o	o	o
e) Regulations governing transit goods	o	o	o	o	o	o
f) Right of ownership of landed property	o	o	o	o	o	o
g) Long-Term Development Plans	o	o	o	o	o	o
h) Uniform strategy for industrial development	o	o	o	o	o	o
i) Priority given to GCC prod. by gov. purchas. policy	o	o	o	o	o	o
j) Allowment to engage in wholesale and retail commerce	o	o	o	o	o	o

Note: in the enterprise questionnaire the word "institution" had been changed into "enterprise"

Table A8: Organizations which Returned the Questionnaire

1. Enterprises:

Bahrain Bedding Factory
Bahrain Light Industries
Saudi Basic Industries Corporation, Riyadh
The National Medical Products Co. Ltd., Riyadh

2. Scientific or governmental institutions:

Arab Planning Institute, Kuwait
Bahrain Centre for Studies & Research
Dubai Chamber of Commerce & Industry
GCC, Secretariat General, Riyadh
Gulf Organization for Industrial Consulting, Doha
Kuwait Institute of Scientific Research
Ministry of Finance, Kuwait
Ministry of Finance and National Economy, Bahrain
The Royal Commission for Jubail & Yanbu, Riyadh
UAE Ministry of Finance and Industry, Abu Dhabi

3. Banks or financial institutions:

Gulf Investment Corporation, Kuwait
National Bank of Kuwait
National Investment Company, Kuwait
The National Commercial Bank, Jeddah

Distribution to and response rate has been as follows:

1. 51 enterprises; response rate: 8% (i.e., 4 questionnaires)

2. 18 scientific or governmental institutions; response rate: 56% (due to multiple responses from some institutions, the total questionnaire return was 20)

3. 4 banks or investment institutions; response rate: 100% (one institution returned 2 questionnaires, therefore the total was 5)

Table A9: Intra-GCC Trade Matrix, 1977-1990 ($ million), Part I: data derived from export statistics; trade flows from country in italics to partner

	1977	1978	1979	1980	1981	1982	1983	1984	1985	1986	1987	1988	1989	1990
(a) Bahrain														
Kuwait	13.3	16.8	48.1	32.3	67.2	117	14.5	12.9	y11.6	y9.7	y9.8	y9.7	y11.2	y6.8
Oman	11	22.3	54.1	78.6	161.1	157.4	18.7	13.1	y11.8	y9.8	y10	y9.9	y11.4	y16.1
Qatar	11.5	6	17.9	33.4	73	79.1	104.7	26.3	y23.7	y19.6	y20	y19.8	y22.8	y20.5
SA	482.7	99.6	144.7	104.9	143.1	185.2	130.5	89.8	y80.8	y67.1	y68.3	y67.4	y77.7	y87.3
UAE	170.7	283.4	476.3	635.5	782.2	482.3	508.1	598.4	y538.3	y446.8	y455	y449.3	y517.7	y361.2
(b) Kuwait														
Bahrain	13	17	10	5	10	11	16	15	10	y3	y3	y3	y3	y2
Oman	5	4	4	4	4	5	8	10	9	*4	*7	*6	*9	*7
Qatar	28	21	21	25	28	30	21	14	13	*4	*4	*6	*8	*6
SA	435	405	441	506	564	448	394	337	294	*100	*102	*98	*122	*70
UAE	94	77	140	411	213	376	195	109	95	*15	*29	*37	*38	*35
(c) Oman														
Bahrain			0.1	0.1	0.2	0.3	*1.7			41.9	39.3	46.8	53.4	41.8
Kuwait		0.1	0.1	0.1	0.6	0.8	*1.2			44.8	26.6	79.2	91.4	46.1
Qatar			0.1	0.3	0.3	1				38.6	36.5	45	58.6	43.3
SA	0.2	0.8	0.9	1.8	5.5	9.1	*3.3			141.8	185.5	188	397.5	335.8
UAE	3.1	4.7	6	7.6	13.9	13	*0.8			1170.5	1441.3	1871	2127	2135.7
(d) Qatar														
Bahrain	2.3		1.1	2.6	0.2	*0.9	*1.9	y0.2	y0.1	y2.6	y2.9	y2.9	y3.2	y3.7
Kuwait	0.1		25.1	19.8	40.8	*4.5	*13.4	y34.1	y26.8	*31.8	*33.1	*53.6	*45.8	y29.4
Oman	0.2		0.9	1.1	0.3	*0.1	*0.3	y0.2	y0.2	*8.1	*3.5	*2.5	*8.9	*9.5
SA	8.2		62.9	57.7	62.3	*67.2	*71.3	y52	y40.9	*61.5	*52.5	*85.8	*65.8	*47.4
UAE	2.3		19.7	30.8	16.8	*29.7	*27.4	y14	y11	*41.8	*45.5	*42.7	*88.2	*117.3
(e) Saudi Arabia														
Bahrain	969	881	1243	2012	2544	1932	1396	1395	1166	879	1141	980	1250	1753
Kuwait	8	33	34	50	191	221	68	95	81	111	163	205	269	199
Oman	17	11	18	14	19	10	4	8	13	14	22	21	37	76
Qatar	3	4	18	15	23	31	31	22	31	36	33	44	54	123
UAE	6	9	25	35	78	70	60	73	143	271	223	293	461	804
(f) UAE														
Bahrain	8	9	26	35	43	49	*32	y41	y41	y23	y25	y25	y28	y33
Kuwait	16	18	25	38	62	68	*39	y57	y56	*55	*94	*140	*90	*58
Oman	10		11	108	28	10	9	y8	y8	*407	*348	*420	*497	*565
Qatar	71	64	76	100	126	155	*32	y130	y129	*31	*31	*36	*53	*46
SA	88	115	202	232	290	320	*138	y270	y267	*127	*108	*119	*127	*151

Notes: * = derived solely from partner record; y = estimates without use of own records, sometimes with partner's record

Source: International Monetary Fund (1992a)

Table A9: Intra-GCC Trade Matrix, 1977-1990 ($ million), Part II: data derived from import statistics; trade flows from country in italics to partner

	1977	1978	1979	1980	1981	1982	1983	1984	1985	1986	1987	1988	1989	1990
(a) Bahrain														
Kuwait	1	2	6	20	7	6	9	8	6	14	18	37	41	y7
Oman	23.1	26.2	29.6	76.9	170.4	173.9	5.9	7.6	14.1	10.8	14.1	6.6	12.9	24.3
Qatar	9	4.4	5	6.1	6.1	4.9	3.2	2.2	2	1.7	1.6	6.3	9.8	16.2
SA	216	46	55	90	161	217	123	63	117	64	63	115	128	107
UAE	77	51	464	406	724	369	294	384	238	130	116	79	96	133
(b) Kuwait														
Bahrain	5.9	10.6	4.2	2.1	2.9	4.8	4.3	4.3	y3.8	y2.9	y3.2	y3.2	y3.6	y2.2
Oman	3.2	2.1	3.1	6.7	19.9	23.9	2.1	4.3	6.5	4.7	7.3	6.4	10.1	7.8
Qatar	26	11.4	10.3	15	12	8.3	5.7	3.9	4.6	4.1	4.9	6.5	9.3	6.9
SA	652	106	146	118	145	157	151	134	143	110	113	108	134	77
UAE	49	38	92	46	134	196	143	53	36	16	32	41	42	39
(c) Oman														
Bahrain	1	1.8	1.9	2.4	0.9	1.7	1.8	3.6	y3.2	y2.4	y2.7	y2.7	y3	y21
Kuwait		1	1	7	2	2	1	1	1	1	2	6	9	*51
Qatar	0.1	0.6			0.2									3.9
SA	3	4	6	3	3	5	4	7	9	9	13	17	27	35
UAE	1					1	1	5	8	7	6	10	2	8
(d) Qatar														
Bahrain	2.5	4.1	1.2	2.8	1.4	0.9	2.1	4.2	y3.8	y2.9	y3.2	y3.2	y3.5	y4.1
Kuwait		3	28	22	4	5	15	34	25	35	36	59	50	y32
Oman	0.3	0.3	1	1.2	0.5	0.1	0.3	5.7	24.6	8.9	3.8	2.7	9.8	10.4
SA	9	15	69	63	76	74	79	69	62	68	58	94	72	52
UAE	3	5	22	34	48	33	30	30	40	46	50	47	97	129
(e) Saudi Arabia														
Bahrain	916	886	1261	1997	2493	1747	1439	1661	y1485	y1132	y1253	y1257	y1388	y1662
Kuwait	4	14	18	24	26	31	37	45	58	100	166	225	284	*219
Oman	2	0.1	1.1	0.5	4.6	6.5	1.4	6.3	8.2	14.7	20.5	29.3	45.5	58.2
Qatar	5.1	2.8	5.5	9.9	4.3						30.1	37.7	37.9	68.9
UAE	123	74	6	16	40	48	67	62	129	188	183	219	298	415
(f) UAE														
Bahrain	21.7	26.2	20.9	22.2	24.6	34.7	35.6	36.7	y32.8	y25	y27.7	y27.8	y30.7	y35.8
Kuwait	2	5	11	13	19	35	43	62	28	61	103	154	99	y64
Oman	128.3	148.8	188	299.6	364.7	374.8	437.2	489.1	665.2	447.8	382.5	462.3	546.5	621.6
Qatar	56.7	15.3	22.4	42.4	37.3	49	34.6	32.8	30	33.8	33.8	39.2	58.4	50.3
SA	108	26	52	59	95	104	152	164	169	139	119	131	140	166

Notes: * = derived solely from partner record; y = estimates without use of own records, sometimes with partner's record

Source: International Monetary Fund (1992a)

Table A10: GCC Countries' GDP ($ million); GCC Countries' Total Exports ($ million); Intra-GCC Exports as % of GCC's GDP and as % of GCC's Total Exports (bold), 1977-1990

(a) Yi	1977	1978	1979	1980	1981	1982
Bahrain	1946.175	2342.425	2668.295	3071.86	3467.852	3645.78
Kuwait	14046.45	15504.76	24842.5	28688.07	25254.52	21585.57
Oman	2741.17	2741.459	3734.511	5927.331	7213.376	7569.774
Qatar	3617.594	4052.137	5773.802	7829.433	8661.413	7596.834
S. Arabia	58171.4	66301.92	97265.53	147575.7	165889.1	133632.8
UAE	16243.08	15679.89	20939.8	29616.44	32988.29	30618.36

1983	1984	1985	1986	1987	1988	1989	1990
3735.142	3905.623	3704.557	3186.733	3169.711	3358.809	3470.7	3643.6
20870.16	21706.86	21453.35	17612.55	22090.4	20024.69	23081.82	15282.6
7935.437	8823.683	9999.421	7330.89	7809.103	7609.623	8402.081	10621.59
6467.694	6704.511	6153.403	5053.109	5446.522	6038.291	6488.024	7380.621
108220.4	99721.89	86673.48	73202.28	73551.4	76141.52	82995.99	93082.3
28030.51	27730.86	27077.09	21656.22	23780.99	23726.51	27512.94	33778.26

(b) Xi, World Total	1977	1978	1979	1980	1981	1982
Bahrain	1845.3	1623.5	2491.9	3610	4347.4	3789.2
Kuwait	9802	10466	18449	20402	16300	10863
Oman	1574.8	1512.4	2165.6	3294.1	4447.9	4115
Qatar	2324.1	2318	3598	5310.9	5389.1	4466.2
S. Arabia	44961	37816	58652	102012	113230	75839
UAE	9637	9125	13652	21618	21238	16837

1983	1984	1985	1986	1987	1988	1989	1990
3200.1	3138.8	2823.7	2343.9	2386.7	2356.6	2715.7	2846.6
11538	12274	10821	7381	10300	8359	11044	8149
4042	3932	4704.5	2923.5	3222.8	4030.6	4362.9	4583.9
3533.6	4516.8	3542.5	2968.6	1994.7	2078.2	2490.4	3291.7
45862	37521	27480	20184	22602	23737	27741	44416
18698	17985	14043	12395	14178	13935	17591	23539

(c) Summary	1977	1978	1979	1980	1981	1982
Intra-GCC X	2476.6	2101.7	3152	4596.6	5590.5	4883.6
Sum GCC Yi	96765.87	106622.6	155224.4	222708.8	243474.6	204649.1
Sum Xi WorldTotal	70144.2	62860.9	99008.5	156247	164952.4	115909.4
X/SumGCCYi *100	**2.56**	**1.97**	**2.03**	**2.06**	**2.30**	**2.39**
X/XiWorldTot *100	**3.53**	**3.34**	**3.18**	**2.94**	**3.39**	**4.21**

1983	1984	1985	1986	1987	1988	1989	1990
3340.8	3425	3101.2	4216.4	4762.8	5406.6	6626.6	7229.9
175259.4	168593.4	155061.3	128041.8	135848.1	136899.4	151951.6	163789
86873.7	79367.6	63414.7	48196	54684.2	54496.4	65945	86826.2
1.906203	**2.031514**	**2.00**	**3.29**	**3.51**	**3.95**	**4.36**	**4.41**
3.845583	**4.315363**	**4.89**	**8.75**	**8.71**	**9.92**	**10.05**	**8.33**

(d) Summary, Without Exports from Oman to the UAE and vice versa

	1977	1978	1979	1980	1981	1982
Intra-GCC X	2463.5	2097	3135	4481	5548.6	4860.6
Sum GCC Yi	96765.87	106622.6	155224.4	222708.8	243474.6	204649.1
Sum Xi WorldTotal	70131.1	62856.2	98991.5	156131.4	164910.5	115886.4
X/SumGCCYi *100	**2.55**	**1.97**	**2.02**	**2.01**	**2.28**	**2.38**
X/XiWorldTot *100	**3.51**	**3.34**	**3.17**	**2.87**	**3.36**	**4.19**

1983	1984	1985	1986	1987	1988	1989	1990
3331	3417	3093.2	2638.9	2973.5	3115.6	4002.6	4529.2
175259.4	168593.4	155061.3	128041.8	135848.1	136899.4	151951.6	163789
86863.9	79359.6	63406.7	46618.5	52894.9	52205.4	63321	84125.5
1.90	**2.03**	**1.99**	**2.06**	**2.19**	**2.28**	**2.63**	**2.77**
3.83	**4.31**	**4.88**	**5.66**	**5.62**	**5.97**	**6.32**	**5.38**

Sources: Arab Monetary Fund (1991a); International Monetary Fund (1992a; 1992c); World Bank (1992)

Table A11: Intra-GCC Trade Matrix of Products of National Origin, 1986-1989 ($ million)

a) Bahrain

	Indust. X of Prod. of Nat.Orig.				Indust. M of Prod. of Nat.Orig.			
	1986	1987	1988	1989	1986	1987	1988	1989
Kuwait	9.47	13.54	28.37	14.96	5.53	7.65	11.17	15.95
Oman	8.76	4.36	5.52	6.64	1.34	1.33	1.96	6.21
Qatar	1.49	1.56	5.25	4.71	0.84	1.35	4.61	3.21
SA	21.07	56.92	111.86	122.96	14.60	26.56	44.95	67.49
UAE	0.73	3.04	4.56	5.84	21.81	26.73	35.00	44.63
GCC	41.52	79.42	155.56	154.84	44.12	63.62	97.69	137.49
GCC[a,b]	41.75	79.57	156.18	156.51	49.84	69.73	108.03	150.73
	total X incl. re-exp. & transit				total M incl. re-exp. & transit			
GCC	553.0	563.1	556.1	640.8	1165.5	1289.7	1293.7	1428.4
World	2343.9	2386.7	2356.6	2715.7	2402.7	2658.5	2666.8	2944.4

Notes: [a] total national commodities (i.e., industrial products plus agricultural and animal products plus natural resources products); the difference between this row and the GCC row is mainly due to imports of natural resources products from the UAE (1986: 3.67, 1987: 3.31, 1988: 4.87, 1989: 5.55) and of agricultural and animal products from Saudi Arabia (1986: 1.36, 1987: 1.72, 1988: 4.29, 1989: 6.64)
[b] without imports of crude oil from Saudi Arabia
Sources: GCC, Secretariat General (1991); Internat. Monetary Fund (1992a)

b) Kuwait

	Indust. X of Prod. of Nat.Orig.				Indust. M of Prod. of Nat.Orig.			
	1986	1987	1988	1989	1986	1987	1988	1989
Bahr.	6.32	7.45	10.83	15.47	9.00	14.15	37.50	41.04
Oman	3.30	5.84	6.31	9.45	0.28	1.23	5.33	7.79
Qatar	4.59	4.79	5.94	8.18	21.79	33.12	57.64	49.68
SA	118.16	107.15	104.68	111.40	66.69	129.63	192.68	238.84
UAE	7.39	13.00	26.90	27.40	43.60	80.80	139.04	94.8
GCC	139.76	138.23	154.66	171.90	141.36	258.93	432.19	432.15
GCC [a]	141.82	139.30	156.00	173.53	181.60	295.50	478.77	487.77
	total X incl. re-exp. & transit				total M incl. re-exp. & transit			
GCC	126	145	150	180	211	325	481	483
World	7383	8264	7661	11476	5717	5493	6143	6295

Notes: [a] total national commodities (i.e., industrial products plus agricultural and animal products plus natural resources products); the difference between this row and the GCC row is mainly due to imports of agricultural and animal products from Saudi Arabia (1986: 28.47, 1987: 22.25, 1988: 21.17, 1989: 41.8) and the UAE (1986: 3.93, 1987: 4.5, 1988: 3.86, 1989: 4.56) and of natural resources products from the UAE (1986: 4.95, 1987: 7.2, 1988: 11.08, 1989: 3.55) and Saudi Arabia (1986: 1.45, 1987: 1.71, 1988: 3.06, 1989: 4.36)
Sources: GCC, Secretariat General (1991); Internat. Montary Fund (1992a)

c) Oman

	Indust. X Prod. of Nat.Orig.				Indust. M of Prod. of Nat.Orig.			
	1986	1987	1988	1989	1986	1987	1988	1989
Bahr.	n.a.	1.00	2.59	3.29	n.a.	2.66	4.22	7.10
Kuwait	n.a.	1.42	4.97	7.25	n.a.	4.69	4.69	8.06
Qatar	n.a.	0.95	1.85	1.91	n.a.	2.10	1.56	8.69
SA	n.a.	3.67	14.30	32.76	n.a.	10.91	20.52	33.18
UAE	n.a.	15.36	29.56	33.57	n.a.	57.12	65.50	90.00
GCC	n.a.	22.40	53.27	78.78	n.a.	77.48	96.49	147.03
GCC[a]	n.a.	50.19	79.44	112.12	n.a.	78.57	97.87	147.81
	total X incl. re-exp. & transit				total M incl. re/exp. & transit			
GCC	1437.6	1729.2	2230.0	2727.9	486.9	428.2	507.3	624.8
World	2923.5	3222.8	4030.6	4362.9	2560.8	1958.8	2201.5	2257.5

Notes: [a] total national commodities (i.e., industrial products plus agricultural and animal products plus natural resources products); the difference between this row and the GCC row is mainly due to exports of agricultural and animal products from Oman to the UAE (1987: 19.45, 1988: 20.5, 1989: 26.22) and Saudi Arabia (1987: 6.32, 1988: 3.48, 1989: 4.48)

Sources: GCC, Secretariat General (1991); Internat. Monetary Fund (1992a)

d) Qatar

	Indust. X of Prod. of Nat.Orig.				Indust. M of Prod. of Nat.Orig.			
	1986	1987	1988	1989	1986	1987	1988	1989
Bahr.	n.a.	n.a.	n.a.	7.71	1.51	1.49	4.79	6.77
Kuwait	n.a.	n.a.	n.a.	12.67	3.33	3.97	5.28	7.15
Oman	n.a.	n.a.	n.a.	7.35	0.08	0.29	1.43	2.51
SA	n.a.	n.a.	n.a.	66.61	13.65	17.20	22.97	27.67
UAE	n.a.	n.a.	n.a.	93.99	26.40	25.81	28.87	43.34
GCC	n.a.	n.a.	n.a.	188.33	44.97	48.76	63.34	87.44
GCC[a]	n.a.	n.a.	n.a.	207.23	63.40	71.19	92.25	119.91
	total X incl. re-exp. & transit				total M incl. re-exp. & transit			
GCC	145.8	137.5	187.2	211.9	39.6	70.4	89.7	115.4
World	2068.6	1994.7	2078.2	2490.4	1098.8	1133.8	1267.0	1326.0

Notes: [a] total national commodities (i.e., industrial products plus agricultural and animal products plus natural resources products); the main factors contributing to the difference in this row and the GCC row are on the one hand exports of natural resources products to the UAE (18.5), on the other hand imports of agricultural and animal products from Saudi Arabia (1986: 8.68, 1987: 11.66, 1988: 13.49, 1989: 8.62) and the UAE (1986: 3.76, 1987: 4.18, 1988: 5.07, 1989: 8.06) and of natural resources products from the UAE (1986: 3.6, 1987: 3.72, 1988: 5.17, 1989: 6.92)

Sources: GCC, Secretariat General (1991); Internat. Monetary Fund (1992a)

e) Saudi Arabia

	Indust. X of Prod. of Nat.Orig.				Indust. M of Prod. of Nat.Orig.			
	1986	1987	1988	1989	1986	1987	1988	1989
Bahr.	9.85	25.28	54.89	67.82	62.78	62.41	114.19	122.24
Kuwait	37.67	102.17	143.54	178.64	96.32	95.93	88.47	111.83
Oman	4.10	10.27	16.30	32.36	0.63	1.98	6.42	12.90
Qatar	12.30	16.03	23.38	31.99	66.77	57.27	173.69	72.04
UAE	39.67	78.93	120.48	427.29	116.10	102.38	110.00	116.26
GCC	103.59	232.68	358.59	738.10	342.60	319.97	492.77	435.27
GCC[a,b]	183.96	474.29	631.09	910.70	385.34	363.57	544.76	500.57
	total X incl. re-exp. & transit				total M incl. re-exp. & transit			
GCC	1311	1582	1543	2071	390	366	465	501
World	20184	22602	23737	27741	19112	20110	21784	21153

Notes: [a] total national commodities (i.e., industrial products plus agricultural and animal products plus natural resources products)
[b] without exports of crude oil to Bahrain, which amounted to about US$ 1000 million (1988: 908.02, 1989: 1160.5)
Sources: GCC, Secretariat General (1991); Internat. Monetary Fund (1992a)

f) United Arab Emirates

	Indust. X of Prod. of Nat.Orig.				Indust. M of Prod. of Nat.Orig.			
	1986	1987	1988	1989	1986	1987	1988	1989[a]
Bahr.	17.13	26.75	35.38	40.32	n.a.	n.a.	n.a.	0.17
Kuwait	44.85	60.05	70.36	57.87	n.a.	n.a.	n.a.	5.60
Oman	56.42	51.15	63.48	64.97	n.a.	n.a.	n.a.	0.02
Qatar	39.53	36.19	41.46	45.15	n.a.	n.a.	n.a.	19.78
SA	88.98	88.09	110.00	113.39	n.a.	n.a.	n.a.	18.51
GCC	246.91	262.23	320.68	321.80	n.a.	n.a.	n.a.	107.08
GCC[b]	258.03	272.49	334.83	331.61	n.a.	n.a.	n.a.	108.13
	total X incl. re-exp. & transit				total M incl. re-exp. & transit			
GCC	643	606	740	795	387	387	396	535
World	12395	14178	13935	17591	6431	6901	8526	9559

Notes: [a] 1989 imports only for Abu Dhabi
[b] total national commodities (i.e., industrial products plus agricultural and animal products plus natural resources products)
Sources: GCC, Secretariat General (1991); Internat. Monetary Fund (1992a)

Table A12: Summary Statistics of Products of National Origin, 1986-89 ($ million): (a) Intra-GCC Trade; (b) Intra-GCC Industrial Trade

(a) Intra-GCC Trade of Products of National Origin; Own Data versus Partner Data

Bahrain	X89	M89pa	X88	M88pa	X87	M87pa	X86	M86pa
Kuwait	14.96	*41.04	28.37	*37.5	13.54	14.15	9.47	9
Oman	6.64	7.1	5.52	4.22	4.36	*2.66	8.76	
Qatar	4.71	6.77	5.25	4.79	1.56	1.49	1.49	1.51
Saudi A.	122.96	122.24	111.86	114.19	56.92	62.41	21.07	*62.78
UAE	5.84	†0.17	4.56		3.04		0.73	
	M89	X89pa	M88	X88pa	M87	X87pa	M86	X86pa
Kuwait	15.95	15.47	11.17	10.83	7.65	7.45	5.53	6.32
Oman	6.21	*3.29	1.96	2.59	1.33	1	1.34	
Qatar	3.21	*7.71	4.61		1.35		0.84	
Saudi A.	67.49	67.82	44.95	54.89	26.56	25.28	14.6	9.85
UAE	44.36	40.32	35	35.38	26.73	26.75	21.81	17.13
Kuwait	X89	M89pa	X88	M88pa	X87	M87pa	X86	M86pa
Oman	9.45	8.06	6.31	4.69	5.84	4.69	3.3	
Qatar	8.18	7.15	5.94	5.28	4.79	3.97	4.59	3.33
Saudi A.	111.4	111.83	104.68	*88.47	197.15	*95.93	118.16	*96.32
UAE	27.4	†5.6	26.9		13		7.39	
	M89	X89pa	M88	X88pa	M87	X87pa	M86	X86pa
Oman	7.79	7.25	5.33	4.97	1.23	1.42	0.28	
Qatar	49.68	*12.67	57.64		33.12		21.79	
Saudi A.	238.84	*178.64	192.68	*143.54	129.63	*102.17	66.69	*37.67
UAE	94.8	*57.87	139.04	*70.36	80.8	*60.05	43.6	44.85
Oman	X89	M89pa	X88	M88pa	X87	M87pa	X86	M86pa
Qatar	1.91	2.51	1.85	1.43	0.95	*0.29		0.08
Saudi A.	32.76	*12.9	14.3	*6.42	3.67	*1.98		0.63
UAE	33.57	†0.02	29.56		15.36			
	M89	X89pa	M88	X88pa	M87	X87pa	M86	X86pa
Qatar	8.69	7.35	1.56		2.1			
Saudi A.	33.18	32.36	20.52	16.3	10.91	10.27		4.1
UAE	90	*64.97	65.5	63.48	57.12	51.15		56.42
Qatar	X89	M89pa	X88	M88pa	X87	M87pa	X86	M86pa
Saudi A.	66.61	72.04		173.69		57.27		66.77
UAE	93.99	†19.8						
	M89	X89pa	M88	X88pa	M87	X87pa	M86	X86pa
Saudi A.	27.67	31.99	22.97	23.38	17.2	16.03	13.65	12.3
UAE	43.34	45.15	28.87	*41.46	25.81	*36.19	26.4	*39.53
Saudi A.	X89	M89pa	X88	M88pa	X87	M87pa	X86	M86pa
UAE	427.29	†18.5	120.48		78.93		39.67	
	M89	X89pa	M88	X88pa	M87	X87pa	M86	X86pa
UAE	116.26	113.39	110	110	102.38	*88.09	116.1	*88.98

Notes: X, M exports from and imports by **bold country** (own data); Mpa, Xpa imports by and exports to partner country (partner's data); * higher value is more than 50% and/or $10 million above lower value's level; † only Abu Dhabi

(b) Intra-GCC Industrial Trade of Products of National Origin

	EXPORTS				IMPORTS;	UAE 1989 ONLY ABU DHABI		
	1986	1987	1988	1989	1986	1987	1988	1989
Bahrain	41.52	79.42	155.56	154.84	44.12	63.62	97.69	137.49
Kuwait	139.76	138.23	154.66	171.9	141.36	258.93	432.19	432.15
Oman		50.19	79.44	112.12		78.57	97.87	147.81
Qatar				207.23	63.4	71.19	92.25	119.91
Saudi A.	103.59	232.68	358.59	738.1	342.6	319.97	492.77	435.27
UAE	246.91	262.23	320.68	321.8				107.08
Total	**531.78**	**762.75**	**1068.93**	**1705.99**	**591.48**	**792.28**	**1212.77**	**1379.71**
w/o O,Q:	531.78	712.56	989.49	1386.64				
				w/o Oman,UAE:	591.48	713.71	1114.9	1124.82
				without UAE:		792.28	1212.77	1272.63

Source: GCC, Secretariat General (1991)

F. References

Note: References which start with an abbreviation in italics refer to official documents of the GCC which are published by the GCC Secretariat General in Riyadh. The dates refer to the date of coming into effect. For a chronological list see Table 11 in section B.3.1.

Adebahr, Hubertus / Maennig, Wolfgang (1987): Außenhandel und Weltwirtschaft, Duncker & Humblot: Berlin

Aghevli, Bijan B. / Khan, Moshin S. / Montiel, Peter J. (1991): Exchange Rate Policies in Developing Countries: Some Analytical Issues, International Monetary Fund: Occasional Paper, No. 78, Washington, D.C.

Agricultural Policy (1985), Joint Agricultural Policy for the GCC, 3-6 November

Aitken, Norman D. (1973): The Effect of the EEC and EFTA on European Trade: A Temporal Cross-Section Analysis, American Economic Review, Vol. 63, No. 5, pp. 881-892

Al-Attiyah, Abdulla bin Hamad (1992): Speech delivered at the GCC-EC Second Industrial Conference, 25-27 October, Doha

Al Bassam, Mohammed (1992): Interview with the Author, Dubai

Al-Fayez, Khaled (1992): Rationale & Methods of Promoting Joint GCC-EC Projects, GCC-EC Second Industrial Conference, 25-27 October, Doha

Al Hajjar, B. / Presley, J.R. (1991): Managerial Inefficiency in Small, Manufacturing Businesses in Saudi Arabia: A Constraint Upon Economic Development, in: Brismes Proceedings of the 1991 International Conference on Middle Eastern Studies, School of Oriental and African Studies: London, pp. 102-114

Al Jafary, Abdul Rahman (1992): Investment Opportunities in the Gulf: Manufacturing Industry Joint Venture Opportunities. Introductory Speech, Second GCC-EC Industrial Conference, 25-27 October, Doha

Al-Khalaf, Khaled Y. (1992): Standards and Metrology in G.C.C. Countries, Speech Delivered at Second GCC-EC Industrial Conference, 25-27 October, Doha

Al-Marzook, Salah (1988): Towards a Regional Capital Market in the Gulf Area, in: Henry T. Azzam (ed.): Gulf Financial Markets, Gulf International Bank: Manama, pp. 35-44

Al-Naqeeb, Khaldoun Hasan (1990): Society and State in the Arab Gulf Peninsula. A Different Perspective, Routledge: London

Al-Sharhan, Rasheed (1992): Interview with the Author, Kuwait

Al-Yousuf, Ala'a (1986): Industrialisation and Economic Integration in the Arab Gulf, The Arab Gulf Journal, Vol. 6, No. 1, April, pp. 25-31

Albach, Horst [1986]: Organization and Coordination, Lecture Notes, Koblenz

Alkazaz, Aziz (1990): Struktur und Integrationsprozeß der Märkte in den arabischen Golfstaaten, in: Henning von Boehmer (ed.): Deutsche Unternehmen in den arabischen Golfstaaten. Leitfaden für die Rechts- und Wirtschaftspraxis, Schäffer: Stuttgart, pp. 1-72

Amelung, Torsten (1990): Explaining Regionalization of Trade in Asia Pacific: A Transaction Cost Approach, Kiel Working Paper No. 423, Kiel Institute of World Economics, June 1990

Amin, S.H. (1984): Political and Strategic Issues in the Persian-Arabian Gulf, Royston

Apex Publishing (1986): The Sultanate of Oman Business Directory 1986/87, 6th edition, Muscat

Arab-British Chamber of Commerce (1990): Arab-UK Business Yearbook 1990-91, 9th edition, London

Arab Communicators [1989]: Bahrain Business Directory. Abstract, 9th edition 1988-89, Manama

Arab Monetary Fund (1981): Annual Report 1980, Abu Dhabi

—— (1991a): Arab Countries: Economic Indicators 1980-1990, Abu Dhabi

—— (1991b): National Accounts of Arab Countries 1980-1990, Abu Dhabi

—— (1992a): Annual Report 1991 (in Arabic), Abu Dhabi

—— (1992b): AMF's Program in the Area of Creation and Development of Arab Capital Markets (in Arabic), Abu Dhabi

Arab News (various dates), daily newspaper, Jeddah

Arab Petroleum Research Center (1992): Arab Oil & Gas Directory 1992, Paris

Arabian Gulf University [1991]: Catalogue 1991-1993, Bahrain

Arikat, Harby Mohammad Mousa (1986): Arab Economic Co-operation and Integration in the Eyes of Arab Intelligentsia. An Opinion Survey, Centre for Middle Eastern and Islamic Studies, Economic Research Paper No. 16, Durham

Askari, Hossein / Dastmaltschi, Babak (1987): Evolution of a GCC Oil Policy, in: John A. Sandwick (ed.): The Gulf Cooperation Council. Moderation and Stability in an Interdependent World, Westview Press: Boulder, pp. 85-105

As-Sudais, Abdulaziz Ali Sulaiman (1985): The Applicability of Customs Unions to the Case of the Cooperation Council for the Arab States of the Gulf (the GCC), Boulder: University of Colorado, Ph.D. thesis

As-Sultan, Yusuf Yaaqub / Al-Matruk, Faisal Turki (1992): The Technological Cooperation Between the GCC and EC – Status Quo and Prospects, Kuwait Institute for Scientific Research (KISR), paper presented at Second GCC-EC Industrial Conference, 25-27 October, Doha

Atalla, Naji A. (1992): Some Petrochemical Potential Joint Venture Projects Researched by GOIC, Second GCC-EC Industrial Conference, 25-27 October, Doha

Bahrain Chamber of Commerce & Industry [1990]: Bahrain Chamber of Commerce & Industry Directory 1990-1991, Manama

Bahrain Marketing & Promotions Office [1992]: Bahrain. Gateway to the Middle East. A Businessman's Guide, Manama

Balassa, Bela (1961a): The Theory of Economic Integration, George Allen & Unwin: London

—— (1961b): Towards a Theory of Economic Integration, Kyklos, Vol. 14, pp. 1-17

Balassa, Bela / Stoutjesdijk, Ardy (1974): Economic Integration Among Developing Countries, International Bank for Reconstruction and Development, Bank Staff Working Paper No. 186

Baldwin, Robert E. (1992): Are Economists' Traditional Trade Policy Views Still Valid? Journal of Economic Literature, Vol. 30, No. 2, June, pp. 804-829

Bauer, Susanne / Oehme, Joachim (1989): Arabische Institutionen. Datenblätter über arabische Entwicklungsbanken und multilaterale arabische Institutionen, DSE: Bonn

Benjamin, Nancy C. / Devarajan, Shantayanan / Weiner, Robert J. (1989): The 'Dutch' Disease in a Developing Country. Oil Reserves in Cameroon, Journal of Development Economics, Vol. 30, pp. 71-92

Berglas, Eitan (1979): Preferential Trading Theory: The n Commodity Case, Journal of Political Economy, Vol. 87, No. 21, pp. 315-331

Bhagwati, Jagdish N. (1982): Directly Unproductive, Profit-Seeking (DUP) Activities, Journal of Political Economy, Vol. 90, No. 5, October, pp. 988-1002

Bild, Peter / Cranfield, John (1990): Oil in the Middle East and North Africa, in: The Middle East and North Africa 1991, Europa Publications: London, pp. 127-166

Bingaradi, Faris T. (1992): Interview with the Author, Abu Dhabi

Bishara, Abdulla Yacoub (1984): The Gulf Cooperation Council: Achievements and Challenges, American-Arab Affairs, No. 7, Winter 1983-84, pp. 40-44

—— (1992): Address to the GCC-EC Second Industrial Conference, 25 October, Doha

Bsaisue, Fo'ado (1984): Development Cooperation Among the GCC Countries, Beirut: Arab Unity Studies Center

Cain, Michael / Al-Badri, Kais (1989): An Assessment of the Trade and Restructuring Effects of the Gulf Co-operation Council, International Journal of Middle East Studies, Vol. 21, February, pp. 57-69

Carter, J.R.L. (1979): Leading Merchant Families of Saudi Arabia, Scorpion Publication: London

—— (1981): Investors in Saudi Arabia. A Reference to Private Investment, Scorpion Publications: London

Charter (1981), Charter of the Cooperation Council for the Arab States of the Gulf, 25 May

Christie, John (1984): The First Steps Forward, in: Aramco Services Company: Aramco World, Vol. 35, No. 1, January-February, pp. 26-33

—— (1990): GCC: The Next Decade, in: Aramco Services Company: Aramco World, Vol. 41, No. 4, July-August, pp. 32-37

Cline, William R. (1982): 'Reciprocity': A New Approach to World Trade Policy? Policy Analyses in International Economics No. 2, September, Institute for International Economics, Washington, D.C.

Council of Saudi Chambers of Commerce & Industry (1992): Means of Development of the Trading Exchanges Among the GCC-EC Countries. Executive Summary, in cooperation with Federation of GCC Chambers, Second GCC-EC Industrial Conference, 25-27 October, Doha

Crystal, Jill (1991): Oil and Politics in the Gulf: Rulers and Merchants in Kuwait & Qatar, Cambridge Studies in the Middle East, No. 24

Decision to Establish (1981), Decision to Establish the Gulf Cooperation Council, 14 February

Development Plans (1985), Common Objectives and Policies of the Development Plans and Programs in the GCC, 17-19 March

Deutsche Bundesbank (1992): Internationale Organisationen und Gremien im Bereich von Währung und Wirtschaft, Sonderdruck No. 3, Frankfurt/Main

Dietl, Gulshan (1988): The GCC Economic Negotiations with the European Community, the USA and Japan, in: Proceedings of the Conference on Industrial and Techno-Economic Cooperation Between the F.R.G. and the Arab Gulf Region, Würzburg, 24-25 September 1987, published in Doha, pp. 357-378

Directorate of Industry Protection & Registration, Ministry of Development and Industry (1991): Industrial Companies Guide, Manama

Doha Declaration (1992). Communique issued after the 2nd GCC-EC Industrial Conference, 25-27 October, Doha

Dornbusch, Rudiger (1992): The Case for Trade Liberalization in Developing Countries, Journal of Economic Perspectives, Vol. 6, No. 1, Winter, pp. 69-85

Dubai Chamber of Commerce & Industry, Department of Industrial Affairs (1991): Dubai Industrial Directory 1991-92, Dubai

Dubai Chamber of Commerce & Industry [1992a]: Establishing Business in Dubai, Dubai

—— [1992b]: Opportunities and Venues of Industrial Investment in Dubai, Dubai

Dubai Ports & Customs, Airport Section, Customs (1992): List of Exemption-Codes, 28 January, Dubai

Eckaus, Richard S. (1989): Absorptive Capacity, in: John Eatwell / Murray Milgate / Peter Newman (eds.): The New Palgrave. Economic Development, Macmillan: London, pp. 18-20

Economic Agreement (1982), Unified Economic Agreement of the Cooperation Council for the Arab States of the Gulf, 1 November; signed by Supreme Council 11 November 1981

Economic Declaration (1987), Economic Declaration of the Riyadh Summit of the Supreme Council, 29 December

[The] Economist Intelligence Unit (1992): Saudi Arabia, No. 1

Education (1985), Role of Education in the Integration of the States of the GCC, 3-6 November

Edwards, Sebastian / van Wijnbergen, Sweder (1989): Disequilibrium and Structural Adjustment, in: H. Chenery / T.N. Srinivasan (eds.): Handbook of Development Economics, Vol. II, Elsevier, pp. 1481-1533

EEC-GCC Cooperation Agreement (1989), signed 15 June 1988, effective end of 1989; published in: Europäische Gemeinschaften: Amtsblatt, L 54, Vol. 32, 25 February 1989 (in German)

Egyptian Gazette (various dates), daily newspaper, Kairo

El-Kuwaiz, Abdullah (1984): The Gulf Cooperation Council and the Concept ot Economic Integration, American-Arab Affairs, No. 7, Winter 1983/84, pp. 45-49

—— (1987): Economic Integration of the Cooperation Council of the Arab States of the Gulf: Challenges, Achievements and Future Outlook, in: John A. Sandwick (ed.): The Gulf Cooperation Council. Moderation and Stability in an Interdependent World, Westview Press: Boulder, pp. 71-83

—— (1988): Monetary Integration in the GCC Countries, in: Henry T. Azzam (ed.): Gulf Financial Markets, Gulf International Bank: Manama, pp. 225-231

—— (1990): Investment Processes in the Gulf Cooperation Council States, in: Said El-Naggar (ed.): Investment Policies in the Arab Countries. Papers presented at a Seminar Held in Kuwait. 11-13 December 1989, International Monetary Fund: Washington, D.C., pp. 188-199

El-Shagi, El-Shagi (1991): Wohlfahrt durch Wettbewerb. Die Unterentwicklung und ihre Überwindung, in: Deutsches Institut für Fernstudien an der Universität Tübingen (ed.): Funkkolleg Humanökologie, Studienbrief 5, Beltz: Weinheim, pp. 11-47

Enders, Klaus / Herberg, Horst (1983): The Dutch Disease: Causes, Consequences, Cures and Calmatives, Weltwirtschaftliches Archiv, Vol. 119, pp. 473-497

Entwicklung und Zusammenarbeit, E+Z (1984): Cheikh Hissam M. Nazer – der 'Architekt der saudischen Entwicklung,' No. 12, pp. 16f

Environment (1985), General Policies and Principles for Protecting the Environment in the GCC, 3-6 November

Ernst & Whinney International (1989a): Doing Business in Kuwait, New York

—— (1989b): Doing Business in Saudi Arabia, New York

Ernst & Young (1990a): Doing Business in Oman, New York

—— (1990b): Doing Business in Qatar, New York

—— (1990c): Doing Business in the United Arab Emirates, New York

—— (1992): Worldwide Corporate Tax Guide and Directory, 1992 edition, New York

European Community (1992): KOM(92) 508 end., 14 December, Brussels

Falcon Directory Publications [1991]: The Gulf Directory 1991-92, 13th edition, Manama

Fayez, Rihan Mubarak (1992): Interview with the Author, Abu Dhabi

Feenstra, Robert C. (1992): How Costly is Protectionism? Journal of Economic Perspectives, Vol. 6, No. 3, Summer, pp. 159-178

Final Communiqué (several years): Final Communiqué of the Meeting of the Supreme Council of the States of the Cooperation Council; 1981a: Abu Dhabi 26 May; 1981b: Riyadh 11 November; 1982: Manama 11 November; 1983: Doha 9 November; 1984: Kuwait 29 November; 1985: Muscat 6 November; 1986: Abu Dhabi 5 November; 1987: Riyadh 29 December; 1988: Manama December; 1989: Muscat December; 1990: Doha 25 December; 1991: Kuwait 25 December; 1992: Abu Dhabi 23 December; 1993: Riyadh 22 December

Financial Times (1991): Oil and Gas International Year Book 1992, Longman: Harlow

Firms (1983), Permission to Establish Firms and to Work Therein in the Fields of Industry, Agriculture, Animal and Fish Resources, and Contracting, 1 March

Firms (1984), Permission to Establish Firms and to Work Therein in the Fields of Gastronomy, Hotel Industry and Maintenance, 1 March

Fischer Stanley (1993): Socialist Economic Reform: Lessons of the First Three Years, American Economic Review, Papers and Proceedings, Vol. 83, No. 2, May, pp. 390-395

Frankel, Jeffrey A. / MacArthur, Alan T. (1987): Political vs. Currency Premia in International Real Interest Differentials: A Study of Forward Rates for 24 Countries, Cambridge: National Bureau of Economic Research, Working Paper Series, No. 2309

Free Trade (1983), Exemption of Products of National Origin from Customs Tariffs and Charges Having Equivalent Effects, 1 March

Gald, Federico (1988): The Prospects of Economic Coöperation with Gulf Countries, Kooperation, Autumn, pp. 25-27

GCC (Cooperation Council for the Arab States of the Gulf), Secretariat General (1985): The Resource Base for Industrialization in the Member States of Co-operation Council of the Arab States of the Gulf, Riyadh

—— (1988): Guide to Manufacturing Companies in the GCC (in Arabic), Riyadh

—— (1988): Decrees Which Have Been Issued and Measures Which Have Been Adopted in Implementing the Unified Economic Agreement, 2nd edition, Riyadh

—— [1988]: Joint Enterprises of GCC Countries (in Arabic), Riyadh

—— (1990): Economic Bulletin, Vol. 5, Riyadh

—— [1990]: Draft of the Uniform Customs Tariff of the GCC countries (in Arabic), Riyadh

—— (1991): Economic Bulletin, Vol. 6, Riyadh

—— [1992]: Draft of Unified Regulations for the Practise of Accountant (in Arabic), Riyadh

General Agreement on Tariffs and Trade (1992): GATT Activities 1991, Geneva

Girgis, Maurice (1992): Interview with the Author, Manama

Government Purchasing (1987), Unified Regulations Granting Priority in Government Purchasing to National Products and Products of National Origin, 1 March

Grain Silos & Flous Mills Organization, Kingdom of Saudi Arabia (1989): Saudi Wheat in International Markets, Riyadh

Guide Foreign Investment (1989), Unified GCC Foreign Capital Investment Regulations. Guide Law, 5-7 March

Gulf Economic & Financial Report (various issues), editor: Henry T. Azzam, published monthly by Gulf International Bank in the 1980s, Manama

Gulf Industrial Focus (various issues): quarterly journal, published by Gulf Organization for Industrial Consulting, Doha

Gulf International Bank (1990): Annual Report and Accounts 1989, Manama

—— (1991): Annual Report and Accounts 1990, Manama

Gulf Investment Corporation (1982a): Agreement of Incorporation, 10 November, reprinted in: Erik R. Peterson (1988): The Gulf Cooperation Council. Search for Unity in a Dynamic Region, Westview Press: Boulder, pp. 270-274

—— (1982b): Articles of Association, 10 November, reprinted in: Erik R. Peterson (1988): The Gulf Cooperation Council. Search for Unity in a Dynamic Region, Westview Press: Boulder, pp. 274-286

—— (1990): Annual Report and Accounts 1989, Kuwait

—— (1991): Annual Report and Accounts 1990, Kuwait

—— (1992): Annual Report and Accounts 1991, Kuwait

Gulf News (various dates), daily newspaper, United Arab Emirates

Gulf Organization for Industrial Consulting (various years): Annual Report 1980; 1981; 1983; 1984; 1987; 1988; 1989; 1990; 1992 [reports have been published in the following year; thus, (1981) refers to the 1980 Report]

Hablutzel, R. (1981): Development Prospects of the Capital-Surplus Oil-Exporting Countries, World Bank Staff Working Paper, No. 483, Washington, D.C.

Harberger, Arnold C. (1993): The Search for Relevance in Economics, American Economic Review, Papers and Proceedings, May, pp. 1-16

Hartwick, John M. (1989): Non-Renewable Resources: Extraction Programs and Markets, Harwood: Chur and London

Heynitz, Achim von (1989): Die Beziehungen zwischen dem Gulf Cooperation Council und der Europäischen Gemeinschaft, unter besonderer Berücksichtigung des Problems des Marktzugangs für petrochemische Produkte, mimeographed

Hitiris, Theodore / Hoyle, Michael H. (1986): Monetary Integration in the GCC: An Evaluation, The Arab Gulf Journal, Vol. 6, No. 1, April, pp. 33-42

Horndasch, Georg (1990): The Economic Future of the Petrochemical Industry in the States of the Gulf Cooperation Council, Industrial Cooperation in the Arab Gulf States, No. 39, January, pp. 143-159

Hummer, Waldemar (1993): Allgemeines Präferenzsystem (APS), in: Dieter Nohlen (ed.): Lexikon Dritte Welt. Länder, Organisationen, Theorien, Begriffe, Personen, Rowohlt: Hamburg, pp. 37f

Industrial Strategy (1985), Uniform Strategy for the Industrial Development of the GCC States, 3-6 November

Institut der deutschen Wirtschaft Köln (1991): Zahlen zur wirtschaftlichen Entwicklung der Bundesrepublik Deutschland, Deutscher Instituts-Verlag: Köln

Institute of Banking Studies (1989): GCC Banks Financial Report (1986-1988), Kuwait

International Monetary Fund (1982): Annual Report on Exchange Arrangements and Exchange Restrictions, Washington, DC

—— (1991a): Balance of Payments Statistics Yearbook, Washington, DC

—— (1991b): Exchange Arrangements and Exchange Restrictions, Annual Report, Washington, DC

—— (1991c): Government Finance Statistics Yearbook, Washington, DC

—— (1992a): Direction of Trade Statistics Yearbook, Washington, DC

—— (1992b): International Financial Statistics, October, Washington, DC

—— (1992c): International Financial Statistics Yearbook, Washington, DC

—— (1992d): Press Release No. 92/82, 11.11.

International Petroleum Encyclopedia [1992], Energy Group of PennWell: Tulsa, Oklahoma

Jebel Ali Free Zone Authority (1992a): Investor's Guide, Dubai

—— (1992b): Who is in the Jebel Ali Free Zone, Dubai

Jordan Times (various issues), daily newspaper, Amman

Kassem, M. Sami (1989): A Note on the Arab Airline Industry, Chapter 4.1 of M. Sami Kassem / Ghazi Habib / et al. (1989): Strategic Management of Services in the Arab Gulf States. Company and Industry Cases, Walter de Gruyter: Berlin and New York, pp. 35-68

Kassem, M. Sami / Habib, Ghazi / et al. (1989): Strategic Management of Services in the Arab Gulf States. Company and Industry Cases, Walter de Gruyter: Berlin and New York

King Fahd University of Petroleum & Minerals (1991): G.C.C. Main Economic Indicators 1991, Dhahran

Kingdom of Saudi Arabia, Ministry of Commerce [1988]: A Guide to Doing Business in the Kingdom of Saudi Arabia, Riyadh

Kloten, Norber / Grosch, Ulrich (1993): Europäische Wirtschafts- und Wählrungsunion, in: Norbert Kloten / Johann Heinrich von Stein (eds.): Obst/Hintner. Geld-, Bank- und Börsenwesen, 39th ed., Schäffer-Poeschel: Stuttgart, pp. 161-183

Knipe, Michael (1993): Gulf Cooperation Council in Asia, Far Eastern Economic Review, June 24, pp. 39-49

Koppers, Simon (1991): Development Planning in East and Southeast Asian Economies, in: Simon Koppers / Susanne Dingens / Alberto Klaas / Hans-Erich Wermuth (eds.): Growth Determinants in East and Southeast Asian Economies, Duncker & Humblot: Berlin, pp. 41-57

—— (1991): Saudi Arabia's Industrialization Strategy in Theory and Practice, in: Brismes Proceedings of the 1991 International Conference on Middle Eastern Studies, School of Oriental and African Studies: London, pp. 115-123

—— (1992): Some Aspects of the Gulf Co-operation Council's Relationship with LDACs, in: Kunibert Raffer / M.A. Mohamed Salih (eds.): The Least Developed and the Oil-Rich Arab Countries. Dependence, Interdependence or Patronage? Macmillan: London, pp. 31-48

Krueger, Anne O. (1974): The Political Economy of the Rent-Seeking Society, American Economic Review, Vol. 64, No. 3, June, pp. 291-303

Küppers, Norbert F. (1990): Aufenthalts- und Arbeitsrecht in den arabischen Golfstaaten, in: Henning von Boehmer (ed.): Deutsche Unternehmen in den arabischen Golfstaaten. Leitfaden für die Rechts- und Wirtschaftspraxis, Schäffer: Stuttgart, pp. 437-464

Kuwait Scientific Research Institute (1992): The Technological Co-operation Between The GCC States and EC. Status Quo and Prospects. A Summary, GCC-EC Second Industrial Conference, 25-27 October, Doha

Kuwait Times (various dates), newspaper, Kuwait

Land Ownership (1985), Right of Ownership of Landed Property, 1 March

Langhammer, Rolf J. / Hiemenz, Ulrich (1990): Regional Integration Among Developing Countries. Opportunities, Obstacles and Options, Kieler Studien, Institut für Weltwirtschaft an der Universität Kiel, No. 232, Tübingen: Mohr

League of Arab States (1945): The Pact of the League of Arab States

Lee, Il Houng (1992): Interview with the Author, 10 November, Washington, D.C.

Linnemann, Hans (1966): An Econometric Study of International Trade Flows, North-Holland Publishing Co.: Amsterdam

Lipsey, R.G. (1960): The Theory of Customs Unions: A General Survey, The Economic Journal, September, pp. 496-513

Loans (1987), Equal Treatment in Obtaining Loans from Banks and Industrial Development Funds, 1 March

Local Agent (1986), Permission to Export National Products Which Have Been Produced in Another Member State to Any Member State Without Appointing a Local Agent, 1 March

Looney, Robert E. (1989): Saudi Arabia's Development Strategy: Comparative Advantage vs. Sustainable Growth, Orient, Vol. 30, No. 1, pp. 75-96

MEED (Middle East Economic Digest, 1992): The EC's New Middle East Strategy, 15 May

Meyer-Laucke, Wilfried / Meyer-Reumann, Rolf (1990): Der gewerbliche Rechtsschutz in den arabischen Golfstaaten, in: Henning von Boehmer (ed.): Deutsche Unternehmen in den arabischen Golfstaaten. Leitfaden für die Rechts- und Wirtschaftspraxis, Schäffer: Stuttgart, pp. 501-554

Michaely, Michael (1976): The Assumptions of Jacob Viner's Theory of Customs Unions, Journal of International Economics, Vol. 6, pp. 75-93

(The) Middle East and North Africa 1991 (1990), Europa Publications: London

Ministry of Industry and Electricity, Kingdom of Saudi Arabia (1992): Industrial Investment Opportunities in the Kingdom of Saudi Arabia, presented at the GCC-EC Second Industrial Conference, 25-27 October, Doha

Mohie El-Din, Badr I. (1984): An Econmic Strategy for Arab Gulf Co-operation in Industrialization, The Arab Gulf Journal, Vol. 4, No. 1, April, pp. 37-49

Mohyuddin, Badr I. (1984): Joint Projects and Regional Cooperation: A Study of the Experiences and Future Opportunities in the Gulf, Industrial Cooperation in the Arab Gulf States, No. 16, pp. 4-27

Moore, Philip (1990): Guaranteeing GCC Trade, Trade Finance & Banker International, No. 87, July, pp. 21-23

Mühlen, Alexander (1989): Basic Structures and Techniques of International Negotiations, Bundesakademie für öffentliche Verwaltung, Werkpapier 25E, Bonn

Müller, Klaus H.F. (1990): Interview with the Author, Manama

Mundell, Robert A. (1961): A Theory of Optimum Currency Areas, American Economic Review, Vol. 51, September, pp. 657-665

Murtfeld, Martin / Azzam, Henry T. (1990): Förderung ausländischer Direktinvestitionen und regionale Finanzierung in den arabischen Golfstaaten, in:

Henning von Boehmer (ed.): Deutsche Unternehmen in den arabischen Golfstaaten. Leitfaden für die Rechts- und Wirtschaftspraxis, Schäffer: Stuttgart, pp. 73-85

Nakhleh, Emile A. (1982): The Persian Gulf and American Policy, Praeger: New York

—— (1986): The Gulf Cooperation Council. Policies, Problems and Prospects, Praeger: New York

NCB Economist (various dates), editor: Henry T. Azzam, published monthly by National Commercial Bank since September 1991, Jeddah

New Arabia (various dates), published fortnightly by Kuwait Research & Advertising Co., London

Nicholson, Mark (1991): Bahrain Opens Door to Foreign Businesses, Financial Times, 3 July

Nienhaus, Volker (1987): Integration Theory and the Problems of Integration Policy in the Third World, Intereconomics, January/February, pp. 41-48

North, Douglass C. (1984): Transaction Costs, Institutions, and Economic History, Zeitschrift für die gesamte Staatswissenschaft, Vol. 140, No. 1, March, pp. 7-19

Okogu, Bright E. / Birol, Fatih (1992): Curbing CO_2 Emissions by Axing EC Coal Subsidies, OPEC Bulletin, Vol. 23, No. 10, November/December, pp. 7-20

Palma, J.G. (1989a): Prebisch, Raúl, in: John Eatwell / Murray Milgate / Peter Newman (eds.): The New Palgrave. Economic Development, Macmillan: London, pp. 291-294

—— (1989b): Structuralism, in: John Eatwell / Murray Milgate / Peter Newman (eds.): The New Palgrave. Economic Development, Macmillan: London, pp. 316-322

Peterson, Erik R. (1988): The Gulf Cooperation Council. Search for Unity in a Dynamic Region, Westview Press: Boulder

Posner, Richard A. (1975): The Social Costs of Monopoly and Regulation, Journal of Political Economy, Vol. 83, No. 4, August, pp. 807-827

Professions (1983), Permission to Engage in the Professions of Medicine, Law, Accounting, Engineering, and Consulting, 1 March

Professions (1984), Permission to Engage in Pharmacy and other professions, 1 March

Retail Commerce (1987), Permission to Engage in Retail Commerce, 1 March

Rieger, Hans Christoph (1991): Basic Issues of ASEAN Economic Co-operation, in: Koppers, Simon et al. (eds.): Growth Determinants in East and Southeast Asian Economies, Duncker & Humblot: Berlin, pp. 215-238

Riyadh Communiqué (1981), Foreign Ministers' Statement on the Founding of the Gulf Cooperation Council, 4 February

Rules Disputes (1981), Rules of Procedures of the Commission for the Settlement of Disputes, 25 May

Rules Ministerial Council (1981), Rules of Procedures of the Ministerial Council, 25 May

Rules Supreme Council (1981), Rules of Procedures of the Supreme Council, 25 May

Salter, W.E.G. (1959): International and External Balance: The Role of Price and Expenditure Effects, Economic Record, Vol. 35, August 1959, pp. 226-238

Samuelson, Paul A. (1948): International Trade and Equalization of Factor Prices, Economic Journal, Vol. 58, June, pp. 163-184

Sapir, André (1981): Trade Benefits under the EEC Generalized System of Preferences, European Economic Review, Vol. 15, pp. 339-355

Saudi Basic Industries Corporation (SABIC, 1991): Annual Report 1990, Riyadh

Saudi British Bank (1991): Saudi Arabia, Business Profile Series, 5th edition, Hong Kong

Saudi Consulting House, Ministry of Industry and Electricity (1988): Industrial Structural [sic] and Opportunities in Saudi Arabia, Kooperation, Vol. 3, No. 6, Autumn, pp. 77-92

Saudi Economic Survey (various dates), Weekly Review of Saudi Arabian Economic and Business Activity, Jeddah

Saudi Export Development Center, Saudi Chambers' Council (1990): Saudi Export Directory, 1st edition, Riyadh

Saudi Gazette (various dates), newspaper, Jeddah

Schaub, Alexander (1992): The European Single Market, Speech at the Second GCC-EC Industrial Cooperation Conference, 25-27 October, Doha

Schlesinger, Helmut (1993): Die Wirtschaft im vereinten Deutschland – Herausforderungen an die Geld- und Finanzpolitik, speech delivered before the 'American Chamber of Commerce', Berlin, 19 March

Singer, Hans W. (1989): Terms of Trade and Economic Development, in: John Eatwell / Murray Milgate / Peter Newman (eds.): The New Palgrave. Economic Development, Macmillan: London, pp. 323-328

—— (1991): Terms of Trade: New Wine *and* New Bottles? Development Policy Review, Vol. 9, No. 4, December, pp. 339-351

Soufi, Wahib Abdulfattah / Mayer, Richard T. (1991): Saudi Arabian Industrial Investment. An Analysis of Government-Business Relationships, Quorum: Westport

Stournaras (1985): Is the Industrialisation of the Arab Gulf a Rational Policy? The Arab Gulf Journal, Vol. 5, No. 1, April, pp. 21-27

Students and Certificates (1986), Equal Treatment of Students and Acceptance of Study Certificates, 1 March

Subroto (1992): Outlining the Organization's Response to the Rio Agenda, OPEC Bulletin, Vol. 23, No. 8, September, pp. 4-10

Swan, T.W. (1955): Longer Run Problems of the Balance of Payments, A.N.Z.A.A.S. paper

Tehran Times (various dates), daily newspaper, Tehran

Tim (1992): Interview with the Author, Doha

Tinbergen, Jan (1962): Shaping the World Economy. Suggestions for an International Economic Policy, The Twentieth Century Fund: New York

Torre, Augusto de la / Kelly, Margaret R. (1992): Regional Trade Arrangements, IMF Occasional Paper, No. 93, March, Washington DC

Transit Goods (1983), Rules and Regulations Governing Transit Goods in the GCC, 1 March

Tullock, Gordon (1980): Efficient Rent Seeking, in: James M. Buchanan / Robert D. Tollison / Gordon Tullock (eds.): Toward a Theory of the Rent-Seeking Society, Texas A&M University Press: College Station, pp. 97-112

—— (1988): Future Directions of Rent-Seeking Research, in: Charles K. Rowley / Robert D. Tollison / Gordon Tullock (eds.): The Political Economy of Rent-Seeking, Kluwer Academic Publishers, pp. 465-480

Twinam, Joseph Wright (1992): The Gulf, Cooperation and The Council. An American Perspective, Middle East Policy Council: Washington, D.C.

Uniform Tariff Range (1983), Establishment of a Minimum External Customs Tariff of 4 Percent and a Maximum Tariff of 20 Percent, 1 September

United Nations Development Programme (1992): Human Development Report 1992

van Wijnbergen, Sweder (1984): The 'Dutch Disease': A Disease After All? The Economic Journal, March, pp. 41-55

—— (1986): Macroeconomic Aspects of the Effectiveness of Foreign Aid: On the Two-Gap Model, Home Goods Disequilibrium and Real Exchange Rate Misalignment, Journal of International Economics, Vol. 21, pp. 123-136

Varghese, Paul (1992): Interview with the Author, Doha

Viner, Jacob (1950): The Customs Union Issue, Carnegie Endowment for International Peace: New York

Weigel, Dale (1990): Foreign Direct Investment: The Role of Joint Ventures and Investment Authorities, in: Said El-Naggar (ed.): Investment Policies in the Arab Countries. Papers presented at a Seminar Held in Kuwait. 11-13 December 1989, International Monetary Fund: Washington, D.C., pp. 70-88

Westerich, Burghart (1990): Aufenthalts- und Arbeitsrecht in Saudi-Arabien, in: Henning von Boehmer (ed.): Deutsche Unternehmen in den arabischen Golfstaaten. Leitfaden für die Rechts- und Wirtschaftspraxis, Schäffer: Stuttgart, pp. 465-468

Wholesale Commerce (1990), Permission to Engage in Wholesale Commerce, 1 March

Williamson, John (1983): The Open Economy and the World Economy, Basic Books: New York

Wonnacott, Paul / Lutz, Mark (1989): Is There a Case for Free Trade Areas? in: Jeffrey J. Schott (ed.): Free Trade Areas and U.S. Trade Policy, Institute for International Economics: Washington, DC, pp. 59-84

Working Paper (1981), GCC Working Paper, 26 May

World Bank (1983): World Development Report 1984, Oxford University Press: New York

—— (1984): World Development Report 1984, Oxford University Press: New York

—— (1988): World Development Report 1988, Oxford University Press: New York

—— (1989): World Development Report 1989, Oxford University Press: New York

—— (1990): World Development Report 1990, Oxford University Press: New York

—— (1992): World Development Report 1992, Oxford University Press: New York

World Customs Clearing (1992): Interview with the Author, Manama

Yang, Chun-Lei (1993): Efficiency in Rent-Seeking Games: The Role of Dynamics and Asymmetry, mimeographed, University of Dortmund, July

Zaidi, Iqbal (1990): Monetary Coordination Among the Gulf Cooperation Council Countries, World Development, Vol. 18, No. 5, pp. 759-768

FSC
www.fsc.org
MIX
Papier | Fördert
gute Waldnutzung
FSC® C083411

Kolibri 360 GmbH
Ferdinand-Jühlke-Straße 7
99095 Erfurt, Deutschland
produktsicherheit@kolibri360.de

Druck:
CPI Druckdienstleistungen GmbH
im Auftrag der
Kolibri 360 GmbH
Ferdinand-Jühlke-Str. 7
99095 Erfurt